McCormack's Guides, updated annually, are written to make life in Alameda County easier, happier and understandable. Our goal is to present useful and accurate information in a readable, entertaining style.

School Rankings, including the latest academic rankings (STAR test) for public schools, college placements by high school, SAT scores, a directory of private schools.

Community profiles. Home prices, rents. Descriptions of cities, towns and neighborhoods.

The perfect guide for parents or people shopping for homes or apartments or just interested in finding out more about Alameda County, its schools and its communities.

"Alameda County 2004" describes the local weather.

Hospital services and medical care. Directory of hospitals.

Child Care. Directory of infant-care and day-care centers. Most popular names for babies.

Places to visit, things to do.

Local Colleges and Unemployment Figures.

Vital statistics. Population and income by town. Republicans and Democrats. Presidential votes. Crime, history, trivia and much more.

McCormack's Guides, edited by former newspaper reporters and editors, was established in 1984 and publishes the most popular general-interest guides to California counties. For a list of our other guides and an order form, see the last page. Or visit: www.mccormacks.com

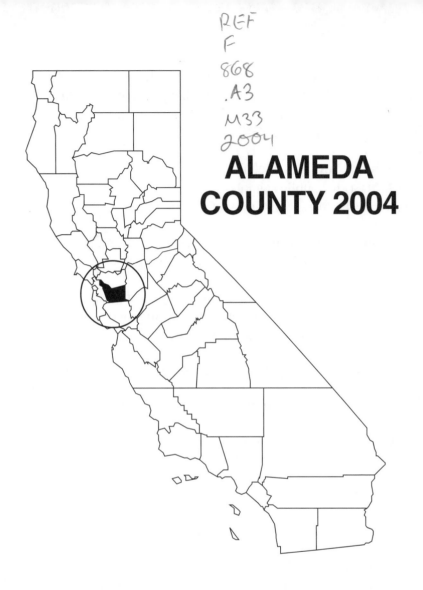

ALAMEDA
COUNTY 2004

Edited by Don McCormack

3211 Elmquist Court, Martinez, CA 94553
Phone: (800) 222-3602 & Fax: (925) 228-7223
bookinfo@mccormacks.com • www.mccormacks.com

Publisher and editor Don McCormack formed McCormack's Guides in 1984 to publish annual guides to California counties. A graduate of the University of California-Berkeley, McCormack joined the Contra Costa Times in 1969 and covered police, schools, politics, planning, courts and government. Later with the Richmond Independent and Berkeley Gazette, he worked as a reporter, then editor and columnist.

Maps illustrator Louis Liu attended the Academy of Art College in San Francisco, where he majored in illustration.

Ad graphics by T Graphics, Antioch, California

Many thanks to the people who write, edit, layout and help publish McCormack's Guides: Theresa Bailey, Martina Bailey, Tammy Demler, Mary Jennings, Arlis Johnson, Meghan McCormack, John VanLandingham.

Indexed   ISBN 1-929365-45-4

Contents

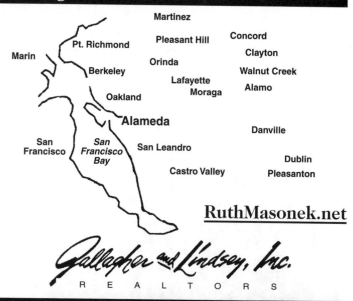

On the Cover:
Chabot Space and Science Center, located in the Oakland hills.

Alameda County

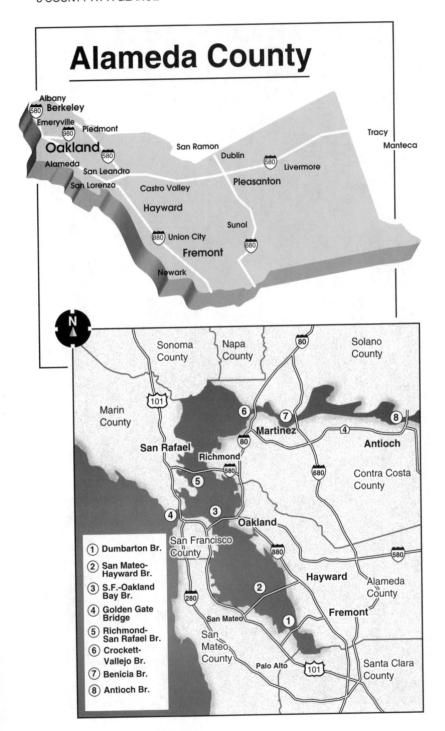

1. Dumbarton Br.
2. San Mateo-Hayward Br.
3. S.F.-Oakland Bay Br.
4. Golden Gate Bridge
5. Richmond-San Rafael Br.
6. Crockett-Vallejo Br.
7. Benicia Br.
8. Antioch Br.

Chapter 1

County at a Glance

ENERGETIC, INTELLECTUAL AND DIVERSE, Alameda County is located across the bay from San Francisco and counts 1,496,200 residents, the great majority of them residing in 14 cities and two unincorporated towns.

Alameda County also includes — a point of confusion — a city called "Alameda."

Just north of Alameda County is Contra Costa County. Together the two counties make up what is known locally as the East Bay.

In land, Alameda encompasses 733 square miles, about one-third the size of Delaware. North to south, the county runs from Albany to Fremont and east to west from Oakland to Livermore and the edge of the San Joaquin Valley. Discovery Peak, located south of Livermore-Pleasanton, is the highest mountain, 3,841 feet.

With the exception of Livermore, Pleasanton, Dublin and the hamlet of Sunol, all cities are located on or near the Bay. Tall hills divide the Bay cities from the inland towns and create different weather patterns.

Temperate with a Punch

The weather is balmy, one of the great attractions of the region. Rarely do temperatures roast or freeze. Rarely does humidity cause discomfort. Many shore cities, however, are too cool for outdoor pools. On some summer days, when the fog barrels through the Golden Gate, the Oakland hills can be plain cold. If you travel a few miles inland, over the ridge into Dublin-Pleasanton, you're in swimming pool country.

In the fall, dry winds called Diablos occasionally roar through the Berkeley-Oakland hills. In 1991, a Diablo-blown fire killed 25 and destroyed 2,500 homes and apartments, a loss of about $1.5 billion.

Fingertip Facts

Three bridges connect Alameda County with the "Peninsula" (San Francisco and San Mateo counties). They are the Bay, the San Mateo and the Dumbarton. Of the three, the Bay, with its spectacular views of San Francisco, is by far the prettiest.

The East Bay

CONTRA COSTA & ALAMEDA COUNTIES

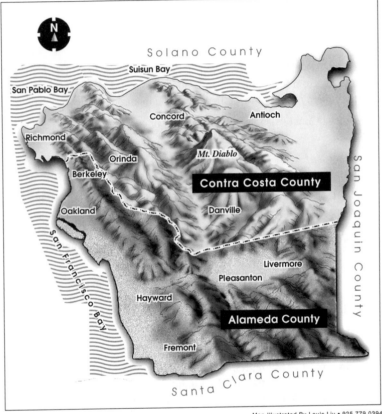

Map Illustrated By Louis Liu • 925.779.0394

But if you commute to San Francisco, you may come to hate the Bay Bridge, a notorious bottleneck, and about to become a bigger pain. Over the next few years, the east span is to be replaced and the west span overhauled and rewired.

The largest and most populous city is Oakland. The richest is Piedmont, the smallest, Emeryville, the most exciting and stimulating, Berkeley, with Oakland a close second.

Alameda County Population

City or Area	1990	2000	2003*
Alameda	76,459	72,259	74,900
Albany	16,327	16,444	16,800
Berkeley	102,724	102,743	104,600
Castro Valley	48,619	57,292	NA
Dublin	23,229	29,973	35,550
Emeryville	5,740	6,882	7,550
Fremont	173,339	203,413	209,000
Hayward	111,498	140,030	144,700
Livermore	56,741	73,345	78,000
Newark	37,861	42,471	43,950
Oakland	372,242	399,484	412,200
Piedmont	10,602	10,952	11,150
Pleasanton	50,553	63,654	67,000
San Leandro	68,223	79,452	81,400
San Lorenzo	19,987	21,898	NA
Union City	53,762	66,869	70,300
Countywide	1,279,18	1,443,741	1,496,200

Source: 1990 census, 2000 census. *City population estimates by California Dept. of Finance, 2003.

Berkeley is home to one of the most successful universities on the planet, the University of California at Berkeley, enrollment about 31,000 (grads and undergrads). The university is called "Cal." Its mascot is a Golden Bear. When fans urge Cal players to get hopping, they chant, "Go Bears." Cal's colors are blue and gold. Its alumni are Old Blues. Cal's arch rival is Stanford University, down and across the Bay. Colors: red. Nicknamed: The Cardinal. When Cal beats Stanford, especially in football or basketball, the hearts of young and old Blues go thumpety-thump in a lively way.

Berkeley's politics are quite liberal and to some people "Berkeley" epitomizes the zaniness of California. The town makes no apologies its politics or its policies. If you think that you are secure in your beliefs, Berkeley will offer someone who will differ, in a challenging way. The town, in lesser numbers, also has its conservatives and its moderates.

Alameda County is generally considered suburbia but 100-percent bedroom communities are few: Piedmont and maybe Castro Valley and San Lorenzo.

The other communities blend business, industry or government with residential, and this helps shorten the commute for many.

Oakland has an international airport that specializes in economy airlines (Southwest, Jet Blue), one of the busiest shipping ports in the nation and a high-rise downtown.

On its south, Alameda County borders Santa Clara County, home of the original Silicon Valley. Short of space, Silicon Valley jumped its borders about 30 years ago and started building offices, plants and research facilities throughout Alameda County, particularly at Fremont, Hayward, Union City, Dublin and Pleasanton.

In the local economy, the university, which employs about 20,000 full and part timers, has been enormously beneficial. Berkeley graduates staff or manage thousands of firms, high tech to high finance, and government institutions. Biotech, one of the coming industries, has a firm hold in the East Bay, thanks in large measure to the university.

At Livermore, the university manages a large laboratory, 8,000 employees, that researches and develops weapons. The lab has its critics and its supporters.

In politics, Alameda County, foremost Berkeley and Oakland, is quite liberal and invariably goes head-over-heels for anyone the Democrats trot out as president. But many people approach politics in a pragmatic and sometimes contradictory way. The communities welcome jobs but often argue over residential development. Both put more cars on the road, a sore point, but housing is considered more intrusive.

Protecting the environment is a big thing in Alameda County. Over the past 40 years, pollution laws have been tightened, development controls installed and hundreds of millions spent to clean up the Bay. Quality-of-life issues are also big. Berkeley blocks many of its residential streets to force motorists onto arterial boulevards. Suburbanites argue for open space to keep the country feeling that they find so pleasing.

In its annual tally of housing, the state counted 551,137 residential units in Alameda County. This included 296,683 single homes, 38,786 single attached, 208,018 apartments or condos and 7,650 mobile homes.

A Diverse Lot

The residents are a diverse lot: all sorts of colors and creeds, rich and poor but mostly middle class, home-owners and renters, white collars and blue, homeless and Nobel winners. Thanks to the university and its labs, the county boasts a large collection of Big Brains.

The 2000 census tallied 215,598 African Americans, 9,146 American Indians, 309,013 Asians, 591,095 Caucasians, 273,910 Hispanics, and 9,142 Native Hawaiian or Pacific Islanders.

Schools, churches, businesses and government agencies do a good job of encouraging everyone to respect and celebrate differences. There are, and probably always will be, arguments over policies such as profiling and affirmative action. Alameda County is very much of the modern world but this said, the county and its residents strongly favor inclusive politics and practices to bring people together.

Average Household Income

City	1990	2000	2005*
Alameda	$70,600	$85,500	$87,200
Albany	60,900	75,900	79,300
Berkeley	63,500	76,100	79,300
Castro Valley	76,200	93,200	95,100
Dublin	83,400	101,700	102,900
Emeryville	61,300	76,600	80,200
Fremont	85,200	103,100	104,600
Hayward	61,200	72,300	74,000
Livermore	78,500	97,800	99,800
Newark	77,700	88,100	90,600
Oakland	54,800	65,500	67,400
Piedmont	180,800	218,800	230,800
Pleasanton	98,100	121,500	123,900
San Leandro	59,800	71,400	72,400
San Lorenzo	63,200	73,400	75,500
Union City	74,800	84,100	88,300
Remainder	115,700	150,400	180,500
Countywide	68,000	82,500	84,200

Source: Association of Bay Area Governments, "*Projections 2002*" Average income per household includes wages and salaries, dividends, interest, rent and transfer payments such as Social Security or public assistance. *Projections.

Charm, Beauty, Amusements

The Bay charms the eye. The hills command sweeping views. If you wish to swim, boat, fish, hit a baseball or a softball or a golf ball or a tennis ball, if you wish to shoot or weave a basket, if you wish to watch the best (or near best) in basketball or baseball or football, if you wish to study painting, or paint a nude or paint the town, Alameda County can accommodate. All the towns field sports for the kids and the adults. Soccer is particularly popular.

If you wish to pursue your ambitions, Alameda County offers the chance. Besides the University of California, the county boasts a state university, two large private universities, seven community colleges, an arts college and many vocational and specialty schools.

California Cuisine was invented in Alameda County, specifically by Alice Waters in her Berkeley restaurant Chez Panisse. Berkeley, Albany and Oakland are loaded with first-class restaurants and recently restaurants that pride themselves on fine cooking have moved out into the suburbs. Livermore and Pleasanton are noted for their wines.

Oakland has a first-class museum and three professional teams — the Warriors (basketball), the Athletics (baseball) and the Raiders (football) — a zoo and a first-class night life built around Jack London Village. For college football and basketball, there's the university. The Sharks (professional hockey) play in San Jose, the Giants and the Forty Niners in San Francisco.

Top 30 Baby Names

Alameda County

Boys

Michael	127
Joshua	118
Daniel	116
Andrew	111
Jacob	105
Kevin	104
Ethan	102
Anthony	94
Matthew	94
Alexander	92
Jose	91
Jonathan	89
David	88
Joseph	87
Nicholas	87
Justin	82
Christopher	79
Ryan	78
William	78
Brandon	73
Benjamin	70
Jason	65
James	63
Christian	61
Samuel	61
Adrian	60
Gabriel	59
Zachary	59
Brian	58
Luis	58

Girls

Emily	86
Isabella	85
Sarah	81
Jessica	78
Jennifer	67
Samantha	64
Sophia	64
Olivia	59
Jasmine	58
Hannah	56
Natalie	55
Stephanie	55
Andrea	53
Lauren	53
Alyssa	49
Nicole	49
Ashley	48
Amanda	47
Emma	47
Alexis	45
Maria	45
Kayla	43
Abigail	42
Elizabeth	42
Grace	41
Isabel	41
Rachel	41
Brianna	39
Michelle	39
Madison	38

California

Boys

Daniel	4,099
Anthony	3,753
Jose	3,533
Andrew	3,521
Jacob	3,351
Joshua	3,343
Michael	3,205
David	3,162
Matthew	3,080
Angel	2,907
Christopher	2,884
Jonathan	2,714
Joseph	2,674
Alexander	2,377
Kevin	2,339
Ryan	2,279
Christian	2,253
Brandon	2,251
Ethan	2,249
Nicholas	2,190
Juan	2,042
Luis	1,970
Jesus	1,969
Nathan	1,934
Justin	1,926
Gabriel	1,783
Carlos	1,767
Adrian	1,671
Bryan	1,652
Jason	1,595

Girls

Emily	3,012
Ashley	2,667
Samantha	2,534
Jessica	1,991
Jennifer	1,976
Isabella	1,875
Alyssa	1,870
Elizabeth	1,696
Jasmine	1,657
Natalie	1,633
Alexis	1,577
Sarah	1,548
Madison	1,525
Hannah	1,486
Stephanie	1,463
Brianna	1,457
Andrea	1,338
Sophia	1,321
Maria	1,301
Emma	1,285
Michelle	1,276
Vanessa	1,253
Victoria	1,208
Kimberly	1,207
Leslie	1,206
Lauren	1,204
Kayla	1,184
Abigail	1,177
Olivia	1,088
Mia	1,080

Source: California Department of Health Services, 2002 birth records. Number of children with the given name. Some names would move higher on the list if the state grouped essentially same names with slightly different spellings, for example, Sarah and Sara. But state computer goes by exact spellings.

Plays, regular movies, offbeat movies, night clubs, jazz clubs, dance recitals, art galleries and art museums, chamber orchestras, symphonies, operas — they are all there. Many of high culture events are presented in Berkeley or Oakland but art and culture groups are found throughout the other cities.

The East Bay is hip enough and populous enough to attract the top acts — Madonna, McCartney, Dylan — touring the country. What the East Bay doesn't have, San Francisco does.

Voter Registration

City	Demo.	Repub.	NP
Alameda	19,719	8,915	6,621
Albany	5,937	1,059	1,551
Berkeley	45,451	5,431	13,845
Dublin	5,253	4,852	2,170
Emeryville	2,130	415	717
Fremont	39,019	23,607	16,297
Hayward	28,242	9,180	7,138
Livermore	14,525	15,191	5,935
Newark	8,785	4,013	2,811
Oakland	125,439	16,676	29,887
Piedmont	3,637	2,516	1,043
Pleasanton	12,936	15,224	5,452
San Leandro	21,896	7,978	5,428
Union City	13,205	4,632	4,533
Unincorporated	34,238	17,428	8,895
Countywide	551,778	159,403	156,197

Source: Registrar of voters, Alameda County, 2000. **Key**. Demo. (Democrat); Repub. (Republican). NP (Non-Partisan) Note: voter registration peaks at presidential elections, then falls off, often sharply, and changes from election to election. These figures are from the presidential election.

Presidential Voting in Alameda County

Year	Democrat	D-Votes	Republican	R-Votes
1948	Truman*	154,549	Dewey	150,588
1952	Stevenson	173,583	Eisenhower*	192,941
1956	Stevenson	174,033	Eisenhower*	192,911
1960	Kennedy*	217,172	Nixon	183,354
1964	Johnson*	283,833	Goldwater	142,988
1968	Humphrey	219,545	Nixon*	153,285
1972	McGovern	259,254	Nixon*	201,862
1976	Carter*	235,988	Ford	155,280
1980	Carter	201,720	Reagan*	158,531
1984	Mondale	282,041	Reagan*	192,408
1988	Dukakis	273,780	Bush*	139,618
1992	Clinton*	314,761	Bush	100,574
1996	Clinton*	303,702	Dole	106,534
2000	Gore	310,519	Bush*	106,137

Source: County Registrar of Voters. * Election winner.

Problems

Alameda County's elementary and secondary schools score among the top in the state and among the lowest. In 2003, Oakland school district, having lost track of its finances, was forced to declare bankruptcy. The state loaned it $100 million and put its own administrator in charge of the district.

In recent years, the state and local voters have greatly increased school funding and adopted programs that, all hope, will help students learn more. Many suburban schools score well above the 50th percentile.

In the early 1990s, Alameda County was recording over 200 homicides a year. Later in the decade, homicides dropped sharply but several years ago made a comeback. In 2001, the county counted 108 homicides; in 2002, the number was 144.

In the 1990s, billions were spent to improve local freeways and mass transit. BART (suburban rail) runs trains to San Francisco and San Mateo County and down to Fremont. The line also runs up to Richmond and Pittsburg and out to Dublin-Pleasanton. The Altamont Commuter Express (a new rail service) carries passengers from the inland cities down to San Jose.

In 2003, BART began service to San Francisco International Airport, a plus for penny-pinching travelers and for people who work at or near the airport.

Also in 2003, Oakland got to work on renovating its airport. The city for years has been improving access roads to and from the airport. The result: a smoother, easier drive to the airport.

But no matter how much money is spent, traffic jams don't go away. The main reason: more people, more cars. In 2000, the state tallied within Alameda County 878,450 cars, 199,767 trucks, 75,298 trailers, and 21,958 motorcycles — a total 1,175,473 vehicles. If you take out everyone under age 16 and over age 85, you come up with about 1.1 million people (Census 2000). Just about one vehicle for every functioning adult. And yes, your hunch is probably right: as soon as you get on the road, they all get on the road.

With the economy souring, rents have softened but, perversely, thanks to low interest rates, home prices have risen. Alameda County offers lower home prices and rents than San Francisco, Santa Clara and San Mateo counties. But it's easy to spend $350,000 on a modest home and fork over $1,200 a month on a one-bedroom apartment. Newcomers to California are shocked by the home prices and rents.

Alameda County has its rich neighborhoods and its poor neighborhoods but the great majority of the housing was built for the middle class or upper middle. Because of the hills, many homes have views of the Bay.

Quakes a Fact of Life

The Hayward and Calaveras faults run right through the county. A major earthquake is not a matter of if. It's a matter of when. For some good information about preparing for a quake and what to do in one, read the beginning of your phone directory.

In the quake of 1989, many Oakland buildings were damaged, about 40 people were killed, a portion of a freeway collapsed, and the Bay Bridge, the main connection to San Francisco, was knocked out of service. A section of the top deck fell to the lower deck. The freeway has been redesigned; the part of the Bay Bridge that collapsed is being replaced.

A Little History

The Spanish arrived in 1772, the expedition led by Lt. Pedro Fages and Father Juan Crespi. European diseases (cholera, measles and smallpox) and settler hostility and indifference obliterated the Indians and almost all their culture.

Then followed the Ranchero interlude, 1820 to about 1860. To secure California for Spain and later Mexico, large land grants were made to soldiers and civil servants.

Luis Peralta got Berkeley, Albany and Oakland; Jose Estudillo, San Leandro; Don Guillermo Castro, the Castro Valley and Hayward; Jose Amador, Dublin; Juan and Augustin Bernal, Pleasanton.

Superb horsemen, the dons raised cattle, staged rodeos and lived in the grand style. Their parties lasted for days, their hospitality was renown.

But few in number and only recently endowed (the Castro and Estudillo grants were not made until the 1840s), they were unable to resist the Yankee invasion. What they didn't sell, they lost to swindlers, squatters and lawyers.

Gold Fever

Gold lured the Yankees to California, but the many who did not strike it rich turned to farming and commerce. Within a few decades of statehood (1850), Alameda County was well on its way to modern life. Horace Carpentier, sly lawyer, and friends incorporated Oakland as a city in 1852, much to surprise of rest of community. In 1853, the county of Alameda was formed, population 3,000. The first county seat was at Union City, the second at San Leandro. Finally, Oakland's votes carried the seat to that city in 1873.

Berkeley

"Westward the course of empire takes its way." Written by Bishop George Berkeley, the words charmed Frederick Billings. Billings was a trustee of the College of California, opened in 1860 in wild Oakland.

Favoring a more secluded and peaceful spot, trustees purchased land north of Oakland and, at Billings' suggestion, named the town "Berkeley." A few years later the college was offered to the state as the cornerstone of a public university system. The University of California at Berkeley went on to become one of the finest universities in the world.

Meanwhile, the trading posts and ranches in the hinterland were growing into small towns that would later burgeon into suburban cities.

The 20th Century

Ships and electric trains, planes and automobiles. The early 20th century saw many changes in Alameda County transportation. Borax Smith, of 20-mule-team fame, for a while beat Southern Pacific at the commuting race to San Francisco. His electrified trains, with the aid of ferries, crossed the Bay in 35 minutes.

In 1926, Oakland purchased 692 acres on Bay Farm Island for an airport.

Bridges

The first bridge was the railroad Dumbarton (Newark to Redwood City), 1910; the second, automotive Dumbarton, 1927. On Oct. 23, 1936, the last rivet was driven on the Bay Bridge. In 1967, Hayward and San Mateo were joined by the San Mateo Bridge. Finally, the Dumbarton, which used to infuriate motorists by raising the drawbridge during rush hour, was replaced with a higher bridge in 1982.

The bridges, World War II and the freeways changed the face of modern Alameda County. War brought people who liked what they saw. The bridges and freeways allowed them to spread over the countryside and travel long distances to work. In World War II, UC-Berkeley helped build the A-bomb dropped on Nagasaki.

How Residents Make Their Money

City or Town	MAN-PRO	SERV	SAL-OFF	FARM	CON	MANU-TRANS
Alameda City	48%	12%	26%	0%	6%	8%
Albany	64	7	21	0	4	4
Berkeley	61	10	20	0	4	5
Castro Valley	41	11	29	0	9	10
Dublin	47	11	29	0	7	7
Emeryville	56	10	22	0	3	10
Fremont	50	8	25	0	6	11
Hayward	27	14	30	0	11	19
Livermore	42	12	26	0	10	9
Newark	32	12	29	0	9	18
Oakland	39	16	25	0	7	12
Piedmont	71	5	20	0	3	2
Pleasanton	52	9	29	0	5	6
San Leandro	33	12	32	0	9	15
San Lorenzo	28	13	31	0	10	18
Union City	36	11	27	0	7	19
Alameda County	42	12	26	0	8	12

Source: 2000 Census. Figures are percent, rounded off, of working civilians over age 16. **Key**: MAN-PRO (managers, professionals); SERV (service); SAL-OFF (sales people, office workers); FARM (farming, fishing, forestry); CONSTRUCTION (building, maintenance, mining), MANU-TRANS (manufacturing, distribution, transportation).

Wild Years

Sixties and Seventies. Free speech. Student protests. Vietnam. War protests and marches. Black Panthers. Hell's Angels. People's Park. Marijuana and LSD. Super Bowl and World Series victories. BART (commuter rail) begins service. Port of Oakland, containerized, takes off. Symbionese Liberation Army. Oakland school superintendent assassinated. Patty Hearst kidnapped. Oakland elects first black mayor.

The Eighties. Raiders depart. Smoking down, cocaine up. Yuppies. Business follows people to suburbs (Pleasanton, Fremont). Japanese, GM join hands in NUMMI auto plant in Fremont. Gene splicing. Herpes and AIDS. Wild sex out, safe sex in. Babies in. Money in. Food in. U.S. veers right, Berkeley stays left but tilts toward center. Drug abuse remains a problem.

Oct. 17, 1989, the earthquake that won't be forgotten for a long time.

The county's demographics change. Revisions in the federal law greatly increased the number of immigrants from the Philippine Islands, China, India and Southeast Asia. The new Alameda County is much more international, cosmopolitan.

The Nineties

Oakland rebuilds from the earthquake.

BART in 1997 extended its line and opened stations in Castro Valley and Dublin, welcome alternatives to congested freeways.

The military pulls out of the Bay Area, the logical outcome to the end of the Cold War. Alameda Naval Air Station, home for decades to the giant carriers, closes and is now being uses for civilian purposes. Lawrence Livermore National Lab survives the shutdowns and finds ways to prove its peacetime benefits.

In 1995, cold-shouldered by L.A., the Raiders return to Oakland and after years of losing seem to have found their winning ways. They made it to the Super Bowl in 2002 but lost. The A's made the playoffs in 2000, 2001 and 2002 and 2003.

2000 Plus

In the late 1990s and in 2000, the California economy boomed and millions were allocated to reduce class sizes and improve instruction.

In 2002, people were saying that many schools were in the best shape they have been in 25 years.

In 2003, with the state deficit hitting $38 billion and Sacramento warning of steep cuts coming to schools, colleges and universities, the cheering turned to fretting. As mentioned, the Oakland school district declared bankruptcy.

Retrospectively, the failings seem obvious but in the heady days of 2000 and 2001, Oakland may have assumed that the good-time dollars would keep rolling in.

When the U.S. invaded Iraq, many in Berkeley protested but the days of sustained protests seem over. The hippies of old are now in their 50s; the younger generation perhaps less interested in politics.

Suburbs and Small Towns

In the suburbs and smaller towns, conservative or middle-of-the-road politics hold greater appeal but many a Democrat resides in towns like Fremont, Union City, Hayward and San Leandro. Growth and development tend to dominate suburban politics because billions of dollars and thousands of jobs ride on development and because the builders are the great moneybags of local politics.

With the passage of Prop. 13, the funding base of local agencies, especially schools, shifted to Sacramento. Each year, heated arguments fill the Sacramento air as local groups try to squeeze money out of the governor and legislature.

Here are the groups making and carrying out local policy in the county:

Education Level of Population Age 25 & Over
(Percent of Population)

City or Town	ND	HS	SC	AA	BA	Grad
Alameda City	8%	7%	23%	7%	27%	15%
Albany	4	11	14	5	30	34
Berkeley	4	9	15	4	30	34
Castro Valley	8	24	26	8	20	11
Dublin	11	21	25	8	24	9
Emeryville	8	11	20	5	28	25
Fremont	7	17	20	8	27	17
Hayward	14	26	3	7	14	5
Livermore	7	20	29	9	20	12
Newark	11	23	25	7	17	7
Oakland	13	18	20	6	18	13
Piedmont	1	4	12	5	37	41
Pleasanton	4	15	24	9	32	16
San Leandro	11	26	25	8	17	7
San Lorenzo	12	33	26	7	11	4
Union City	10	21	22	8	21	8
Alameda County	10	19	22	7	21	14

Source: 2000 Census. Figures are percent of population age 25 and older, rounded to the nearest whole number. **Key:** ND (Less than 9th grade or some high school but no degree); HS (adults with high school diploma or GED only, no college); SC (adults with some college education); AA (adults with an associate degree); BA (adults with a bachelor's degree only); Grad (adults with a master's or higher degree).

The Board of Supervisors

Five members are elected countywide but by districts (Oakland votes for its supervisor, the Fremont area for its supervisor, and so on.) Supervisors are regional and municipal governors. They control spending for courts, social services and public health, including hospitals for the poor.

In their municipal hats, they build roads, decide zonings and, through the sheriff, provide police protection for unincorporated areas.

If you live in Castro Valley, San Lorenzo or outside any city limits, you will be governed from Oakland, seat of the county government, but often county officials follow the advice of local leaders.

City Councils

Generally, five members (Berkeley has nine) are elected, one council for each of the county's 14 cities. Some cities (Berkeley, Oakland) have directly elected mayors who share power with the councils. Councils are responsible for repairing roads, keeping neighborhoods safe, maintaining parks, providing recreation and doing other municipal chores.

Utility Districts

California grew so fast and chaotically that some regional needs, such as sewer and water, were met on an emergency basis by forming taxing districts with their own elected directors. The East Bay Municipal Utility District provides water to large portions of Alameda and Contra Costa counties and sewage treatment to six Alameda cities.

East Bay Regional Parks

If the park is big, chances are it's owned by the East Bay Regional Park District, one of the most successful park agencies nationally. The district, through its elected board, manages parks in Alameda and Contra Costa counties. Cities and special districts manage the small, municipal parks.

School Boards

Generally composed of five persons. There are 20 school districts in Alameda County, each with an elected school board.

Members hire or fire principals and superintendents, negotiate teacher salaries and decide policy matters and how much should be spent on computers and shop. The everyday running of schools is left to superintendents. Major funding decisions are made in Sacramento.

BART & Other Transit Districts

Elected Bay Area Rapid Transit District (BART) directors are responsible for making the trains run on time, providing parking at the stations and deciding where to extend BART.

Other transit agencies, such as AC Transit, run buses.

Regional Governments

As the Bay Area grew, it became apparent that many political boundaries either didn't make sense or else were too restrictive to solve regional problems, such as air and water pollution. Regional agencies were formed to deal with these problems.

Among the more important are, the Bay Conservation and Development Commission (shore protection), the Bay Area Air Quality Management District, the Regional Water Quality Control Board, the Association of Bay Area Governments and the Metropolitan Transportation Commission.

Chapter 2

National School Rankings

HERE ARE THE RESULTS for Alameda county of the 2003 STAR test as administered by the California Dept. of Education in spring 2003 to almost all public school students.

STAR is based on a national norm. The people who developed the test gave it to students of diverse backgrounds who supposedly represented U.S. students in general. From these results, national standards were drawn up.

Grades two to eleven were tested. Elementary pupils were tested in reading, math, language and spelling. High school students were tested in reading, math, language and science. We have coded the subjects as follows: reading (Rd), math (Ma), language (Lg), spelling (Sp) and science (Sci). Other subjects were tested; see the school or district for results.

The highest score is 99, the lowest is 1. A score of 50 is considered average. A school scoring 75 means that it has done better than about 75 percent of the other schools in the nation. If a school scores 25, it means that about 75 percent of the other schools in the nation have scored higher. Scores for grade levels with low enrollments will often not be reported.

STAR has its shortcomings. Only a small percentage of the students tested to come up with the national norm spoke little or no English. California schools have about 20 percent limited English speaking.

For this reason, the national sampling, representative of the nation, is not representative of California. If the national sampling were representative of California schools, many of our scores would be higher.

Critics contend that standardized tests are inherently flawed.

Parents and Realtors should interpret these scores cautiously, especially when a school has enrolled many students with a limited command of English. When combined with other data carried in McCormack's Guides, STAR will give you a more rounded picture of the schools.

See Chapter 2b for comparisons between California schools. See end of Chapter 3 for list of school districts and the towns they serve.

Scores range from 1-99, with 50 the national average. A school scoring 75 has done better than 75 percent of other public schools in the U.S. **Key:** Rd (Reading), Ma (Math), Lg (Language), Sp (Spelling), Sci (Science)

Alameda City Unified School Dist.

Alameda High

Grade	Rd	Ma	Lg	Sp	Sci
9	51	58	51	54	
10	50	66	61	54	
11	46	68	54	58	

Andersen Comm. Learning

Grade	Rd	Ma	Lg	Sp	Sci
7	78	74	77	80	
8	60	54	62	66	
9	78	77	87		75
10	71	71	81		66
11	80	83	80		83

Bay Area School

Grade	Rd	Ma	Lg	Sp	Sci
9	65	50	56		46
10	66	16	51		29

Bay Farm Elem.

Grade	Rd	Ma	Lg	Sp	Sci
2	81	91	80	84	
3	71	92	76	80	
4	70	78	73	76	
5	80	88	82	82	
6	83	80	84	64	

Chipman Middle

Grade	Rd	Ma	Lg	Sp	Sci
6	36	37	33	48	
7	36	38	38	44	
8	38	32	37	41	

Earhart Elem.

Grade	Rd	Ma	Lg	Sp	Sci
2	69	86	75	76	
3	68	76	67	74	
4	70	91	80	83	
5	71	86	75	75	
6	72	77	80	63	

Edison Elem.

Grade	Rd	Ma	Lg	Sp	Sci
2	86	92	80	80	
3	76	75	71	75	
4	58	60	55	69	
5	71	72	74	58	

Encinal High

Grade	Rd	Ma	Lg	Sp	Sci
9	53	54	54		45
10	43	40	45		35
11	43	42	45		40

Franklin Elem.

Grade	Rd	Ma	Lg	Sp	Sci
2	71	83	66	61	
3	61	72	63	67	
4	45	56	47	60	
5	74	63	68	52	

Haight Elem.

Grade	Rd	Ma	Lg	Sp	Sci
2	46	54	43	59	
3	46	59	40	65	
4	45	56	39	59	
5	39	45	40	53	

Island High (Cont.)

Grade	Rd	Ma	Lg	Sp	Sci
11	13	9	18		24

Lincoln Middle

Grade	Rd	Ma	Lg	Sp	Sci
6	63	75	72	69	
7	66	68	66	73	
8	56	60	57	73	

Longfellow Elem.

Grade	Rd	Ma	Lg	Sp	Sci
2	42	57	56	64	
3	28	48	31	51	
4	29	35	28	49	
5	46	62	41	57	

Lum Elem.

Grade	Rd	Ma	Lg	Sp	Sci
2	59	76	65	82	
3	48	74	48	74	
4	47	70	45	74	
5	48	62	45	56	

Miller Elem.

Grade	Rd	Ma	Lg	Sp	Sci
2	48	77	51	59	
3	35	68	46	48	
4	55	72	50	70	
5	33	32	40	54	

Otis Elem.

Grade	Rd	Ma	Lg	Sp	Sci
2	56	78	50	62	
3	59	68	54	64	
4	62	78	68	72	
5	60	59	65	67	

Paden Elem.

Grade	Rd	Ma	Lg	Sp	Sci
2	67	72	70	70	
3	52	72	51	62	
4	50	43	44	52	
5	54	60	65	63	
6	46	52	56	58	
7	46	46	47	57	
8	66	64	54	83	

Washington Elem.

Grade	Rd	Ma	Lg	Sp	Sci
2	35	42	27	41	
3	45	71	48	69	
4	43	50	40	67	
5	31	39	45	59	

Wood Middle

Grade	Rd	Ma	Lg	Sp	Sci
6	42	47	41	58	
7	47	44	45	60	
8	43	47	44	62	

Woodstock Elem.

Grade	Rd	Ma	Lg	Sp	Sci
2	39	54	44	60	
3	28	44	34	60	
4	36	49	36	58	
5	35	55	37	42	

Alameda Co. Off. of Education

Alt./Opportunity

Grade	Rd	Ma	Lg	Sp	Sci
9	10		24		
10	13	9	19		3
11	23	12	22		18

Juvenile Hall/Court

Grade	Rd	Ma	Lg	Sp	Sci
8	14	5	9	18	
9	6	7	6		3
10	7	7	8		8
11	5	9	7		6

Albany City Unified School Dist.

Albany High

Grade	Rd	Ma	Lg	Sp	Sci
9	78	84	83		77
10	72	86	81		77
11	69	85	70		77

Scores range from 1-99, with 50 the average. A school scoring 75 has done better than 75 percent of other public schools in the U.S. **Key:** Rd (Reading), Ma (Math), Lg (Language), Sp (Spelling), Sci (Science)

Grade	Rd	Ma	Lg	Sp	Sci
Albany Middle					
6	74	82	84	74	
7	79	80	80	69	
8	70	79	74	73	
Cornell Elem.					
2	62	78	58	67	
3	71	84	69	71	
4	66	76	78	75	
5	69	70	79	65	
MacGregor High (Cont.)					
11	22	16	13		22
Marin Elem.					
2	83	91	76	72	
3	85	90	73	72	
4	74	71	83	69	
5	79	67	85	69	
Ocean View Elem.					
2	72	82	73	72	
3	69	85	71	72	
4	76	75	83	81	
5	81	82	82	76	
Berkeley Unified School Dist.					
Berkeley Alt.					
9	7	3	8		
10	15		18		
Berkeley High					
9	50	57	56		42
10	56	65	68		61
11	66	82	73		82
Cragmont Elem.					
2	59	88	62	41	
3	45	64	55	44	
4	46	54	46	65	
5	46	38	53	45	
Emerson Elem.					
2	68	70	60	64	
3	50	66	57	59	
4	61	62	59	65	
5	60	79	75	45	
Jefferson Elem.					
2	60	78	53	51	
3	58	75	48	67	
4	79	76	85	72	
5	47	43	43	44	
King Middle					
6	53	48	54	52	
7	54	50	49	51	
8	57	53	53	58	
Leconte Elem.					
2	37	57	38	36	
3	56	60	42	56	
4	66	58	54	61	
5	47	49	58	35	
Longfellow Arts & Tech					
6	43	47	39	47	
7	51	51	54	55	
8	47	54	49	70	

Grade	Rd	Ma	Lg	Sp	Sci
Malcolm X Elem.					
2	44	54	42	44	
3	56	76	60	52	
4	44	54	42	46	
5	32	33	30	34	
Muir Elem.					
2	55	68	67	65	
3	54	73	62	61	
4	68	79	64	77	
5	35	59	45	53	
Oxford Elem.					
2	68	69	76	62	
3	58	72	51	58	
4	59	63	62	50	
5	48	74	59	45	
Parks Magnet					
2	36	62	31	33	
3	27	42	28	41	
4	17	31	21	36	
5	19	31	27	36	
Thousand Oaks Elem.					
2	39	65	39	42	
3	30	60	39	40	
4	40	51	39	54	
5	28	56	35	39	
Washington Elem.					
2	55	65	43	54	
3	40	51	41	51	
4	35	62	34	41	
5	34	54	45	45	
Whittier/Arts Elem.					
2	56	53	63	55	
3	39	51	47	55	
4	54	61	64	71	
5	47	52	44	65	
6	78	73	80	77	
Willard Middle					
6	46	40	42	43	
7	56	48	49	54	
8	42	39	40	47	
Calif. School for the Deaf					
Calif School for the Deaf					
2	4	7	1	33	
3	9	12	7	40	
4	3	8	2	13	
5	8	18	12	22	
6	5	9	4	25	
7	6	2	3	13	
8	7	8	11	23	
9	3	6	7		
10	7	11	8		
11	4	10	5		9
Castro Valley Unified School Dist.					
Canyon Middle					
6	61	73	66	64	
7	68	68	64	58	
8	54	56	54	64	

Scores range from 1-99, with 50 the national average. A school scoring 75 has done better than 75 percent of other public schools in the U.S. **Key:** Rd (Reading), Ma (Math), Lg (Language), Sp (Spelling), Sci (Science)

Castro Valley Elem.

Grade	Rd	Ma	Lg	Sp	Sci
2	44	65	50	61	
3	39	68	44	60	
4	43	65	50	65	
5	48	60	52	47	

Castro Valley High

Grade	Rd	Ma	Lg	Sp	Sci
9	57	63	57		68
10	53	67	62		63
11	53	71	59		65

Chabot Elem.

Grade	Rd	Ma	Lg	Sp	Sci
2	68	82	67	66	
3	71	82	68	67	
4	59	71	56	65	
5	61	77	70	56	

Creekside Middle

Grade	Rd	Ma	Lg	Sp	Sci
6	66	75	70	66	
7	73	77	70	57	
8	58	63	58	69	

Independent Elem.

Grade	Rd	Ma	Lg	Sp	Sci
2	68	87	77	75	
3	63	78	69	69	
4	72	90	80	89	
5	77	82	86	78	

Jensen Ranch Elem.

Grade	Rd	Ma	Lg	Sp	Sci
2	76	95	82	85	
3	76	94	80	79	
4	78	90	83	86	
5	84	94	89	85	

Marshall Elem.

Grade	Rd	Ma	Lg	Sp	Sci
2	40	54	42	51	
3	58	75	60	68	
4	62	77	67	72	
5	66	79	76	58	

Palomares Elem.

Grade	Rd	Ma	Lg	Sp	Sci
2	53	78	67	52	
3	58	80	64	69	
4	69	79	65	80	

Proctor Elem.

Grade	Rd	Ma	Lg	Sp	Sci
2	65	76	70	67	
3	71	84	74	73	
4	65	84	72	65	
5	71	76	84	66	

Redwood Alt. (Cont.)

Grade	Rd	Ma	Lg	Sp	Sci
9	31	29	19		21
10	15	22	21		23
11	13	24	15		16

Stanton Elem.

Grade	Rd	Ma	Lg	Sp	Sci
2	48	80	59	51	
3	59	71	61	69	
4	45	74	54	64	
5	50	60	57	51	

Vannoy Elem.

Grade	Rd	Ma	Lg	Sp	Sci
2	73	83	68	65	
3	73	80	68	68	
4	68	79	68	69	
5	76	83	86	67	

Dublin Unified School Dist.

Dougherty Elem.

Grade	Rd	Ma	Lg	Sp	Sci
2	74	88	86	87	
3	76	85	72	84	
4	80	95	83	93	
5	68	79	75	71	

Dublin Elem.

Grade	Rd	Ma	Lg	Sp	Sci
2	62	79	73	62	
3	73	79	67	71	
4	60	58	59	61	
5	63	68	71	59	

Dublin High

Grade	Rd	Ma	Lg	Sp	Sci
9	65	74	64		62
10	62	70	69		63
11	63	74	65		63

Frederiksen Elem.

Grade	Rd	Ma	Lg	Sp	Sci
2	53	75	60	65	
3	55	70	58	64	
4	61	70	70	61	
5	58	73	72	59	

Murray Elem.

Grade	Rd	Ma	Lg	Sp	Sci
2	59	75	55	64	
3	52	77	49	75	
4	76	71	69	73	
5	65	67	69	61	

Nielsen Elem.

Grade	Rd	Ma	Lg	Sp	Sci
2	61	78	62	59	
3	46	75	49	55	
4	61	66	72	67	
5	67	50	69	65	

Valley High (Cont.)

Grade	Rd	Ma	Lg	Sp	Sci
10	26	15	33		34
11	27	20	17		31

Wells Middle

Grade	Rd	Ma	Lg	Sp	Sci
6	66	68	70	66	
7	65	65	65	65	
8	65	70	64	68	

Emery Unified School Dist.

Anna Yates Elem.

Grade	Rd	Ma	Lg	Sp	Sci
2	43	43	36	68	
3	26	34	31	51	
4	28	37	26	58	
5	33	35	35	48	

Emery High

Grade	Rd	Ma	Lg	Sp	Sci
9	22	20	25		16
10	17	12	26		18
11	27	29	30		21

Emery Middle

Grade	Rd	Ma	Lg	Sp	Sci
6	27	26	21	47	
7	41	23	46	51	
8	41	17	45	58	

Fremont Unified School Dist.

American High

Grade	Rd	Ma	Lg	Sp	Sci
9	60	65	58		60
10	60	69	67		65
11	52	67	57		57

Scores range from 1-99, with 50 the average. A school scoring 75 has done better than 75 percent of other public schools in the U.S. **Key:** Rd (Reading), Ma (Math), Lg (Language), Sp (Spelling), Sci (Science)

Grade	Rd	Ma	Lg	Sp	Sci
Ardenwood Elem.					
2	50	73	57	80	
3	59	89	69	81	
4	64	89	80	89	
5	66	82	80	76	
6	67	85	77	80	
Azeveda Elem.					
2	60	53	56	57	
3	40	55	42	69	
4	29	40	33	61	
5	55	74	64	64	
6	57	76	62	67	
Blacow Elem.					
2	17	52	20	29	
3	33	50	32	58	
4	38	57	45	48	
5	40	55	40	41	
6	53	62	53	62	
Brier Elem.					
2	61	75	60	74	
3	47	75	48	68	
4	46	56	55	62	
5	34	45	41	47	
6	48	66	47	56	
Brookvale Elem.					
2	56	82	61	66	
3	42	66	49	60	
4	61	75	64	76	
5	61	69	79	71	
6	53	64	54	67	
Cabrillo Elem.					
2	40	35	36	51	
3	20	28	14	43	
4	26	37	26	53	
5	26	36	32	38	
6	42	48	37	56	
Centerville Jr. High					
7	65	67	65	62	
8	57	62	59	63	
Chadbourne Elem.					
2	83	98	88	94	
3	77	95	84	89	
4	74	92	87	92	
5	86	96	93	92	
6	74	90	86	85	
Circle of Independent Learning					
5	81	52	77	61	
6	63	72	72	60	
7	83	67	71	72	
8	52	35	53	57	
9	46	45	38		43
10	50	28	51		45
Durham Elem.					
2	59	79	62	76	
3	33	60	34	60	
4	41	65	56	62	
5	46	51	43	46	
6	39	68	48	65	

Grade	Rd	Ma	Lg	Sp	Sci
Forest Park Elem.					
2	75	94	80	92	
3	64	92	76	88	
4	66	88	83	92	
5	63	82	77	78	
6	74	90	89	89	
Glenmoor Elem.					
2	68	69	67	76	
3	45	65	47	67	
4	60	76	71	77	
5	54	72	64	57	
6	50	66	49	59	
Gomes Elem.					
2	82	98	88	93	
3	81	96	86	92	
4	83	93	89	93	
5	86	95	92	94	
6	88	97	94	94	
Green Elem.					
2	51	51	41	55	
3	43	60	34	70	
4	53	68	51	65	
5	48	43	40	51	
6	43	43	34	45	
Grimmer Elem.					
2	29	52	22	25	
3	14	35	14	26	
4	19	28	23	29	
5	27	36	32	29	
6	47	57	49	58	
Hirsch Elem.					
2	51	64	57	61	
3	37	67	46	71	
4	44	67	47	72	
5	52	65	56	60	
6	55	69	63	69	
Hopkins Jr. High					
7	87	96	91	86	
8	80	91	86	95	
Horner Jr. High					
7	63	73	66	66	
8	59	69	60	76	
Irvington High					
9	55	62	55		54
10	57	70	62		58
11	53	69	57		61
Kennedy High					
9	41	51	41		39
10	50	58	53		47
11	54	71	57		57
Leitch Elem.					
2	68	87	74	85	
Maloney Elem.					
2	55	71	64	78	
3	46	77	47	75	
4	40	57	57	69	
5	53	60	58	59	
6	52	70	62	68	

Scores range from 1-99, with 50 the national average. A school scoring 75 has done better than 75 percent of other public schools in the U.S. **Key:** Rd (Reading), Ma (Math), Lg (Language), Sp (Spelling), Sci (Science)

Mattos Elem.

Grade	Rd	Ma	Lg	Sp	Sci
2	50	67	46	66	
3	48	64	52	70	
4	32	36	44	53	
5	58	64	60	51	
6	56	69	49	56	

Millard Elem.

Grade	Rd	Ma	Lg	Sp	Sci
2	58	81	62	65	
3	51	82	61	74	
4	40	60	52	66	
5	53	62	63	60	
6	43	55	48	59	

Mission San Jose Elem.

Grade	Rd	Ma	Lg	Sp	Sci
2	82	96	86	91	
3	76	93	83	91	
4	85	95	92	96	
5	82	96	93	88	
6	87	97	94	98	

Mission San Jose High

Grade	Rd	Ma	Lg	Sp	Sci
9	85	97	88		93
10	88	95	92		91
11	81	95	85		88

Mission Valley Elem.

Grade	Rd	Ma	Lg	Sp	Sci
2	78	95	87	91	
3	76	95	80	88	
4	75	92	85	89	
5	81	95	91	91	
6	78	90	87	87	

Niles Elem.

Grade	Rd	Ma	Lg	Sp	Sci
2	70	84	73	80	
3	60	79	63	73	
4	63	82	75	79	
5	67	67	66	61	
6	65	76	66	71	

Oliveira Elem.

Grade	Rd	Ma	Lg	Sp	Sci
2	59	59	54	74	
3	29	58	34	56	
4	35	56	37	54	
5	26	47	44	51	
6	59	64	58	59	

Parkmont Elem.

Grade	Rd	Ma	Lg	Sp	Sci
2	75	90	82	80	
3	68	90	73	81	
4	67	80	74	73	
5	62	72	66	67	
6	60	80	73	75	

Patterson Elem.

Grade	Rd	Ma	Lg	Sp	Sci
2	51	65	56	67	
3	36	65	44	64	
4	49	57	58	66	
5	43	46	54	50	
6	55	60	56	59	

Robertson High (Cont.)

Grade	Rd	Ma	Lg	Sp	Sci
9	26	23	28		29
10	15	16	18		26
11	28	16	20		14

Thornton Jr. High

Grade	Rd	Ma	Lg	Sp	Sci
7	55	62	58	61	
8	59	70	59	76	

Vallejo Mill Elem.

Grade	Rd	Ma	Lg	Sp	Sci
2	62	79	67	72	
3	43	78	48	67	
4	46	55	50	61	
5	58	57	70	66	
6	65	64	66	66	

Walters Jr. High

Grade	Rd	Ma	Lg	Sp	Sci
7	51	51	52	51	
8	49	47	47	52	

Warm Springs Elem.

Grade	Rd	Ma	Lg	Sp	Sci
3	69	90	76	86	
4	65	84	74	86	
5	73	89	80	76	
6	68	83	73	83	

Warwick Elem.

Grade	Rd	Ma	Lg	Sp	Sci
2	61	79	67	77	
3	47	70	50	76	
4	62	76	73	79	
5	56	68	67	71	
6	51	69	52	73	

Washington High

Grade	Rd	Ma	Lg	Sp	Sci
9	61	64	58		58
10	63	71	70		62
11	59	69	58		55

Weibel Elem.

Grade	Rd	Ma	Lg	Sp	Sci
2	80	94	87	93	
3	74	94	81	90	
4	81	93	90	92	
5	82	93	92	92	
6	85	98	94	98	

Hayward Unified School Dist.

Bowman Elem.

Grade	Rd	Ma	Lg	Sp	Sci
2	26	45	22	27	
3	28	49	30	48	
4	21	33	24	37	
5	22	28	29	43	
6	38	33	32	34	

Brenkwitz High (Cont.)

Grade	Rd	Ma	Lg	Sp	Sci
10	4	7	8		4
11	7	8	6		5

Bret Harte Middle

Grade	Rd	Ma	Lg	Sp	Sci
7	41	38	42	42	
8	41	39	37	56	

Burbank Elem.

Grade	Rd	Ma	Lg	Sp	Sci
2	27	54	23	26	
3	16	45	12	19	
4	19	41	19	37	
5	19	28	22	30	
6	31	34	23	41	

Chavez Middle

Grade	Rd	Ma	Lg	Sp	Sci
7	29	30	30	40	
8	30	29	26	36	

Cherryland Elem.

Grade	Rd	Ma	Lg	Sp	Sci
2	27	48	29	23	
3	16	30	20	29	
4	16	34	19	30	
5	17	31	26	35	
6	27	27	25	34	

Scores range from 1-99, with 50 the average. A school scoring 75 has done better than 75 percent of other public schools in the U.S. **Key:** Rd (Reading), Ma (Math), Lg (Language), Sp (Spelling), Sci (Science)

East Ave. Elem.

Grade	Rd	Ma	Lg	Sp	Sci
2	52	76	60	62	
3	60	82	55	59	
4	49	74	64	61	
5	35	52	35	55	
6	38	46	44	42	

Eden Gardens Elem.

Grade	Rd	Ma	Lg	Sp	Sci
2	41	48	35	54	
3	32	49	33	50	
4	26	42	30	47	
5	30	40	32	58	
6	32	32	25	49	

Eldridge Elem.

Grade	Rd	Ma	Lg	Sp	Sci
2	51	76	55	58	
3	35	66	44	51	
4	47	70	47	57	
5	35	50	40	47	
6	44	58	50	50	

Fairview Elem.

Grade	Rd	Ma	Lg	Sp	Sci
2	32	42	38	56	
3	28	48	37	44	
4	32	29	32	49	
5	23	23	25	47	
6	41	46	44	52	

Glassbrook Elem.

Grade	Rd	Ma	Lg	Sp	Sci
2	24	46	21	25	
3	18	40	22	25	

Harder Elem.

Grade	Rd	Ma	Lg	Sp	Sci
2	26	54	21	23	
3	16	35	17	37	
4	25	38	25	36	
5	23	34	27	40	
6	36	36	32	47	

Hayward High

Grade	Rd	Ma	Lg	Sp	Sci
9	31	35	32		23
10	29	40	35		40
11	25	34	26		26

Hayward Project Elem.

Grade	Rd	Ma	Lg	Sp	Sci
2	21	30	17	17	
3	24	28	27	31	
4	19	30	23	42	
5	43	36	44	38	
6	46	42	54	55	
7	50	45	52	41	
8	42	32	42	38	

Highland Elem.

Grade	Rd	Ma	Lg	Sp	Sci
2	53	79	67	54	
3	23	38	29	50	
4	43	61	47	54	
5	61	56	66	57	
6	57	49	56	60	

King Middle

Grade	Rd	Ma	Lg	Sp	Sci
7	25	30	30	40	
8	35	34	33	41	

Longwood Elem.

Grade	Rd	Ma	Lg	Sp	Sci
2	31	58	36	44	
3	24	37	20	32	
4	18	25	19	36	
5	23	27	22	35	
6	29	30	28	34	

Lorin A. Eden Elem.

Grade	Rd	Ma	Lg	Sp	Sci
2	32	53	34	41	
3	27	49	28	48	
4	36	55	45	61	
5	26	37	33	38	
6	39	46	34	50	

Markham Elem.

Grade	Rd	Ma	Lg	Sp	Sci
2	32	60	36	39	
3	22	37	27	39	
4	22	33	20	37	
5	23	23	26	28	
6	24	30	22	34	

Mt. Eden High

Grade	Rd	Ma	Lg	Sp	Sci
9	31	38	32		29
10	23	39	30		30
11	23	31	25		26

Muir Elem.

Grade	Rd	Ma	Lg	Sp	Sci
2	21	35	22	30	
3	17	32	18	23	
4	30	55	34	44	
5	19	27	15	32	
6	39	42	45	42	

Ochoa Middle

Grade	Rd	Ma	Lg	Sp	Sci
7	35	37	36	46	
8	31	31	32	44	

Palma Ceia Elem.

Grade	Rd	Ma	Lg	Sp	Sci
2	31	57	48	51	
3	30	59	37	55	
4	30	51	34	69	
5	28	30	24	45	
6	28	29	25	51	

Park Elem.

Grade	Rd	Ma	Lg	Sp	Sci
2	32	46	26	27	
3	23	34	21	32	
4	28	38	26	39	
5	23	21	19	35	
6	26	27	23	36	

Ruus Elem.

Grade	Rd	Ma	Lg	Sp	Sci
2	26	44	31	36	
3	27	47	26	46	
4	22	18	20	30	
5	21	27	27	36	
6	20	25	16	29	

Schafer Park Elem.

Grade	Rd	Ma	Lg	Sp	Sci
2	36	51	36	47	
3	29	55	37	38	
4	20	30	29	38	
5	21	43	21	32	
6	33	40	33	51	

Shepherd Elem.

Grade	Rd	Ma	Lg	Sp	Sci
2	13	42	13	14	
3	18	32	17	24	

Southgate Elem.

Grade	Rd	Ma	Lg	Sp	Sci
2	39	60	43	55	
3	28	38	30	55	
4	27	39	32	51	
5	30	35	32	39	
6	44	43	40	54	

Scores range from 1-99, with 50 the national average. A school scoring 75 has done better than 75 percent of other public schools in the U.S. **Key:** Rd (Reading), Ma (Math), Lg (Language), Sp (Spelling), Sci (Science)

Grade	Rd	Ma	Lg	Sp	Sci
Strobridge Elem.					
2	37	36	26	26	
3	33	47	39	56	
4	36	44	46	62	
5	28	34	24	41	
6	38	27	39	40	
Tennyson High					
9	15	25	16		15
10	11	20	13		16
11	14	23	16		18
Treeview Elem.					
2	49	60	45	50	
3	31	49	30	48	
4	30	42	30	42	
5	40	43	49	52	
6	43	45	44	46	
Tyrrell Elem.					
4	22	32	21	31	
5	21	32	18	31	
6	27	34	31	35	
Winton Middle					
7	24	34	25	34	
8	28	31	28	27	

Livermore Valley Jt. Unified School Dist.

Grade	Rd	Ma	Lg	Sp	Sci
Almond Ave. Elem.					
2	71	87	70	67	
3	65	84	60	72	
4	82	81	81	76	
5	82	87	83	70	
Altamont Creek Elem.					
2	65	84	66	62	
3	55	72	49	55	
4	63	73	67	68	
5	60	54	54	50	
Arroyo Mocho Elem.					
2	68	82	76	66	
3	76	87	77	71	
4	63	80	75	70	
5	63	72	60	64	
Arroyo Seco Elem.					
2	69	77	68	68	
3	64	81	62	72	
4	69	76	74	70	
5	66	76	75	58	
Christensen Middle					
6	55	61	61	58	
7	56	56	52	58	
8	58	63	54	72	
Croce Elem.					
2	62	81	67	66	
3	57	69	55	67	
4	50	67	55	65	
5	58	56	60	59	
Del Valle Cont. High					
11	20	32	24		31

Grade	Rd	Ma	Lg	Sp	Sci
East Ave. Middle					
6	60	67	61	60	
7	58	61	56	63	
8	61	71	58	76	
Granada High					
9	65	68	64		62
10	70	73	73		69
11	62	73	63		66
Jackson Ave. Elem.					
2	59	73	53	68	
3	57	82	54	60	
4	46	50	55	68	
5	63	62	71	46	
Junction Ave. Middle					
6	43	39	41	42	
7	51	50	50	59	
8	49	53	47	60	
Livermore High					
9	58	63	57		59
10	58	63	64		57
11	46	60	56		54
Marylin Ave. Elem.					
2	27	41	25	30	
3	34	44	33	53	
4	32	37	34	45	
5	39	33	37	29	
Michell Elem.					
2	53	57	48	46	
3	38	60	43	56	
4	43	56	49	57	
5	50	54	61	51	
Phoenix High (Cont.)					
10	10	19	10		11
11	19	13	20		18
Portola Elem.					
2	32	44	22	26	
3	33	59	32	40	
4	34	49	40	43	
5	46	39	45	33	
Rancho Las Positas Elem.					
2	57	78	51	47	
3	64	78	56	65	
4	46	61	54	59	
5	53	61	54	43	
Smith Elem.					
2	76	85	68	60	
3	63	82	61	62	
4	59	65	64	68	
5	73	80	79	63	
Sunset Elem.					
2	70	83	71	74	
3	69	78	69	74	
4	70	76	76	73	
5	73	77	82	67	

Scores range from 1-99, with 50 the average. A school scoring 75 has done better than 75 percent of other public schools in the U.S. **Key:** Rd (Reading), Ma (Math), Lg (Language), Sp (Spelling), Sci (Science)

Vineyard Alt.

Grade	Rd	Ma	Lg	Sp	Sci
7	73	70	73	78	
8	31	35	29	44	
9	32	50	38		37
10	40	31	28	35	
11	34	37	38	32	

William Mendenhall Middle

Grade	Rd	Ma	Lg	Sp	Sci
6	62	67	68	61	
7	74	71	68	60	
8	67	70	62	76	

New Haven USD (Union City)

Alvarado Elem.

Grade	Rd	Ma	Lg	Sp	Sci
2	33	58	35	44	
3	34	74	37	54	
4	37	61	39	54	
5	37	50	39	47	

Alvarado Middle

Grade	Rd	Ma	Lg	Sp	Sci
6	45	59	45	57	
7	48	58	54	57	
8	51	58	51	56	

Barnard-White Middle

Grade	Rd	Ma	Lg	Sp	Sci
6	33	49	29	41	
7	36	42	35	40	
8	42	48	40	43	

Cabello Elem.

Grade	Rd	Ma	Lg	Sp	Sci
2	41	67	43	53	
3	29	77	33	56	
4	36	68	37	53	
5	40	60	42	51	

Chavez Middle

Grade	Rd	Ma	Lg	Sp	Sci
6	46	59	42	53	
7	45	59	44	54	
8	47	54	45	58	

Eastin Elem.

Grade	Rd	Ma	Lg	Sp	Sci
2	63	89	70	67	
3	51	85	58	68	
4	49	74	62	71	
5	51	74	64	60	

Emanuele Elem.

Grade	Rd	Ma	Lg	Sp	Sci
2	40	68	42	46	
3	32	72	33	49	
4	30	49	30	41	
5	31	42	31	42	

Hillview Crest Elem.

Grade	Rd	Ma	Lg	Sp	Sci
2	34	63	32	35	
3	39	69	38	40	
4	28	51	37	38	
5	36	50	40	41	

James Logan High

Grade	Rd	Ma	Lg	Sp	Sci
9	48	56	46		44
10	52	64	55		51
11	50	63	54		51

Kitayama Elem.

Grade	Rd	Ma	Lg	Sp	Sci
2	51	75	57	60	
3	45	78	46	61	
4	48	70	55	61	
5	49	65	56	52	

Pioneer Elem.

Grade	Rd	Ma	Lg	Sp	Sci
2	58	76	61	77	
3	57	81	60	76	
4	54	76	57	68	
5	65	84	74	72	

Searles Elem.

Grade	Rd	Ma	Lg	Sp	Sci
2	46	52	39	51	
3	42	75	49	53	
4	27	42	34	43	
5	42	59	45	45	

Newark Unified School Dist.

Bridgepoint High (Cont.)

Grade	Rd	Ma	Lg	Sp	Sci
10	16	31	26		43
11	22	17	22		26

Bunker Elem.

Grade	Rd	Ma	Lg	Sp	Sci
2	49	67	53	64	
3	48	72	49	63	
4	52	62	63	58	
5	34	39	35	48	
6	45	55	45	48	

Crossroads High (Alt.)

Grade	Rd	Ma	Lg	Sp	Sci
10	14	11	21		26
11	27	15	22		27

Graham Elem.

Grade	Rd	Ma	Lg	Sp	Sci
2	32	61	41	43	
3	34	49	32	47	
4	19	36	25	36	
5	33	44	32	43	
6	38	55	39	42	

Kennedy Elem.

Grade	Rd	Ma	Lg	Sp	Sci
2	50	63	53	54	
3	56	68	54	60	
4	57	60	67	68	
5	62	62	64	56	
6	63	70	64	66	

Lincoln Elem.

Grade	Rd	Ma	Lg	Sp	Sci
2	41	71	42	41	
3	43	61	43	63	
4	53	70	58	68	
5	36	60	47	46	
6	45	51	47	57	

Milani Elem.

Grade	Rd	Ma	Lg	Sp	Sci
2	33	67	38	43	
3	27	51	24	48	
4	32	60	35	68	
5	34	42	40	41	
6	48	62	44	50	

Musick Elem.

Grade	Rd	Ma	Lg	Sp	Sci
2	43	64	38	44	
3	29	60	38	62	
4	40	48	38	57	
5	35	39	35	54	
6	44	56	38	54	

Newark Jr. High

Grade	Rd	Ma	Lg	Sp	Sci
7	37	47	38	42	
8	37	48	36	43	

Scores range from 1-99, with 50 the national average. A school scoring 75 has done better than 75 percent of other public schools in the U.S. **Key:** Rd (Reading), Ma (Math), Lg (Language), Sp (Spelling), Sci (Science)

Newark Memorial High

Grade	Rd	Ma	Lg	Sp	Sci
9	47	53	46		56
10	42	48	48		54
11	31	43	37		44

Schilling Elem.

Grade	Rd	Ma	Lg	Sp	Sci
2	33	46	41	43	
3	38	65	36	55	
4	23	23	19	28	
5	22	33	27	33	
6	46	57	43	49	

Snow Elem.

Grade	Rd	Ma	Lg	Sp	Sci
2	51	69	51	52	
3	43	66	46	52	
4	48	52	45	47	
5	47	51	51	52	
6	54	79	62	51	

Oakland Military (Charter)
Oakland Military

Grade	Rd	Ma	Lg	Sp	Sci
7	36	27	31	41	
8	39	36	40	45	

Oakland Unified School Dist.
Allendale Elem.

Grade	Rd	Ma	Lg	Sp	Sci
2	26	48	26	35	
3	22	37	27	51	
4	16	25	23	48	
5	19	19	18	37	

American Indian Public Charter

Grade	Rd	Ma	Lg	Sp	Sci
6	52	66	54	48	
7	46	41	51	57	
8	32	44	33	53	
9	61	59	56		54

Arts (Alt.)

Grade	Rd	Ma	Lg	Sp	Sci
5	31	24	34	35	
6	22	17	19	25	
7	45	27	44	24	
8	30	20	27	34	

ASCEND

Grade	Rd	Ma	Lg	Sp	Sci
3	17	43	25	35	
5	39	60	30	40	
6	25	44	27	36	
7	39	41	34	41	

Bella Vista Elem.

Grade	Rd	Ma	Lg	Sp	Sci
2	39	65	38	74	
3	27	57	30	65	
4	19	38	22	58	
5	27	44	25	55	

Brewer Middle

Grade	Rd	Ma	Lg	Sp	Sci
6	28	28	24	39	
7	27	33	30	41	
8	28	36	30	41	

Brookfield Village Elem.

Grade	Rd	Ma	Lg	Sp	Sci
2	27	38	26	31	
3	18	33	21	35	
4	16	22	13	36	
5	19	19	20	30	

Burbank Elem.

Grade	Rd	Ma	Lg	Sp	Sci
2	16	26	14	22	
3	12	14	19	37	
4	14	10	10	26	
5	13	23	14	36	

Burchhalter Elem.

Grade	Rd	Ma	Lg	Sp	Sci
2	91	94	84	91	
3	40	79	47	75	
4	44	77	59	78	
5	23	29	18	31	

Carter Middle

Grade	Rd	Ma	Lg	Sp	Sci
6	15	16	14	27	
7	18	15	18	26	
8	27	24	22	38	

Castlemont Sr. High

Grade	Rd	Ma	Lg	Sp	Sci
9	8	15	8		14
10	7	13	9		18
11	8	20	10		17

Chabot Elem.

Grade	Rd	Ma	Lg	Sp	Sci
2	73	80	71	73	
3	73	85	73	72	
4	85	79	84	78	
5	77	70	83	72	

Claremont Middle

Grade	Rd	Ma	Lg	Sp	Sci
6	32	31	34	44	
7	40	34	39	47	
8	38	33	35	49	

Cleveland Elem.

Grade	Rd	Ma	Lg	Sp	Sci
2	68	94	81	91	
3	51	82	57	78	
4	38	67	48	67	
5	39	54	43	50	

Cole Elem.

Grade	Rd	Ma	Lg	Sp	Sci
4	13	15	18	36	
5	22	19	20	30	
6	14	13	12	28	
7	19	16	19	30	
8	24	17	21	32	

Cox Elem.

Grade	Rd	Ma	Lg	Sp	Sci
2	15	24	12	21	
3	20	31	20	43	
4	11	19	13	32	
5	16	21	14	37	

Crocker Highlands Elem.

Grade	Rd	Ma	Lg	Sp	Sci
2	76	77	69	75	
3	79	81	76	69	
4	77	81	74	62	
5	61	61	63	54	

Dewey/Baymart Sr. High

Grade	Rd	Ma	Lg	Sp	Sci
9	5	6	5		6
10	7	5	8		9
11	5	4	8		5

E. Bay Consv. Corps Charter

Grade	Rd	Ma	Lg	Sp	Sci
2	27	48	22	41	
3	43	47	42	38	
4	48	42	37	43	
5	46	53	39	64	

Scores range from 1-99, with 50 the average. A school scoring 75 has done better than 75 percent of other public schools in the U.S. **Key:** Rd (Reading), Ma (Math), Lg (Language), Sp (Spelling), Sci (Science)

Grade	Rd	Ma	Lg	Sp	Sci	Grade	Rd	Ma	Lg	Sp	Sci
Elmhurst Middle						**Harte Middle**					
6	13	12	10	29		6	26	27	23	46	
7	12	12	14	29		7	33	33	34	45	
8	17	16	19	30		8	36	41	34	52	
Emerson Elem.						**Havenscourt Middle**					
2	39	62	47	62		6	10	8	9	23	
3	28	41	31	64		7	13	16	15	34	
4	6	11	13	28		8	20	21	20	28	
5	13	11	18	26		**Hawthorne Elem.**					
Far West (Cont.)						2	15	26	9	21	
9	22	22	18		16	3	14	24	14	25	
10	30	17	31		26	4	14	28	17	28	
11	20	29	14		12	5	23	30	22	33	
Foster Elem.						**Highland Elem.**					
2	19	20	17	24		2	10	15	5	13	
3	8	12	11	28		3	7	18	8	19	
4	8	8	10	32		4	9	9	8	23	
5	13	18	12	38		5	14	13	19	28	
Franklin Elem.						**Hillcrest Elem.**					
2	23	58	21	46		2	80	85	76	76	
3	31	67	28	61		3	87	90	84	81	
4	20	38	19	47		4	85	95	91	89	
5	22	31	20	41		5	84	84	86	62	
Fremont Sr. High						6	87	78	85	58	
9	14	15	15		9	7	81	82	81	60	
10	10	16	14		11	8	76	66	71	85	
11	16	20	17		11	**Hoover Elem.**					
Frick Middle						2	38	45	47	64	
6	15	14	12	28		3	16	33	22	40	
7	18	19	22	30		4	14	28	17	37	
8	23	18	27	28		5	21	24	18	30	
Fruitvale Elem.						**Howard Elem.**					
2	41	65	56	66		2	44	56	56	70	
3	24	40	28	60		3	41	50	46	65	
4	25	44	30	59		4	35	38	44	56	
5	33	33	35	63		5	30	37	20	60	
Garfield Elem.						**Huerta Learning Acad.**					
2	26	57	32	45		2	5	32	19	12	
3	17	38	18	40		3	6	8	3	8	
4	13	26	17	37		4	16	32	14	21	
5	17	25	16	33		5	15	21	14	33	
Glenview Elem.						6	14	11	15	32	
2	42	72	50	73		7	19	29	12	40	
3	58	68	52	72		8	21	40	28	32	
4	38	35	41	50		**International Comm.**					
5	43	49	40	56		2	25	63	17	12	
Golden Gate Elem.						3	20	30	14	29	
2	33	31	21	75		4	25	61	41	50	
3	17	19	18	49		5	19	21	16	29	
4	15	23	22	47		**Jefferson Elem.**					
5	20	23	19	27		2	16	26	14	21	
Grass Valley Elem.						3	13	25	13	23	
2	43	63	51	53		4	11	12	12	19	
3	51	68	49	76		5	15	16	12	28	
4	53	56	41	74							
5	39	63	34	53							

Scores range from 1-99, with 50 the national average. A school scoring 75 has done better than 75 percent of other public schools in the U.S. **Key:** Rd (Reading), Ma (Math), Lg (Language), Sp (Spelling), Sci (Science)

Kaiser Elem.

Grade	Rd	Ma	Lg	Sp	Sci
2	70	77	73	82	
3	56	83	49	65	
4	62	67	61	58	
5	55	63	61	61	
7	27	38	24	46	

King

Grade	Rd	Ma	Lg	Sp	Sci
2	19	14	17	41	
3	26	30	20	57	

King Estates Middle

Grade	Rd	Ma	Lg	Sp	Sci
6	23	16	18	44	
7	22	16	24	38	
8	19	16	19	23	

KIPP

Grade	Rd	Ma	Lg	Sp	Sci
5	17	20	19	40	

La Escuelita Elem.

Grade	Rd	Ma	Lg	Sp	Sci
2	23	43	37	38	
3	22	43	21	50	
4	19	37	20	48	
5	48	56	49	63	

Lafayette Elem.

Grade	Rd	Ma	Lg	Sp	Sci
2	39	51	41	59	
3	24	26	21	40	
4	16	15	18	37	
5	22	27	16	37	

Lakeview Elem.

Grade	Rd	Ma	Lg	Sp	Sci
2	41	42	42	73	
3	36	36	31	62	
4	26	16	23	65	
5	23	18	20	46	

Laney Middle

Grade	Rd	Ma	Lg	Sp	Sci
6	11	13	15	22	
7	5	5	7	20	
8	10	10	10	28	
9	25	23	19		18
10	32	18	33		23

Laurel Elem.

Grade	Rd	Ma	Lg	Sp	Sci
2	38	62	36	76	
3	33	62	31	70	
4	35	58	45	73	
5	30	34	35	64	

Lazear Elem.

Grade	Rd	Ma	Lg	Sp	Sci
2	28	44	19	34	
3	23	39	27	35	
4	19	25	16	30	
5	21	22	19	33	

LIFE Acad.

Grade	Rd	Ma	Lg	Sp	Sci
9	20	28	19		21
10	29	25	27		32
11	29	25	27		26

Lighthouse

Grade	Rd	Ma	Lg	Sp	Sci
6	26	20	22	37	

Lincoln Elem.

Grade	Rd	Ma	Lg	Sp	Sci
2	67	92	81	93	
3	41	80	42	83	
4	45	76	51	83	
5	52	79	58	73	

Lionel Wilson College Prep.

Grade	Rd	Ma	Lg	Sp	Sci
6	26	37	24	30	
7	9	20	14	35	
8	13	12	11	11	
9	18	17	18		11
10	21	18	24		29

Lockwood Elem.

Grade	Rd	Ma	Lg	Sp	Sci
2	17	54	22	32	
3	12	25	13	40	
4	12	22	12	24	
5	11	16	10	27	

Longfellow Elem.

Grade	Rd	Ma	Lg	Sp	Sci
2	21	16	20	50	
3	24	22	25	67	
4	16	6	24	49	
5	21	20	15	15	

Lowell Middle

Grade	Rd	Ma	Lg	Sp	Sci
6	12	14	10	28	
7	15	16	17	30	
8	20	18	16	31	

Madison Middle

Grade	Rd	Ma	Lg	Sp	Sci
6	15	9	15	23	
7	20	18	22	29	
8	17	13	20	22	

Mann Elem.

Grade	Rd	Ma	Lg	Sp	Sci
2	14	18	19	37	
3	24	37	20	51	
4	12	16	15	21	
5	22	22	20	41	

Manzanita Elem.

Grade	Rd	Ma	Lg	Sp	Sci
2	32	44	30	49	
3	18	30	17	40	
4	15	23	16	37	
5	16	17	14	29	

Markham Elem.

Grade	Rd	Ma	Lg	Sp	Sci
2	21	39	20	22	
3	21	44	24	39	
4	21	32	24	39	
5	23	18	23	38	

Marshall Elem.

Grade	Rd	Ma	Lg	Sp	Sci
2	40	27	45	70	
3	47	49	44	64	
4	42	42	55	62	
5	45	39	44	45	

Maxwell Park Elem.

Grade	Rd	Ma	Lg	Sp	Sci
2	29	17	29	44	
3	20	32	21	47	
4	13	21	16	34	
5	27	26	25	39	

McClymonds Sr. High

Grade	Rd	Ma	Lg	Sp	Sci
9	19	13	14		12
10	17	19	20		15
11	14	14	20		12

Melrose Elem.

Grade	Rd	Ma	Lg	Sp	Sci
2	15	25	10	16	
3	10	21	11	18	
4	12	30	15	16	
5	22	28	22	28	

Scores range from 1-99, with 50 the average. A school scoring 75 has done better than 75 percent of other public schools in the U.S. **Key:** Rd (Reading), Ma (Math), Lg (Language), Sp (Spelling), Sci (Science)

Melrose Leadership Acad.

Grade	Rd	Ma	Lg	Sp	Sci
6	15	17	15	19	
7	30	25	29	34	

Merritt Middle College High

Grade	Rd	Ma	Lg	Sp	Sci
8	10	8	7	19	
9	9	17	12		12
10	12	8	12		11
11	14	11	14		22

Miller Elem.

Grade	Rd	Ma	Lg	Sp	Sci
2	72	94	80	82	
3	76	88	71	77	
4	72	71	69	75	
5	65	70	67	69	

Monarch Acad.

Grade	Rd	Ma	Lg	Sp	Sci
2	27	39	29	33	
3	15	48	21	26	
4	18	31	22	34	
5	21	47	28	47	

Montclair Elem.

Grade	Rd	Ma	Lg	Sp	Sci
2	79	92	80	78	
3	62	82	57	60	
4	71	85	72	71	
5	86	84	89	82	

Montera Middle

Grade	Rd	Ma	Lg	Sp	Sci
6	53	54	61	53	
7	69	61	69	52	
8	48	55	52	55	

Munck Elem.

Grade	Rd	Ma	Lg	Sp	Sci
2	58	72	58	73	
3	28	50	38	60	
4	45	45	40	54	
5	23	27	14	37	

North Oakland Charter

Grade	Rd	Ma	Lg	Sp	Sci
2	68	82	50	51	

Oakland Charter Acad.

Grade	Rd	Ma	Lg	Sp	Sci
6	23	37	22	37	
7	27	33	25	45	
8	19	17	16	23	

Oakland School

Grade	Rd	Ma	Lg	Sp	Sci
9	71	58	76		54

Oakland Sr. High

Grade	Rd	Ma	Lg	Sp	Sci
9	26	34	27		21
10	22	40	26		21
11	30	39	33		31

Oakland Technical Sr. High

Grade	Rd	Ma	Lg	Sp	Sci
9	24	27	24		16
10	23	38	32		29
11	27	44	34		29

Parker Elem.

Grade	Rd	Ma	Lg	Sp	Sci
2	17	23	16	41	
3	26	44	20	59	
4	11	15	9	24	
5	24	37	25	37	

Peralta Elem.

Grade	Rd	Ma	Lg	Sp	Sci
2	68	63	72	73	
3	43	60	54	62	
4	48	62	37	67	
5	33	47	32	39	

Piedmont Ave. Elem.

Grade	Rd	Ma	Lg	Sp	Sci
2	36	46	31	49	
3	42	58	39	61	
4	26	43	24	48	
5	40	41	41	50	

Prescott Elem.

Grade	Rd	Ma	Lg	Sp	Sci
2	33	56	36	37	
3	16	31	15	30	
4	10	14	12	31	
5	19	23	21	35	

Ralph Bunche Acad.

Grade	Rd	Ma	Lg	Sp	Sci
8	13	12	10	15	

Redwood Heights Elem.

Grade	Rd	Ma	Lg	Sp	Sci
2	72	90	73	76	
3	71	93	79	87	
4	61	66	68	68	
5	63	56	64	63	

Reems Acad.

Grade	Rd	Ma	Lg	Sp	Sci
2	20	26	32	36	
3	29	33	23	40	
4	20	16	15	29	
5	24	15	22	31	
6	15	16	18	18	
7	22	20	17	40	
8	34	37	25	32	

Roosevelt Middle

Grade	Rd	Ma	Lg	Sp	Sci
6	25	32	22	41	
7	19	31	20	40	
8	30	47	29	45	

Rudsdale Acad.

Grade	Rd	Ma	Lg	Sp	Sci
8	11	11	9	19	

Santa Fe Elem.

Grade	Rd	Ma	Lg	Sp	Sci
2	43	33	48	62	
3	28	34	33	56	
4	14	25	19	33	
5	20	25	17	34	

School of Social Justice Comm.

Grade	Rd	Ma	Lg	Sp	Sci
9	14	21	20		18
10	14	11	11		19
11	7	17	12		7

Sequoia Elem.

Grade	Rd	Ma	Lg	Sp	Sci
2	35	33	32	63	
3	24	32	26	55	
4	44	47	49	46	
5	42	39	40	35	

Sherman Elem.

Grade	Rd	Ma	Lg	Sp	Sci
2	35	29	33	54	
3	20	33	24	50	
4	19	17	17	27	
5	17	21	12	31	

Simmons Middle

Grade	Rd	Ma	Lg	Sp	Sci
6	11	10	9	23	
7	10	14	12	27	
8	13	16	12	21	

Skyline High

Grade	Rd	Ma	Lg	Sp	Sci
9	38	42	38		24
10	31	42	39		29
11	37	49	38		35

Scores range from 1-99, with 50 the national average. A school scoring 75 has done better than 75 percent of other public schools in the U.S. **Key:** Rd (Reading), Ma (Math), Lg (Language), Sp (Spelling), Sci (Science)

Sobrante Park Elem.

Grade	Rd	Ma	Lg	Sp	Sci
2	29	40	33	34	
3	15	24	17	37	
4	10	5	9	21	
5	16	12	12	40	

Street Acad. (Alt.)

Grade	Rd	Ma	Lg	Sp	Sci
9	27	27	29		23
10	23	20	29		32
11	35	25	36		32

Stonehurst Elem.

Grade	Rd	Ma	Lg	Sp	Sci
2	19	22	10	16	
3	22	42	21	30	
4	14	22	19	36	
5	18	32	15	34	

Swett Elem.

Grade	Rd	Ma	Lg	Sp	Sci
2	32	60	43	61	
3	23	31	21	57	
4	22	23	15	52	
5	22	16	19	30	
6	23	22	22	47	
7	13	22	20	41	
8	38	35	30	32	

Thornhill Elem.

Grade	Rd	Ma	Lg	Sp	Sci
2	86	95	86	84	
3	76	85	80	78	
4	80	83	88	78	
5	81	90	84	72	

Toler Heights Elem.

Grade	Rd	Ma	Lg	Sp	Sci
2	29	39	33	65	
3	12	29	8	23	
4	12	18	12	30	
5	31	39	34	48	

University Prep.

Grade	Rd	Ma	Lg	Sp	Sci
9	33	33	32		21
10	71	84	74		61

Urban Promise

Grade	Rd	Ma	Lg	Sp	Sci
6	27	12	16	34	
7	30	28	36	33	

Washington Elem.

Grade	Rd	Ma	Lg	Sp	Sci
2	43	40	63	66	
3	67	66	64	60	
4	11	16	15	34	
5	33	27	30	41	

Webster Acad. (K-6)

Grade	Rd	Ma	Lg	Sp	Sci
2	18	38	15	23	
3	13	28	12	26	
4	16	23	19	37	
5	11	12	11	25	

West Oakland Comm.

Grade	Rd	Ma	Lg	Sp	Sci
6	44	42	44	40	

Westlake Middle

Grade	Rd	Ma	Lg	Sp	Sci
6	24	28	23	34	
7	24	38	25	39	
8	29	39	33	35	

Whittier Elem.

Grade	Rd	Ma	Lg	Sp	Sci
2	15	30	8	17	
3	7	12	9	18	
4	12	18	15	35	
5	15	21	18	35	

Woodland Elem.

Grade	Rd	Ma	Lg	Sp	Sci
2	20	26	17	16	
3	11	29	12	17	
4	5	14	8	15	
5	4	10	5	16	

Piedmont City Unified School Dist.

Beach Elem.

Grade	Rd	Ma	Lg	Sp	Sci
2	86	90	88	80	
3	80	90	82	80	
4	91	90	85	78	
5	82	87	88	78	

Havens Elem.

Grade	Rd	Ma	Lg	Sp	Sci
2	80	94	78	66	
3	85	87	77	72	
4	81	90	85	85	
5	75	83	86	70	

Piedmont High

Grade	Rd	Ma	Lg	Sp	Sci
9	81	89	87		90
10	89	91	94		94
11	91	96	93		96

Piedmont Middle

Grade	Rd	Ma	Lg	Sp	Sci
6	84	84	89	76	
7	88	88	89	75	
8	83	88	86	86	

Wildwood Elem.

Grade	Rd	Ma	Lg	Sp	Sci
2	82	93	76	66	
3	77	77	71	65	
4	79	83	92	76	
5	76	78	88	72	

Pleasanton Unified School Dist.

Alisal Elem.

Grade	Rd	Ma	Lg	Sp	Sci
2	65	80	66	70	
3	65	81	63	77	
4	70	79	79	83	
5	68	72	73	66	

Amador Valley High

Grade	Rd	Ma	Lg	Sp	Sci
9	75	81	75		70
10	66	73	75		66
11	66	80	68		65

Donlon Elem.

Grade	Rd	Ma	Lg	Sp	Sci
2	84	91	78	79	
3	66	76	62	69	
4	75	79	82	77	
5	73	74	82	72	

Fairlands Elem.

Grade	Rd	Ma	Lg	Sp	Sci
2	74	93	78	77	
3	73	84	74	80	
4	66	69	68	78	
5	68	65	72	62	

Foothill High

Grade	Rd	Ma	Lg	Sp	Sci
9	75	81	74		70
10	72	78	80		73
11	63	72	67		68

Scores range from 1-99, with 50 the average. A school scoring 75 has done better than 75 percent of other public schools in the U.S. **Key:** Rd (Reading), Ma (Math), Lg (Language), Sp (Spelling), Sci (Science)

Hart Middle

Grade	Rd	Ma	Lg	Sp	Sci
6	77	85	80	70	
7	83	80	84	78	
8	76	78	76	85	

Harvest Park Int.

Grade	Rd	Ma	Lg	Sp	Sci
6	73	76	77	70	
7	75	73	78	77	
8	72	72	73	83	

Hearst Elem.

Grade	Rd	Ma	Lg	Sp	Sci
2	75	87	77	71	
3	70	87	68	74	
4	71	82	82	79	
5	81	82	86	77	

Lydiksen Elem.

Grade	Rd	Ma	Lg	Sp	Sci
2	70	86	74	72	
3	65	87	66	72	
4	69	81	76	79	
5	68	77	72	65	

Mohr Elem.

Grade	Rd	Ma	Lg	Sp	Sci
2	79	95	83	83	
3	76	90	78	82	
4	71	79	76	84	
5	82	92	84	80	

Pleasanton Middle

Grade	Rd	Ma	Lg	Sp	Sci
6	75	79	77	69	
7	81	79	82	74	
8	72	76	73	78	

Valley View Elem.

Grade	Rd	Ma	Lg	Sp	Sci
2	77	93	80	70	
3	69	80	62	69	
4	69	82	71	70	
5	78	81	79	65	

Village High

Grade	Rd	Ma	Lg	Sp	Sci
10	35	29	37		32
11	43	32	35		35

Vintage Hills Elem.

Grade	Rd	Ma	Lg	Sp	Sci
2	77	93	81	83	
3	70	88	72	78	
4	78	82	77	83	
5	74	87	82	67	

Walnut Grove Elem.

Grade	Rd	Ma	Lg	Sp	Sci
2	82	92	76	76	
3	71	81	69	69	
4	76	80	79	74	
5	80	89	85	77	

San Leandro Unified School Dist.

Bancroft Middle

Grade	Rd	Ma	Lg	Sp	Sci
6	40	35	42	44	
7	48	40	47	48	
8	42	35	40	40	

Garfield Elem.

Grade	Rd	Ma	Lg	Sp	Sci
2	44	50	47	42	
3	27	39	29	53	
4	33	37	34	48	
5	33	33	40	50	

Jefferson Elem.

Grade	Rd	Ma	Lg	Sp	Sci
2	37	46	34	48	
3	29	50	38	48	
4	25	37	29	48	
5	35	35	35	50	

Lincoln High (Cont.)

Grade	Rd	Ma	Lg	Sp	Sci
10	13	20	11		17
11	19	21	20		20

Madison Elem.

Grade	Rd	Ma	Lg	Sp	Sci
2	44	52	48	59	
3	41	51	41	60	
4	41	47	47	68	
5	43	34	43	45	

McKinley Elem.

Grade	Rd	Ma	Lg	Sp	Sci
2	43	58	51	52	
3	39	67	41	69	
4	38	52	40	53	
5	26	33	34	45	

Monroe Elem.

Grade	Rd	Ma	Lg	Sp	Sci
2	33	61	51	46	
3	34	57	33	51	
4	42	55	48	53	
5	35	42	42	48	

Muir Middle

Grade	Rd	Ma	Lg	Sp	Sci
6	40	40	39	47	
7	36	42	38	46	
8	41	40	39	47	

Roosevelt Elem.

Grade	Rd	Ma	Lg	Sp	Sci
2	63	73	67	75	
3	41	51	42	51	
4	59	69	68	72	
5	55	62	63	48	

San Leandro Charter

Grade	Rd	Ma	Lg	Sp	Sci
2	39	49	37	40	
3	23	40	37	51	
4	38	49	47	50	

San Leandro High

Grade	Rd	Ma	Lg	Sp	Sci
9	43	50	45		39
10	29	46	35		32
11	30	45	37		32

Washington Elem.

Grade	Rd	Ma	Lg	Sp	Sci
2	40	74	47	44	
3	27	37	26	33	
4	23	25	22	27	
5	36	35	37	32	

Wilson Elem.

Grade	Rd	Ma	Lg	Sp	Sci
2	36	46	38	41	
3	24	40	26	44	
4	27	35	33	46	
5	34	39	39	43	

San Lorenzo Unified School Dist.

Arroyo High

Grade	Rd	Ma	Lg	Sp	Sci
9	46	54	47		48
10	42	48	49		49
11	38	52	42		45

Scores range from 1-99, with 50 the national average. A school scoring 75 has done better than 75 percent of other public schools in the U.S. **Key:** Rd (Reading), Ma (Math), Lg (Language), Sp (Spelling), Sci (Science)

Bay Elem.

Grade	Rd	Ma	Lg	Sp	Sci
2	55	81	64	66	
3	36	66	34	55	
4	42	52	52	59	
5	39	53	43	55	

Bohannon Middle

Grade	Rd	Ma	Lg	Sp	Sci
6	33	37	37	43	
7	43	43	43	38	
8	43	39	38	41	

Colonial Acres Elem.

Grade	Rd	Ma	Lg	Sp	Sci
2	33	41	26	49	
3	21	33	25	33	
4	28	37	36	45	
5	28	37	30	41	

Corvallis Elem.

Grade	Rd	Ma	Lg	Sp	Sci
2	40	57	44	56	
3	39	58	48	59	
4	27	43	33	44	
5	36	43	47	53	

Dayton Elem.

Grade	Rd	Ma	Lg	Sp	Sci
2	48	79	47	64	
3	29	50	33	58	
4	39	61	48	70	
5	37	44	42	50	

Del Rey Elem.

Grade	Rd	Ma	Lg	Sp	Sci
2	37	46	42	43	
3	23	39	25	30	
4	37	44	35	49	
5	33	44	39	51	

Edendale Middle

Grade	Rd	Ma	Lg	Sp	Sci
6	21	30	20	37	
7	30	34	30	33	
8	28	34	26	31	

Grant Elem.

Grade	Rd	Ma	Lg	Sp	Sci
2	56	77	58	50	
3	36	49	32	49	
4	34	37	33	53	
5	29	43	30	50	

Hesperian Elem.

Grade	Rd	Ma	Lg	Sp	Sci
2	31	61	29	34	
3	22	37	25	42	
4	20	26	20	45	
5	18	26	23	36	

Hillside Elem.

Grade	Rd	Ma	Lg	Sp	Sci
2	32	33	27	38	
3	24	38	25	44	
4	19	26	17	36	
5	19	20	19	41	

Lorenzo Manor Elem.

Grade	Rd	Ma	Lg	Sp	Sci
2	31	43	30	31	
3	31	47	28	36	
4	28	34	28	47	
5	26	31	26	35	

Royal Sunset (Cont.)

Grade	Rd	Ma	Lg	Sp	Sci
9	24	15	11		19
10	5	5	6		5
11	14	15	11		16

San Lorenzo High

Grade	Rd	Ma	Lg	Sp	Sci
9	29	34	29		31
10	32	41	33		39
11	31	34	30		33

Washington Manor Middle

Grade	Rd	Ma	Lg	Sp	Sci
6	41	53	44	52	
7	43	49	46	46	
8	48	58	47	60	

Sunol Glen Unified School Dist.

B.A.S.I.S.

Grade	Rd	Ma	Lg	Sp	Sci
2	72	72	48	69	
3	49	47	39	37	
4	45	48	48	29	
5	46	36	32	41	
6	69	59	74	67	
7	58	42	54	47	
8	59	37	60	44	
9	64	51	55		50
10	49	31	57		34
11	34	27	47		12

Sunol Glen Elem.

Grade	Rd	Ma	Lg	Sp	Sci
2	56	58	56	51	
3	57	68	64	56	
4	65	77	71	77	
5	79	68	82	67	
6	62	75	73	57	
7	71	62	70	56	
8	78	75	67	83	

Chapter 2b

State School Rankings

• What do these numbers mean?

These percentile rankings, drawn from the scores on the 2003 STAR test, compare California schools and grades, one against the other.

Grades two to eleven were tested. Elementary pupils were tested in reading, math, language and spelling. High school students were tested in reading, math, language and science. We have coded the subjects as follows: reading (Rd), math (Ma), language (Lg), spelling (Sp) and science (Sci).

If a school scores in the 91st percentile, it has done better than 91 percent of the other public schools in the state. If it scores in the 51st percentile, it has done better than 51 percent of the others; the 40th rank, better than 40 percent of the others. If a school scores in the first percentile, 99 percent of the other schools have scored higher.

• How do these numbers differ from the rankings in Chapter 2.

The results broken out in Chapter 2 are based on a comparison against a national norm or standard where the national average is 50.

Although the results in Chapter 2b are based on the same data as the results in Chapter 2, the Chapter 2b approach presents the results in a different way. Chapter 2b isolates California schools and simply ranks them one against the other, without regard to a national standard. These scores have no "average." Readers should interpret the Chapter 2b scores as a rough measure of how California schools compare against one another.

• Do the numbers in this chapter tell whether California education is improving?

No. Ranking systems don't recognize overall gains or losses. If every school in California raised raw scores 20 percent, some schools would still be ranked at the bottom, a few at the top. The same if every raw score dropped. A ranking system shows how one school did against all other schools.

Scores range from 1-99. A school scoring 75 has done better than 75 percent of other public schools in California.

Key: Rd (Reading), Ma (Math), Lg (Language), Sp (Spelling), Sci (Science)

Alameda City Unified School Dist.

Alameda High

Grade	Rd	Ma	Lg	Sp	Sci
9	68	77	70		76
10	72	87	81		77
11	72	90	78		85

Andersen Comm. Learning

Grade	Rd	Ma	Lg	Sp	Sci
7	93	91	94	98	
8	80	67	86	82	
9	97	93	99		95
10	94	92	96		90
11	98	97	98		98

Bay Area School

Grade	Rd	Ma	Lg	Sp	Sci
9	87	66	77		65
10	91	23	68		38

Bay Farm Elem.

Grade	Rd	Ma	Lg	Sp	Sci
2	98	95	96	96	
3	93	98	96	96	
4	92	89	90	91	
5	97	97	94	98	
6	99	91	97	84	

Chipman Middle

Grade	Rd	Ma	Lg	Sp	Sci
6	36	29	33	51	
7	35	37	40	45	
8	40	28	43	38	

Earhart Elem.

Grade	Rd	Ma	Lg	Sp	Sci
2	87	90	92	90	
3	90	80	90	89	
4	92	98	94	96	
5	92	96	90	95	
6	93	87	95	83	

Edison Elem.

Grade	Rd	Ma	Lg	Sp	Sci
2	99	96	96	94	
3	96	78	93	91	
4	80	67	72	83	
5	92	85	89	77	

Encinal High

Grade	Rd	Ma	Lg	Sp	Sci
9	70	72	74		64
10	62	57	58		50
11	65	58	66		61

Franklin Elem.

Grade	Rd	Ma	Lg	Sp	Sci
2	90	86	80	69	
3	82	74	86	78	
4	65	60	62	68	
5	94	75	83	66	

Haight Elem.

Grade	Rd	Ma	Lg	Sp	Sci
2	54	40	45	66	
3	62	54	52	76	
4	65	60	50	67	
5	50	48	46	68	

Island High (Cont.)

Grade	Rd	Ma	Lg	Sp	Sci
11	15	5	22		31

Lincoln Middle

Grade	Rd	Ma	Lg	Sp	Sci
6	83	86	89	90	
7	81	85	85	96	
8	73	76	80	90	

Longfellow Elem.

Grade	Rd	Ma	Lg	Sp	Sci
2	47	44	66	73	
3	32	36	36	48	
4	37	26	30	47	
5	59	75	48	75	

Lum Elem.

Grade	Rd	Ma	Lg	Sp	Sci
2	74	74	79	95	
3	65	77	66	89	
4	67	79	58	89	
5	63	74	55	73	

Miller Elem.

Grade	Rd	Ma	Lg	Sp	Sci
2	57	76	60	66	
3	45	68	61	41	
4	77	82	66	84	
5	37	24	46	70	

Otis Elem.

Grade	Rd	Ma	Lg	Sp	Sci
2	69	77	58	71	
3	80	68	74	73	
4	85	89	86	87	
5	79	70	80	89	

Paden Elem.

Grade	Rd	Ma	Lg	Sp	Sci
2	84	68	86	82	
3	71	74	71	70	
4	72	40	56	53	
5	73	72	80	84	
6	55	54	71	73	
7	52	52	58	77	
8	87	82	75	96	

Washington Elem.

Grade	Rd	Ma	Lg	Sp	Sci
2	33	20	20	34	
3	61	73	66	82	
4	62	52	52	79	
5	33	36	55	78	

Wood Middle

Grade	Rd	Ma	Lg	Sp	Sci
6	48	47	48	73	
7	53	49	54	83	
8	50	54	57	77	

Woodstock Elem.

Grade	Rd	Ma	Lg	Sp	Sci
2	41	40	47	68	
3	32	29	42	65	
4	49	50	45	65	
5	42	65	42	46	

Alameda Co. Off. of Education

Alt./Opportunity

Grade	Rd	Ma	Lg	Sp	Sci
9	10		28		
10	18	9	24		1
11	31	9	29		20

Juvenile Hall/Court

Grade	Rd	Ma	Lg	Sp	Sci
8	6	2	4	4	
9	4	5	6		1
10	9	5	7		5
11	2	5	3		2

Scores range from 1-99. A school scoring 75 has done better than 75 percent of other public schools in California.
Key: Rd (Reading), Ma (Math), Lg (Language), Sp (Spelling), Sci (Science)

Albany City Unified School Dist.

Albany High
Grade	Rd	Ma	Lg	Sp	Sci
9	97	96	98		97
10	94	98	96		96
11	95	97	94		97

Albany Middle
Grade	Rd	Ma	Lg	Sp	Sci
6	95	93	97	95	
7	94	95	95	93	
8	92	95	96	90	

Cornell Elem.
Grade	Rd	Ma	Lg	Sp	Sci
2	79	77	69	78	
3	93	90	92	86	
4	89	86	93	90	
5	90	84	92	87	

MacGregor High (Cont.)
Grade	Rd	Ma	Lg	Sp	Sci
11	29	18	15		27

Marin Elem.
Grade	Rd	Ma	Lg	Sp	Sci
2	98	95	93	85	
3	99	96	95	87	
4	94	81	96	83	
5	96	80	96	91	

Ocean View Elem.
Grade	Rd	Ma	Lg	Sp	Sci
2	91	84	89	85	
3	91	92	93	87	
4	95	85	96	95	
5	97	93	94	96	

Berkeley Unified School Dist.

Berkeley Alt.
Grade	Rd	Ma	Lg	Sp	Sci
9	6	1	9		
10	23		22		

Berkeley High
Grade	Rd	Ma	Lg	Sp	Sci
9	67	75	77		59
10	80	86	87		85
11	93	97	96		98

Cragmont Elem.
Grade	Rd	Ma	Lg	Sp	Sci
2	74	92	75	34	
3	61	62	76	34	
4	66	57	60	76	
5	59	34	66	52	

Emerson Elem.
Grade	Rd	Ma	Lg	Sp	Sci
2	86	66	72	73	
3	68	65	79	64	
4	84	70	77	76	
5	79	91	90	52	

Jefferson Elem.
Grade	Rd	Ma	Lg	Sp	Sci
2	76	77	61	52	
3	78	78	66	78	
4	97	86	97	87	
5	61	45	51	50	

King Middle
Grade	Rd	Ma	Lg	Sp	Sci
6	68	49	69	61	
7	64	61	62	65	
8	74	65	73	71	

Leconte Elem.
Grade	Rd	Ma	Lg	Sp	Sci
2	36	44	38	26	
3	76	56	56	59	
4	89	64	70	70	
5	61	55	72	26	

Longfellow Arts & Tech
Grade	Rd	Ma	Lg	Sp	Sci
6	50	47	44	48	
7	59	62	68	73	
8	59	67	67	86	

Malcolm X Elem.
Grade	Rd	Ma	Lg	Sp	Sci
2	51	40	43	39	
3	76	80	83	50	
4	63	57	55	41	
5	35	26	29	23	

Muir Elem.
Grade	Rd	Ma	Lg	Sp	Sci
2	67	63	81	75	
3	73	76	85	68	
4	90	89	81	92	
5	42	70	55	68	

Oxford Elem.
Grade	Rd	Ma	Lg	Sp	Sci
2	86	64	93	71	
3	78	74	71	62	
4	81	71	79	49	
5	63	88	74	52	

Parks Magnet
Grade	Rd	Ma	Lg	Sp	Sci
2	34	53	26	20	
3	30	26	30	29	
4	12	20	15	20	
5	9	21	23	29	

Thousand Oaks Elem.
Grade	Rd	Ma	Lg	Sp	Sci
2	41	58	40	36	
3	37	56	50	26	
4	57	53	50	57	
5	28	66	38	36	

Washington Elem.
Grade	Rd	Ma	Lg	Sp	Sci
2	67	58	45	57	
3	54	42	54	48	
4	48	70	42	31	
5	40	63	55	52	

Whittier/Arts Elem.
Grade	Rd	Ma	Lg	Sp	Sci
2	69	38	76	60	
3	52	42	63	56	
4	76	68	81	85	
5	61	60	53	87	
6	97	83	95	97	

Willard Middle
Grade	Rd	Ma	Lg	Sp	Sci
6	56	35	50	38	
7	67	57	62	72	
8	47	40	49	52	

Calif. School for the Deaf

Calif School for the Deaf
Grade	Rd	Ma	Lg	Sp	Sci
2	1	1	1	20	
3	1	1	1	26	
4	1	1	1	1	
5	1	3	2	3	
6	1	1	1	5	
7	2	1	1	2	
8	2	3	5	8	
9	1	3	8		
10	9	14	7		
11	1	6	1		5

Scores range from 1-99. A school scoring 75 has done better than 75 percent of other public schools in California.

Key: Rd (Reading), Ma (Math), Lg (Language), Sp (Spelling), Sci (Science)

Castro Valley Unified School Dist.

Canyon Middle

Grade	Rd	Ma	Lg	Sp	Sci
6	81	83	84	85	
7	83	85	82	79	
8	69	71	75	80	

Castro Valley Elem.

Grade	Rd	Ma	Lg	Sp	Sci
2	51	58	58	69	
3	52	68	60	65	
4	62	73	66	76	
5	63	72	64	57	

Castro Valley High

Grade	Rd	Ma	Lg	Sp	Sci
9	75	82	79		91
10	77	88	82		87
11	82	92	87		91

Chabot Elem.

Grade	Rd	Ma	Lg	Sp	Sci
2	86	84	81	76	
3	93	88	91	79	
4	81	81	73	76	
5	80	90	85	73	

Creekside Middle

Grade	Rd	Ma	Lg	Sp	Sci
6	87	86	87	87	
7	89	93	89	77	
8	77	81	81	85	

Independent Elem.

Grade	Rd	Ma	Lg	Sp	Sci
2	86	90	94	89	
3	85	83	92	82	
4	93	97	94	98	
5	96	93	97	97	

Jensen Ranch Elem.

Grade	Rd	Ma	Lg	Sp	Sci
2	94	98	98	97	
3	96	99	98	95	
4	96	97	96	98	
5	98	99	98	99	

Marshall Elem.

Grade	Rd	Ma	Lg	Sp	Sci
2	43	40	43	52	
3	79	78	83	81	
4	85	88	84	87	
5	86	91	91	77	

Palomares Elem.

Grade	Rd	Ma	Lg	Sp	Sci
2	66	77	82	55	
3	79	86	88	82	
4	91	89	83	95	

Proctor Elem.

Grade	Rd	Ma	Lg	Sp	Sci
2	83	74	86	78	
3	93	90	95	89	
4	88	94	89	76	
5	92	89	96	88	

Redwood Alt. (Cont.)

Grade	Rd	Ma	Lg	Sp	Sci
9	35	34	21		23
10	23	31	27		29
11	15	32	17		16

Stanton Elem.

Grade	Rd	Ma	Lg	Sp	Sci
2	57	81	71	52	
3	80	73	84	82	
4	65	84	70	74	
5	66	72	71	64	

Vannoy Elem.

Grade	Rd	Ma	Lg	Sp	Sci
2	92	86	84	75	
3	94	86	91	81	
4	90	89	86	83	
5	95	94	97	89	

Dublin Unified School Dist.

Dougherty Elem.

Grade	Rd	Ma	Lg	Sp	Sci
2	93	92	99	98	
3	96	92	94	98	
4	97	99	96	99	
5	89	91	90	93	

Dublin Elem.

Grade	Rd	Ma	Lg	Sp	Sci
2	79	79	89	71	
3	94	84	90	86	
4	82	64	77	70	
5	83	82	86	78	

Dublin High

Grade	Rd	Ma	Lg	Sp	Sci
9	87	92	88		86
10	87	91	88		87
11	92	93	92		90

Frederiksen Elem.

Grade	Rd	Ma	Lg	Sp	Sci
2	66	72	72	75	
3	74	71	80	73	
4	84	80	88	70	
5	78	87	87	78	

Murray Elem.

Grade	Rd	Ma	Lg	Sp	Sci
2	74	72	65	73	
3	71	82	68	91	
4	95	81	87	88	
5	86	80	84	81	

Nielsen Elem.

Grade	Rd	Ma	Lg	Sp	Sci
2	77	77	75	67	
3	62	78	68	56	
4	84	74	89	79	
5	88	56	84	87	

Valley High (Cont.)

Grade	Rd	Ma	Lg	Sp	Sci
10	37	21	42		49
11	36	26	20		44

Wells Middle

Grade	Rd	Ma	Lg	Sp	Sci
6	87	78	87	87	
7	80	81	84	89	
8	86	88	88	84	

Emery Unified School Dist.

Anna Yates Elem.

Grade	Rd	Ma	Lg	Sp	Sci
2	49	22	34	79	
3	28	13	36	48	
4	36	29	25	65	
5	37	29	38	60	

Emery High

Grade	Rd	Ma	Lg	Sp	Sci
9	23	22	29		15
10	25	15	32		21
11	36	39	40		25

Emery Middle

Grade	Rd	Ma	Lg	Sp	Sci
6	18	14	12	48	
7	44	11	56	66	
8	46	8	59	71	

Scores range from 1-99. A school scoring 75 has done better than 75 percent of other public schools in California.
Key: Rd (Reading), Ma (Math), Lg (Language), Sp (Spelling), Sci (Science)

Fremont Unified School Dist.

American High

Grade	Rd	Ma	Lg	Sp	Sci
9	80	84	81		83
10	85	90	87		89
11	80	89	85		84

Ardenwood Elem.

Grade	Rd	Ma	Lg	Sp	Sci
2	60	70	68	94	
3	80	96	92	97	
4	87	97	94	99	
5	86	93	93	96	
6	88	95	94	98	

Azeveda Elem.

Grade	Rd	Ma	Lg	Sp	Sci
2	76	38	66	62	
3	54	47	56	82	
4	37	34	40	70	
5	74	88	79	85	
6	75	87	79	88	

Blacow Elem.

Grade	Rd	Ma	Lg	Sp	Sci
2	4	36	10	15	
3	42	39	38	62	
4	54	62	58	45	
5	52	65	46	42	
6	68	69	67	82	

Brier Elem.

Grade	Rd	Ma	Lg	Sp	Sci
2	77	72	72	88	
3	64	78	66	81	
4	66	60	72	72	
5	40	48	48	57	
6	59	75	57	70	

Brookvale Elem.

Grade	Rd	Ma	Lg	Sp	Sci
2	69	84	74	76	
3	58	65	68	65	
4	84	85	81	91	
5	80	83	93	93	
6	68	72	69	88	

Cabrillo Elem.

Grade	Rd	Ma	Lg	Sp	Sci
2	43	12	34	52	
3	14	6	4	32	
4	31	29	25	56	
5	23	31	33	34	
6	48	49	40	70	

Centerville Jr. High

Grade	Rd	Ma	Lg	Sp	Sci
7	80	83	84	87	
8	74	79	82	78	

Chadbourne Elem.

Grade	Rd	Ma	Lg	Sp	Sci
2	98	99	99	99	
3	97	99	99	99	
4	94	98	98	99	
5	99	99	99	99	
6	95	98	98	99	

Circle of Independent Learning

Grade	Rd	Ma	Lg	Sp	Sci
5	97	60	91	81	
6	83	82	89	79	
7	97	83	90	95	
8	67	33	73	69	
9	59	59	49		60
10	72	42	68		65

Durham Elem.

Grade	Rd	Ma	Lg	Sp	Sci
2	74	79	75	90	
3	42	56	42	65	
4	59	73	73	72	
5	59	58	51	55	
6	42	78	59	85	

Forest Park Elem.

Grade	Rd	Ma	Lg	Sp	Sci
2	93	97	96	99	
3	86	98	96	99	
4	89	96	96	99	
5	83	93	91	97	
6	95	98	99	99	

Glenmoor Elem.

Grade	Rd	Ma	Lg	Sp	Sci
2	86	64	82	90	
3	61	63	63	79	
4	82	86	88	92	
5	73	85	79	75	
6	63	75	61	77	

Gomes Elem.

Grade	Rd	Ma	Lg	Sp	Sci
2	98	99	99	99	
3	98	99	99	99	
4	98	99	99	99	
5	99	99	99	99	
6	99	99	99	99	

Green Elem.

Grade	Rd	Ma	Lg	Sp	Sci
2	62	34	41	60	
3	59	56	42	84	
4	74	77	67	76	
5	63	45	46	64	
6	50	39	35	43	

Grimmer Elem.

Grade	Rd	Ma	Lg	Sp	Sci
2	21	36	13	10	
3	4	15	4	6	
4	15	14	19	10	
5	27	31	33	12	
6	57	62	61	73	

Hirsch Elem.

Grade	Rd	Ma	Lg	Sp	Sci
2	62	56	67	69	
3	49	67	61	86	
4	63	76	62	87	
5	69	78	69	80	
6	71	79	80	90	

Hopkins Jr. High

Grade	Rd	Ma	Lg	Sp	Sci
7	98	99	99	99	
8	98	99	99	99	

Horner Jr. High

Grade	Rd	Ma	Lg	Sp	Sci
7	77	90	85	90	
8	79	87	83	92	

Irvington High

Grade	Rd	Ma	Lg	Sp	Sci
9	73	80	76		76
10	81	91	82		82
11	82	90	85		89

Kennedy High

Grade	Rd	Ma	Lg	Sp	Sci
9	52	68	56		52
10	72	79	71		68
11	83	92	85		84

Leitch Elem.

Grade	Rd	Ma	Lg	Sp	Sci
2	86	90	91	97	

Scores range from 1-99. A school scoring 75 has done better than 75 percent of other public schools in California.

Key: Rd (Reading), Ma (Math), Lg (Language), Sp (Spelling), Sci (Science)

Maloney Elem.

Grade	Rd	Ma	Lg	Sp	Sci
2	68	67	78	92	
3	62	82	63	91	
4	57	62	74	83	
5	71	72	72	78	
6	66	80	79	89	

Mattos Elem.

Grade	Rd	Ma	Lg	Sp	Sci
2	60	62	51	76	
3	65	62	73	85	
4	43	28	56	56	
5	78	77	75	64	
6	73	79	61	70	

Millard Elem.

Grade	Rd	Ma	Lg	Sp	Sci
2	72	82	75	75	
3	70	88	84	89	
4	57	67	69	77	
5	71	75	78	80	
6	50	58	59	77	

Mission San Jose Elem.

Grade	Rd	Ma	Lg	Sp	Sci
2	98	99	99	99	
3	96	98	99	99	
4	99	99	99	99	
5	98	99	99	99	
6	99	99	99	99	

Mission San Jose High

Grade	Rd	Ma	Lg	Sp	Sci
9	99	99	99		99
10	99	99	99		99
11	99	99	99		99

Mission Valley Elem.

Grade	Rd	Ma	Lg	Sp	Sci
2	96	98	99	99	
3	96	99	98	99	
4	95	98	97	99	
5	97	99	98	99	
6	97	98	98	99	

Niles Elem.

Grade	Rd	Ma	Lg	Sp	Sci
2	88	87	89	94	
3	81	84	86	89	
4	86	92	92	94	
5	88	80	81	81	
6	86	87	84	92	

Oliveira Elem.

Grade	Rd	Ma	Lg	Sp	Sci
2	74	47	63	88	
3	35	52	42	59	
4	48	60	47	57	
5	23	51	53	64	
6	78	72	74	77	

Parkmont Elem.

Grade	Rd	Ma	Lg	Sp	Sci
2	93	94	98	94	
3	90	96	95	97	
4	90	90	91	88	
5	82	85	81	89	
6	79	91	90	95	

Patterson Elem.

Grade	Rd	Ma	Lg	Sp	Sci
2	62	58	66	78	
3	47	63	60	73	
4	70	62	76	77	
5	56	50	68	62	
6	71	66	71	77	

Robertson High (Cont.)

Grade	Rd	Ma	Lg	Sp	Sci
9	28	26	33		34
10	23	23	22		33
11	39	19	25		13

Thornton Jr. High

Grade	Rd	Ma	Lg	Sp	Sci
7	66	78	75	86	
8	79	88	82	92	

Vallejo Mill Elem.

Grade	Rd	Ma	Lg	Sp	Sci
2	79	79	82	85	
3	59	83	66	79	
4	66	59	66	70	
5	78	68	85	88	
6	86	72	84	87	

Walters Jr. High

Grade	Rd	Ma	Lg	Sp	Sci
7	59	63	67	66	
8	62	54	63	60	

Warm Springs Elem.

Grade	Rd	Ma	Lg	Sp	Sci
3	91	96	96	99	
4	88	94	91	98	
5	93	97	93	96	
6	89	94	90	98	

Warwick Elem.

Grade	Rd	Ma	Lg	Sp	Sci
2	77	79	82	91	
3	64	71	69	93	
4	85	86	90	94	
5	75	82	82	93	
6	64	79	65	94	

Washington High

Grade	Rd	Ma	Lg	Sp	Sci
9	81	83	81		81
10	87	92	90		86
11	88	90	86		83

Weibel Elem.

Grade	Rd	Ma	Lg	Sp	Sci
2	97	97	99	99	
3	95	99	98	99	
4	98	99	99	99	
5	98	99	99	99	
6	99	99	99	99	

Hayward Unified School Dist.

Bowman Elem.

Grade	Rd	Ma	Lg	Sp	Sci
2	15	25	13	13	
3	32	38	34	41	
4	21	23	22	23	
5	16	17	28	48	
6	40	23	31	17	

Brenkwitz High (Cont.)

Grade	Rd	Ma	Lg	Sp	Sci
10	3	5	7		1
11	5	3	1		1

Bret Harte Middle

Grade	Rd	Ma	Lg	Sp	Sci
7	44	37	48	39	
8	46	40	43	67	

Burbank Elem.

Grade	Rd	Ma	Lg	Sp	Sci
2	18	40	13	11	
3	7	31	3	2	
4	15	37	11	23	
5	9	17	14	14	
6	26	25	15	33	

Scores range from 1-99. A school scoring 75 has done better than 75 percent of other public schools in California.
Key: Rd (Reading), Ma (Math), Lg (Language), Sp (Spelling), Sci (Science)

Grade	Rd	Ma	Lg	Sp	Sci
Chavez Middle					
7	22	23	25	33	
8	26	22	20	29	
Cherryland Elem.					
2	18	29	23	8	
3	7	8	13	9	
4	10	24	11	12	
5	6	21	22	26	
6	18	15	19	17	
East Ave. Elem.					
2	64	74	72	71	
3	81	88	76	64	
4	70	84	81	70	
5	42	60	38	72	
6	40	45	54	35	
Eden Gardens Elem.					
2	45	29	33	57	
3	40	38	40	45	
4	31	39	33	43	
5	31	39	33	77	
6	27	22	19	53	
Eldridge Elem.					
2	62	74	65	64	
3	45	65	60	48	
4	67	80	62	63	
5	42	56	46	57	
6	52	63	62	55	
Fairview Elem.					
2	27	20	38	61	
3	32	36	46	34	
4	43	15	37	47	
5	17	8	20	57	
6	46	45	54	61	
Glassbrook Elem.					
2	12	27	11	10	
3	10	22	18	5	
Harder Elem.					
2	15	40	11	8	
3	7	15	8	21	
4	30	31	24	20	
5	17	28	23	39	
6	36	27	31	48	
Hayward High					
9	35	43	39		26
10	41	57	44		58
11	33	46	35		34
Hayward Project Elem.					
2	8	7	6	4	
3	23	6	28	12	
4	15	16	19	33	
5	56	31	53	34	
6	56	38	69	68	
7	58	51	67	36	
8	48	28	53	32	
Highland Elem.					
2	66	79	82	57	
3	21	19	32	45	
4	62	68	62	57	
5	80	66	81	75	
6	75	50	71	79	

Grade	Rd	Ma	Lg	Sp	Sci
King Middle					
7	17	23	25	33	
8	35	31	35	38	
Longwood Elem.					
2	25	46	34	39	
3	23	17	13	13	
4	14	9	11	20	
5	17	15	14	26	
6	23	20	25	18	
Lorin A. Eden Elem.					
2	27	38	31	34	
3	30	38	30	41	
4	49	59	58	70	
5	23	33	34	34	
6	42	45	35	55	
Markham Elem.					
2	27	49	34	31	
3	19	17	28	24	
4	22	23	13	23	
5	18	8	22	11	
6	14	20	13	18	
Mt. Eden High					
9	35	47	39		34
10	33	56	37		41
11	31	42	33		34
Muir Elem.					
2	8	12	13	16	
3	9	10	10	4	
4	39	59	42	37	
5	9	15	3	19	
6	42	38	56	35	
Ochoa Middle					
7	34	36	36	50	
8	27	26	33	45	
Palma Ceia Elem.					
2	25	44	55	52	
3	37	54	46	56	
4	39	53	42	83	
5	28	20	18	52	
6	21	17	19	58	
Park Elem.					
2	27	27	17	13	
3	21	13	16	13	
4	36	31	25	27	
5	18	6	9	26	
6	17	15	15	23	
Ruus Elem.					
2	15	23	26	26	
3	30	33	26	38	
4	22	3	13	12	
5	13	15	23	29	
6	8	12	5	9	
Schafer Park Elem.					
2	34	34	34	44	
3	35	47	46	23	
4	18	16	32	25	
5	13	45	12	19	
6	31	35	33	58	

Scores range from 1-99. A school scoring 75 has done better than 75 percent of other public schools in California.

Key: Rd (Reading), Ma (Math), Lg (Language), Sp (Spelling), Sci (Science)

Shepherd Elem.

Grade	Rd	Ma	Lg	Sp	Sci
2	2	20	4	2	
3	10	10	8	4	

Southgate Elem.

Grade	Rd	Ma	Lg	Sp	Sci
2	41	49	45	60	
3	32	19	34	56	
4	34	33	37	51	
5	31	29	33	36	
6	52	39	46	65	

Strobridge Elem.

Grade	Rd	Ma	Lg	Sp	Sci
2	36	13	17	11	
3	42	33	50	59	
4	49	42	60	72	
5	28	28	18	42	
6	40	15	44	31	

Tennyson High

Grade	Rd	Ma	Lg	Sp	Sci
9	15	29	19		13
10	16	29	16		18
11	16	32	19		20

Treeview Elem.

Grade	Rd	Ma	Lg	Sp	Sci
2	59	49	49	51	
3	39	38	34	41	
4	39	38	33	33	
5	52	45	60	66	
6	50	43	54	46	

Tyrrell Elem.

Grade	Rd	Ma	Lg	Sp	Sci
4	22	21	15	13	
5	13	24	7	18	
6	18	25	30	21	

Winton Middle

Grade	Rd	Ma	Lg	Sp	Sci
7	15	30	15	17	
8	23	26	23	13	

Livermore Valley Jt. Unified School Dist.

Almond Ave. Elem.

Grade	Rd	Ma	Lg	Sp	Sci
2	90	90	86	78	
3	87	90	83	87	
4	98	91	95	91	
5	98	97	95	92	

Altamont Creek Elem.

Grade	Rd	Ma	Lg	Sp	Sci
2	83	87	80	71	
3	74	74	68	56	
4	86	83	84	80	
5	79	63	68	62	

Arroyo Mocho Elem.

Grade	Rd	Ma	Lg	Sp	Sci
2	86	84	93	76	
3	96	94	97	86	
4	86	90	92	84	
5	83	85	75	85	

Arroyo Seco Elem.

Grade	Rd	Ma	Lg	Sp	Sci
2	87	76	84	79	
3	86	87	85	87	
4	91	86	91	84	
5	87	89	90	77	

Christensen Middle

Grade	Rd	Ma	Lg	Sp	Sci
6	72	68	78	74	
7	67	70	67	79	
8	77	81	75	89	

Croce Elem.

Grade	Rd	Ma	Lg	Sp	Sci
2	79	82	82	76	
3	77	70	76	79	
4	72	76	72	76	
5	78	66	75	78	

Del Valle Cont. High

Grade	Rd	Ma	Lg	Sp	Sci
11	25	44	31		43

East Ave. Middle

Grade	Rd	Ma	Lg	Sp	Sci
6	79	76	78	79	
7	70	76	72	88	
8	81	89	81	92	

Granada High

Grade	Rd	Ma	Lg	Sp	Sci
9	87	88	88		86
10	93	93	92		93
11	91	93	90		92

Jackson Ave. Elem.

Grade	Rd	Ma	Lg	Sp	Sci
2	74	70	61	79	
3	77	88	74	65	
4	66	52	72	80	
5	83	75	86	55	

Junction Ave. Middle

Grade	Rd	Ma	Lg	Sp	Sci
6	50	33	48	35	
7	60	61	63	82	
8	62	65	63	73	

Livermore High

Grade	Rd	Ma	Lg	Sp	Sci
9	77	82	79		82
10	82	84	84		81
11	72	83	83		81

Marylin Ave. Elem.

Grade	Rd	Ma	Lg	Sp	Sci
2	18	19	16	16	
3	44	29	40	52	
4	43	29	42	39	
5	50	26	42	12	

Michell Elem.

Grade	Rd	Ma	Lg	Sp	Sci
2	66	44	55	43	
3	50	56	58	59	
4	62	61	65	63	
5	66	63	76	64	

Phoenix High (Cont.)

Grade	Rd	Ma	Lg	Sp	Sci
10	14	28	11		9
11	23	11	25		20

Portola Elem.

Grade	Rd	Ma	Lg	Sp	Sci
2	27	23	13	11	
3	42	54	38	26	
4	46	50	52	35	
5	59	36	55	21	

Rancho Las Positas Elem.

Grade	Rd	Ma	Lg	Sp	Sci
2	71	77	60	44	
3	86	83	77	76	
4	66	68	70	67	
5	71	73	68	48	

Smith Elem.

Grade	Rd	Ma	Lg	Sp	Sci
2	94	88	84	68	
3	85	88	84	70	
4	81	73	81	80	
5	93	92	93	84	

Scores range from 1-99. A school scoring 75 has done better than 75 percent of other public schools in California.
Key: Rd (Reading), Ma (Math), Lg (Language), Sp (Spelling), Sci (Science)

Sunset Elem.

Grade	Rd	Ma	Lg	Sp	Sci
2	88	86	87	88	
3	91	83	92	89	
4	92	86	92	88	
5	93	90	94	89	

Vineyard Alt.

Grade	Rd	Ma	Lg	Sp	Sci
7	89	87	91	98	
8	27	33	25	45	
9	37	66	49		50
10	58	45	35		50
11	49	51	53		46

William Mendenhall Middle

Grade	Rd	Ma	Lg	Sp	Sci
6	82	76	85	80	
7	90	88	87	83	
8	89	88	86	92	

New Haven USD (Union City)

Alvarado Elem.

Grade	Rd	Ma	Lg	Sp	Sci
2	28	46	33	39	
3	44	77	46	54	
4	52	68	50	57	
5	46	56	44	57	

Alvarado Middle

Grade	Rd	Ma	Lg	Sp	Sci
6	53	65	56	72	
7	54	72	69	77	
8	65	74	70	67	

Barnard-White Middle

Grade	Rd	Ma	Lg	Sp	Sci
6	31	50	26	33	
7	35	45	34	33	
8	48	56	49	43	

Cabello Elem.

Grade	Rd	Ma	Lg	Sp	Sci
2	45	62	45	56	
3	35	82	40	59	
4	49	77	47	56	
5	52	72	50	64	

Chavez Middle

Grade	Rd	Ma	Lg	Sp	Sci
6	56	65	50	63	
7	50	74	52	72	
8	59	67	59	71	

Eastin Elem.

Grade	Rd	Ma	Lg	Sp	Sci
2	81	93	86	78	
3	70	92	80	81	
4	70	84	79	86	
5	68	88	79	80	

Emanuele Elem.

Grade	Rd	Ma	Lg	Sp	Sci
2	43	63	43	43	
3	40	74	40	43	
4	39	50	33	31	
5	33	43	31	46	

Hillview Crest Elem.

Grade	Rd	Ma	Lg	Sp	Sci
2	31	54	27	24	
3	52	70	48	26	
4	36	53	47	25	
5	44	56	46	43	

James Logan High

Grade	Rd	Ma	Lg	Sp	Sci
9	63	74	63		62
10	75	85	74		73
11	78	86	78		78

Kitayama Elem.

Grade	Rd	Ma	Lg	Sp	Sci
2	62	72	68	68	
3	61	83	61	69	
4	68	80	72	70	
5	64	78	69	66	

Pioneer Elem.

Grade	Rd	Ma	Lg	Sp	Sci
2	72	74	74	91	
3	77	87	83	93	
4	76	86	74	81	
5	86	95	89	94	

Searles Elem.

Grade	Rd	Ma	Lg	Sp	Sci
2	54	36	40	52	
3	58	78	68	52	
4	34	39	42	35	
5	55	70	55	52	

Newark Unified School Dist.

Bridgepoint High (Cont.)

Grade	Rd	Ma	Lg	Sp	Sci
10	24	45	32		62
11	29	20	29		34

Bunker Elem.

Grade	Rd	Ma	Lg	Sp	Sci
2	59	62	61	73	
3	65	74	68	72	
4	73	70	80	65	
5	40	36	38	60	
6	53	59	56	51	

Crossroads High (Alt.)

Grade	Rd	Ma	Lg	Sp	Sci
10	21	14	27		33
11	36	15	29		37

Graham Elem.

Grade	Rd	Ma	Lg	Sp	Sci
2	27	51	41	38	
3	44	38	38	40	
4	15	28	24	20	
5	37	46	33	48	
6	40	59	44	36	

Kennedy Elem.

Grade	Rd	Ma	Lg	Sp	Sci
2	60	54	61	57	
3	76	68	74	65	
4	79	67	84	80	
5	82	75	79	73	
6	83	80	81	87	

Lincoln Elem.

Grade	Rd	Ma	Lg	Sp	Sci
2	45	67	43	34	
3	59	58	58	72	
4	74	80	76	80	
5	44	72	58	55	
6	53	52	57	72	

Milani Elem.

Grade	Rd	Ma	Lg	Sp	Sci
2	28	62	38	38	
3	30	42	21	42	
4	43	67	43	80	
5	40	43	46	43	
6	59	69	54	55	

Musick Elem.

Grade	Rd	Ma	Lg	Sp	Sci
2	49	56	38	39	
3	35	56	48	70	
4	57	48	48	63	
5	42	36	38	70	
6	52	60	42	65	

Scores range from 1-99. A school scoring 75 has done better than 75 percent of other public schools in California.

Key: Rd (Reading), Ma (Math), Lg (Language), Sp (Spelling), Sci (Science)

Grade	Rd	Ma	Lg	Sp	Sci
Newark Jr. High					
7	38	55	40	39	
8	39	56	41	43	
Newark Memorial High					
9	61	71	63		78
10	61	68	63		77
11	43	61	51		68
Schilling Elem.					
2	28	27	41	38	
3	50	63	44	56	
4	25	7	11	8	
5	16	26	23	21	
6	56	62	52	53	
Snow Elem.					
2	62	64	60	55	
3	59	65	61	50	
4	68	55	58	43	
5	61	58	63	66	
6	70	89	79	58	

Oakland Military

Grade	Rd	Ma	Lg	Sp	Sci
Oakland Military					
7	35	17	27	36	
8	42	35	49	47	

Oakland Unified School Dist.

Grade	Rd	Ma	Lg	Sp	Sci
Allendale Elem.					
2	15	29	17	24	
3	19	17	28	48	
4	10	9	19	45	
5	9	5	7	31	
American Indian Public Charter					
6	66	75	69	51	
7	52	44	65	77	
8	31	49	35	62	
9	81	78	78		76
Arts (Alt.)					
5	33	10	36	26	
6	10	4	9	5	
7	50	17	52	4	
8	26	11	22	25	
ASCEND					
3	9	28	23	17	
5	50	72	30	40	
6	15	41	23	23	
7	41	44	32	36	
Bella Vista Elem.					
2	41	58	38	88	
3	30	50	34	76	
4	15	31	17	65	
5	27	46	20	72	
Brewer Middle					
6	21	17	17	29	
7	20	29	25	36	
8	23	35	27	38	

Grade	Rd	Ma	Lg	Sp	Sci
Brookfield Village Elem.					
2	18	14	17	17	
3	10	12	16	17	
4	10	6	3	20	
5	9	5	11	14	
Burbank Elem.					
2	3	4	4	8	
3	2	1	11	21	
4	6	1	1	7	
5	2	8	3	29	
Burchhalter Elem.					
2	99	97	98	99	
3	54	84	64	91	
4	63	88	77	92	
5	18	18	7	18	
Carter Middle					
6	3	4	3	7	
7	8	4	7	6	
8	21	16	13	32	
Castlemont Sr. High					
9	7	16	9		13
10	9	18	9		21
11	6	26	8		19
Chabot Elem.					
2	92	81	87	87	
3	94	92	95	87	
4	99	89	97	92	
5	96	84	95	94	
Claremont Middle					
6	27	21	35	41	
7	43	31	44	55	
8	41	30	39	56	
Cleveland Elem.					
2	86	97	97	99	
3	70	88	79	94	
4	54	76	63	79	
5	50	63	51	62	
Cole Elem.					
4	4	2	9	20	
5	16	5	11	14	
6	3	2	2	8	
7	9	4	7	10	
8	17	8	12	21	
Cox Elem.					
2	3	3	3	7	
3	14	9	13	32	
4	2	4	3	14	
5	5	6	3	31	
Crocker Highlands Elem.					
2	94	76	85	89	
3	97	87	96	82	
4	96	91	91	72	
5	80	73	78	70	
Dewey/Baymart Sr. High					
9	3	3	4		3
10	9	2	7		6
11	2	1	4		1

Scores range from 1-99. A school scoring 75 has done better than 75 percent of other public schools in California.

Key: Rd (Reading), Ma (Math), Lg (Language), Sp (Spelling), Sci (Science)

E. Bay Consv. Corps Charter

Grade	Rd	Ma	Lg	Sp	Sci
2	18	29	13	34	
3	59	33	56	23	
4	68	39	47	35	
5	59	61	44	85	

Elmhurst Middle

Grade	Rd	Ma	Lg	Sp	Sci
6	2	2	2	9	
7	4	3	4	8	
8	8	7	10	17	

Emerson Elem.

Grade	Rd	Ma	Lg	Sp	Sci
2	41	53	53	71	
3	32	24	36	73	
4	1	1	3	8	
5	2	1	7	8	

Far West (Cont.)

Grade	Rd	Ma	Lg	Sp	Sci
9	23	25	20		15
10	43	25	38		33
11	25	39	16		10

Foster Elem.

Grade	Rd	Ma	Lg	Sp	Sci
2	5	2	6	10	
3	1	1	2	8	
4	1	1	1	14	
5	2	3	2	34	

Franklin Elem.

Grade	Rd	Ma	Lg	Sp	Sci
2	11	46	11	43	
3	39	67	30	69	
4	18	31	11	43	
5	16	21	11	43	

Fremont Sr. High

Grade	Rd	Ma	Lg	Sp	Sci
9	13	16	17		6
10	15	23	18		10
11	20	26	20		8

Frick Middle

Grade	Rd	Ma	Lg	Sp	Sci
6	3	3	2	8	
7	8	7	12	10	
8	15	9	22	13	

Fruitvale Elem.

Grade	Rd	Ma	Lg	Sp	Sci
2	45	58	66	76	
3	23	22	30	65	
4	30	42	33	67	
5	37	26	38	84	

Garfield Elem.

Grade	Rd	Ma	Lg	Sp	Sci
2	15	44	27	42	
3	9	19	10	26	
4	4	10	7	23	
5	6	11	5	21	

Glenview Elem.

Grade	Rd	Ma	Lg	Sp	Sci
2	47	68	58	87	
3	79	68	73	87	
4	54	26	53	49	
5	56	55	46	73	

Golden Gate Elem.

Grade	Rd	Ma	Lg	Sp	Sci
2	29	8	11	89	
3	9	2	10	43	
4	7	7	17	43	
5	12	8	9	9	

Grass Valley Elem.

Grade	Rd	Ma	Lg	Sp	Sci
2	49	54	60	56	
3	70	68	68	93	
4	74	61	53	89	
5	50	76	36	68	

Harte Middle

Grade	Rd	Ma	Lg	Sp	Sci
6	17	15	15	46	
7	30	29	32	47	
8	36	43	37	60	

Havenscourt Middle

Grade	Rd	Ma	Lg	Sp	Sci
6	1	1	1	3	
7	4	4	4	17	
8	10	12	11	14	

Hawthorne Elem.

Grade	Rd	Ma	Lg	Sp	Sci
2	3	4	1	7	
3	4	3	4	5	
4	6	14	7	8	
5	18	20	14	21	

Highland Elem.

Grade	Rd	Ma	Lg	Sp	Sci
2	1	1	1	2	
3	1	1	1	2	
4	1	1	1	4	
5	3	1	9	11	

Hillcrest Elem.

Grade	Rd	Ma	Lg	Sp	Sci
2	97	88	93	90	
3	99	96	99	97	
4	99	99	99	99	
5	98	95	97	82	
6	99	88	98	74	
7	96	96	96	83	
8	97	84	94	97	

Hoover Elem.

Grade	Rd	Ma	Lg	Sp	Sci
2	38	25	53	73	
3	7	12	18	26	
4	6	14	7	23	
5	13	10	7	14	

Howard Elem.

Grade	Rd	Ma	Lg	Sp	Sci
2	51	42	66	82	
3	56	39	61	76	
4	48	31	56	61	
5	31	33	11	80	

Huerta Learning Acad.

Grade	Rd	Ma	Lg	Sp	Sci
2	1	9	8	2	
3	1	1	1	1	
4	10	21	4	3	
5	4	6	3	21	
6	3	2	4	14	
7	9	21	3	33	
8	12	41	23	21	

International Comm.

Grade	Rd	Ma	Lg	Sp	Sci
2	14	55	6	2	
3	14	8	4	9	
4	30	68	53	49	
5	10	6	5	12	

Jefferson Elem.

Grade	Rd	Ma	Lg	Sp	Sci
2	3	4	5	7	
3	3	4	4	4	
4	2	1	2	2	
5	4	2	2	11	

Scores range from 1-99. A school scoring 75 has done better than 75 percent of other public schools in California.

Key: Rd (Reading), Ma (Math), Lg (Language), Sp (Spelling), Sci (Science)

Kaiser Elem.

Grade	Rd	Ma	Lg	Sp	Sci
2	88	76	89	95	
3	76	90	68	76	
4	85	76	78	65	
5	74	76	76	81	
7	19	37	14	51	

King

Grade	Rd	Ma	Lg	Sp	Sci
2	5	1	6	34	
3	28	8	13	61	

King Estates Middle

Grade	Rd	Ma	Lg	Sp	Sci
6	12	4	7	41	
7	13	4	14	26	
8	10	7	10	8	

KIPP

Grade	Rd	Ma	Lg	Sp	Sci
5	6	6	9	40	

La Escuelita Elem.

Grade	Rd	Ma	Lg	Sp	Sci
2	11	22	36	29	
3	19	28	16	45	
4	15	29	13	45	
5	63	66	60	84	

Lafayette Elem.

Grade	Rd	Ma	Lg	Sp	Sci
2	41	34	41	66	
3	23	5	16	26	
4	10	2	9	23	
5	16	15	5	31	

Lakeview Elem.

Grade	Rd	Ma	Lg	Sp	Sci
2	45	20	43	87	
3	47	16	36	70	
4	31	2	19	76	
5	18	3	11	55	

Laney Middle

Grade	Rd	Ma	Lg	Sp	Sci
6	2	2	4	3	
7	2	1	2	3	
8	4	4	4	14	
9	26	26	22		18
10	47	27	42		29

Laurel Elem.

Grade	Rd	Ma	Lg	Sp	Sci
2	38	53	34	90	
3	42	60	36	85	
4	48	64	58	88	
5	31	28	38	85	

Lazear Elem.

Grade	Rd	Ma	Lg	Sp	Sci
2	20	23	8	23	
3	21	20	28	17	
4	15	9	5	12	
5	13	8	9	21	

LIFE Acad.

Grade	Rd	Ma	Lg	Sp	Sci
9	20	33	21		23
10	42	36	33		44
11	40	34	36		34

Lighthouse

Grade	Rd	Ma	Lg	Sp	Sci
6	17	7	13	25	

Lincoln Elem.

Grade	Rd	Ma	Lg	Sp	Sci
2	84	96	97	99	
3	56	86	56	98	
4	65	86	67	96	
5	69	91	72	94	

Lionel Wilson College Prep.

Grade	Rd	Ma	Lg	Sp	Sci
6	17	29	17	11	
7	3	8	4	20	
8	5	5	5	2	
9	17	18	20		9
10	30	27	30		39

Lockwood Elem.

Grade	Rd	Ma	Lg	Sp	Sci
2	4	40	13	19	
3	2	4	4	26	
4	3	6	2	5	
5	1	2	1	9	

Longfellow Elem.

Grade	Rd	Ma	Lg	Sp	Sci
2	8	1	10	51	
3	23	2	23	79	
4	10	1	22	47	
5	13	6	4	1	

Lowell Middle

Grade	Rd	Ma	Lg	Sp	Sci
6	2	3	2	8	
7	5	4	6	10	
8	10	9	7	19	

Madison Middle

Grade	Rd	Ma	Lg	Sp	Sci
6	3	1	4	3	
7	11	6	12	8	
8	8	5	11	7	

Mann Elem.

Grade	Rd	Ma	Lg	Sp	Sci
2	2	1	8	27	
3	23	17	13	48	
4	3	2	4	3	
5	16	8	11	43	

Manzanita Elem.

Grade	Rd	Ma	Lg	Sp	Sci
2	27	23	24	49	
3	10	8	8	26	
4	7	7	5	23	
5	5	3	3	12	

Markham Elem.

Grade	Rd	Ma	Lg	Sp	Sci
2	8	16	10	8	
3	17	29	21	24	
4	21	21	22	27	
5	18	3	17	34	

Marshall Elem.

Grade	Rd	Ma	Lg	Sp	Sci
2	43	5	49	83	
3	64	38	60	73	
4	60	39	72	72	
5	58	36	53	52	

Maxwell Park Elem.

Grade	Rd	Ma	Lg	Sp	Sci
2	21	1	23	39	
3	14	10	16	40	
4	4	5	5	17	
5	27	13	20	37	

McClymonds Sr. High

Grade	Rd	Ma	Lg	Sp	Sci
9	19	13	16		11
10	25	28	26		16
11	16	14	25		10

Melrose Elem.

Grade	Rd	Ma	Lg	Sp	Sci
2	3	4	1	3	
3	1	2	2	2	
4	3	16	4	1	
5	16	17	14	11	

Scores range from 1-99. A school scoring 75 has done better than 75 percent of other public schools in California.
Key: Rd (Reading), Ma (Math), Lg (Language), Sp (Spelling), Sci (Science)

Grade	Rd	Ma	Lg	Sp	Sci
Melrose Leadership Acad.					
6	3	4	4	2	
7	24	14	22	17	
Merritt Middle College High					
8	4	3	3	5	
9	9	18	14		10
10	17	7	14		10
11	16	7	16		27
Miller Elem.					
2	91	97	96	95	
3	96	95	93	93	
4	93	81	87	90	
5	86	84	82	91	
Monarch Acad.					
2	18	16	23	20	
3	6	36	16	6	
4	14	20	17	17	
5	13	51	26	57	
Montclair Elem.					
2	96	96	96	92	
3	84	88	79	65	
4	93	95	89	86	
5	99	95	98	98	
Montera Middle					
6	68	57	78	63	
7	84	76	88	68	
8	60	68	72	66	
Munck Elem.					
2	72	68	69	87	
3	32	39	48	65	
4	65	44	52	57	
5	18	15	3	31	
North Oakland Charter					
2	86	84	58	52	
Oakland Charter Acad.					
6	12	29	13	25	
7	20	29	15	47	
8	10	8	7	8	
Oakland School					
9	93	77	96		76
Oakland Sr. High					
9	28	40	31		23
10	32	57	33		26
11	41	54	44		43
Oakland Technical Sr. High					
9	25	31	28		15
10	33	54	40		39
11	36	62	45		40
Parker Elem.					
2	4	3	6	34	
3	28	29	13	64	
4	2	2	1	5	
5	20	33	20	31	
Peralta Elem.					
2	86	55	88	87	
3	59	56	74	70	
4	68	70	47	79	
5	37	51	33	37	

Grade	Rd	Ma	Lg	Sp	Sci
Piedmont Ave. Elem.					
2	34	27	26	49	
3	58	52	50	69	
4	31	40	22	45	
5	52	41	48	62	
Prescott Elem.					
2	29	42	34	27	
3	7	9	6	10	
4	2	1	2	13	
5	10	8	12	26	
Ralph Bunche Acad.					
8	5	5	5	3	
Redwood Heights Elem.					
2	91	94	89	90	
3	93	98	97	99	
4	84	74	86	81	
5	83	66	79	84	
Reems Acad.					
2	7	4	27	26	
3	35	12	19	26	
4	18	2	4	10	
5	20	2	14	18	
6	3	4	7	2	
7	13	8	6	33	
8	33	37	17	21	
Roosevelt Middle					
6	15	22	13	33	
7	9	25	9	33	
8	26	54	25	47	
Rudsdale Acad.					
8	4	4	4	5	
Santa Fe Elem.					
2	49	10	55	71	
3	32	13	40	59	
4	6	9	11	15	
5	12	11	6	24	
School of Social Justice Comm.					
9	13	22	23		18
10	21	14	13		23
11	5	20	12		3
Sequoia Elem.					
2	33	10	27	72	
3	23	10	26	56	
4	63	47	65	41	
5	55	36	46	26	
Sherman Elem.					
2	33	6	29	57	
3	14	12	21	45	
4	15	3	7	8	
5	6	6	2	18	
Simmons Middle					
6	2	2	1	3	
7	3	3	3	7	
8	5	7	5	6	
Skyline High					
9	47	53	49		28
10	46	59	50		39
11	54	69	53		52

Scores range from 1-99. A school scoring 75 has done better than 75 percent of other public schools in California.

Key: Rd (Reading), Ma (Math), Lg (Language), Sp (Spelling), Sci (Science)

Grade	Rd	Ma	Lg	Sp	Sci
Sobrante Park Elem.					
2	21	18	29	23	
3	6	3	8	21	
4	2	1	1	3	
5	5	1	2	40	
St. Acad. (Alt.)					
9	29	31	34		26
10	33	29	36		44
11	51	34	50		46
Stonehurst Elem.					
2	5	3	2	3	
3	19	26	16	10	
4	6	6	11	20	
5	8	24	4	24	
Swett Elem.					
2	27	49	45	69	
3	21	9	16	61	
4	22	7	4	54	
5	16	2	9	14	
6	11	9	13	48	
7	4	10	9	36	
8	40	33	27	21	
Thornhill Elem.					
2	99	98	99	97	
3	96	92	98	94	
4	97	93	98	92	
5	97	98	96	94	
Toler Heights Elem.					
2	21	16	29	75	
3	2	7	1	4	
4	3	3	2	12	
5	33	36	36	60	
University Prep.					
9	39	39	39		23
10	94	97	92		85
Urban Promise					
6	18	2	5	18	
7	24	18	36	14	
Washington Elem.					
2	49	18	76	76	
3	89	65	88	65	
4	2	2	4	17	
5	37	15	29	43	
Webster Acad.					
2	5	14	5	8	
3	3	6	3	6	
4	10	7	11	23	
5	1	1	1	6	
West Oakland Comm.					
6	52	38	54	31	
Westlake Middle					
6	14	17	16	18	
7	15	37	15	28	
8	25	40	35	27	
Whittier Elem.					
2	3	7	1	4	
3	1	1	1	2	
4	3	3	4	18	
5	4	6	7	26	

Grade	Rd	Ma	Lg	Sp	Sci
Woodland Elem.					
2	7	4	6	3	
3	2	7	3	1	
4	1	2	1	1	
5	1	1	1	1	

Piedmont City Unified School Dist.

Grade	Rd	Ma	Lg	Sp	Sci
Beach Elem.					
2	99	94	99	94	
3	98	96	98	96	
4	99	97	97	92	
5	98	97	98	97	
Havens Elem.					
2	97	97	95	76	
3	99	94	97	87	
4	98	97	97	97	
5	95	94	97	92	
Piedmont High					
9	98	98	99		99
10	99	99	99		99
11	99	99	99		99
Piedmont Middle					
6	99	94	99	96	
7	99	98	98	96	
8	99	99	99	98	
Wildwood Elem.					
2	98	97	93	76	
3	97	82	93	76	
4	97	93	99	91	
5	95	91	98	94	

Pleasanton Unified School Dist.

Grade	Rd	Ma	Lg	Sp	Sci
Alisal Elem.					
2	83	81	80	83	
3	87	87	86	93	
4	92	90	94	96	
5	89	85	88	88	
Amador Valley High					
9	95	95	95		93
10	91	93	93		90
11	93	96	93		91
Donlon Elem.					
2	99	95	95	93	
3	88	81	85	82	
4	95	89	96	92	
5	93	88	94	94	
Fairlands Elem.					
2	93	97	95	91	
3	94	90	95	96	
4	89	78	86	92	
5	89	78	87	82	
Foothill High					
9	95	95	94		93
10	94	95	96		95
11	92	92	93		93
Hart Middle					
6	96	95	95	92	
7	97	95	97	98	
8	97	95	96	97	

Scores range from 1-99. A school scoring 75 has done better than 75 percent of other public schools in California.
Key: Rd (Reading), Ma (Math), Lg (Language), Sp (Spelling), Sci (Science)

Grade	Rd	Ma	Lg	Sp	Sci
Harvest Park Int.					
6	94	87	94	92	
7	91	90	95	97	
8	94	89	95	96	
Hearst Elem.					
2	93	90	94	84	
3	92	94	91	89	
4	93	92	96	94	
5	97	93	97	97	
Lydiksen Elem.					
2	88	90	91	85	
3	87	94	89	87	
4	91	91	92	94	
5	89	90	87	87	
Mohr Elem.					
2	96	98	98	96	
3	96	96	97	97	
4	93	90	92	97	
5	98	98	96	97	
Pleasanton Middle					
6	95	89	94	90	
7	96	95	97	96	
8	94	93	95	94	
Valley View Elem.					
2	95	97	96	83	
3	91	86	85	82	
4	91	92	88	84	
5	96	93	93	87	
Village High					
10	50	42	47		44
11	65	44	46		52
Vintage Hills Elem.					
2	95	97	97	96	
3	92	95	94	94	
4	96	92	93	96	
5	94	97	94	89	
Walnut Grove Elem.					
2	98	96	93	90	
3	93	87	92	82	
4	95	90	94	89	
5	97	97	96	97	

San Leandro Unified School Dist.

Grade	Rd	Ma	Lg	Sp	Sci
Bancroft Middle					
6	44	26	50	41	
7	54	42	58	59	
8	48	33	49	35	
Garfield Elem.					
2	51	32	53	36	
3	30	20	32	52	
4	45	29	42	45	
5	37	26	46	62	
Jefferson Elem.					
2	36	27	31	48	
3	35	40	48	42	
4	30	29	32	45	
5	42	29	38	62	

Grade	Rd	Ma	Lg	Sp	Sci
Lincoln High (Cont.)					
10	18	29	13		19
11	24	28	25		23
Madison Elem.					
2	51	36	55	66	
3	56	42	54	65	
4	59	47	62	81	
5	56	28	51	52	
McKinley Elem.					
2	49	46	60	55	
3	52	67	54	82	
4	54	55	52	56	
5	23	26	36	52	
Monroe Elem.					
2	29	51	60	43	
3	44	50	40	48	
4	60	59	63	56	
5	42	43	50	60	
Muir Middle					
6	44	35	44	48	
7	35	46	40	51	
8	46	41	47	52	
Roosevelt Elem.					
2	81	70	82	89	
3	56	42	56	48	
4	81	78	86	87	
5	74	75	78	60	
San Leandro Charter					
2	41	31	36	32	
3	21	22	46	48	
4	54	50	62	49	
San Leandro High					
9	55	66	61		53
10	42	64	44		44
11	41	63	51		46
Washington Elem.					
2	43	71	53	39	
3	30	17	26	14	
4	25	9	17	8	
5	44	29	42	20	
Wilson Elem.					
2	34	27	38	34	
3	23	22	26	34	
4	34	26	40	41	
5	40	36	44	48	

San Lorenzo Unified School Dist.

Grade	Rd	Ma	Lg	Sp	Sci
Arroyo High					
9	59	72	65		67
10	61	68	65		70
11	57	73	60		69
Bay Elem.					
2	68	82	78	76	
3	47	65	42	56	
4	60	55	69	67	
5	50	61	51	72	

Scores range from 1-99. A school scoring 75 has done better than 75 percent of other public schools in California.

Key: Rd (Reading), Ma (Math), Lg (Language), Sp (Spelling), Sci (Science)

Grade	Rd	Ma	Lg	Sp	Sci
Bohannon Middle					
6	31	29	40	38	
7	47	47	50	26	
8	50	40	44	39	
Colonial Acres Elem.					
2	29	19	17	49	
3	17	12	23	14	
4	36	29	45	39	
5	28	33	30	43	
Corvallis Elem.					
2	43	44	47	61	
3	52	52	66	64	
4	34	40	40	37	
5	44	45	58	68	
Dayton Elem.					
2	57	79	53	73	
3	35	40	40	62	
4	56	68	63	84	
5	46	46	50	62	
Del Rey Elem.					
2	36	27	43	38	
3	21	20	23	10	
4	52	42	44	47	
5	37	46	44	64	
Edendale Middle					
6	10	20	10	25	
7	24	31	25	14	
8	23	31	21	19	
Grant Elem.					
2	69	76	69	51	
3	47	38	38	43	
4	46	29	40	56	
5	30	45	30	62	
Hesperian Elem.					
2	25	51	23	23	
3	19	17	23	31	
4	18	10	13	39	
5	8	13	17	29	
Hillside Elem.					
2	27	10	20	29	
3	23	19	23	34	
4	15	10	7	20	
5	10	6	9	43	

Grade	Rd	Ma	Lg	Sp	Sci
Lorenzo Manor Elem.					
2	25	22	24	17	
3	39	33	30	19	
4	36	24	30	43	
5	23	21	22	26	
Royal Sunset (Cont.)					
9	25	16	13		20
10	5	2	4		2
11	16	15	11		17
San Lorenzo High					
9	32	40	34		39
10	47	58	42		56
11	43	46	40		49
Washington Manor Middle					
6	46	55	54	61	
7	47	59	56	51	
8	60	74	63	73	

Sunol Glen Unified School Dist.

Grade	Rd	Ma	Lg	Sp	Sci
B.A.S.I.S.					
2	91	69	55	82	
3	67	33	50	21	
4	65	48	63	10	
5	59	31	33	43	
6	90	65	92	88	
7	70	46	69	56	
8	79	37	84	45	
9	86	68	76		70
10	71	45	76		49
11	49	37	69		10
Sunol Glen Elem.					
2	69	46	66	52	
3	77	68	88	59	
4	88	88	88	92	
5	96	82	94	89	
6	82	86	90	72	
7	87	78	89	75	
8	97	92	91	96	

Chapter 3

How Public Schools Work

SCORES MEASURE academic success but they have their shortcomings. Some students know the material but are not adept at taking tests and some tests are so poorly designed that they fail to assess what has been taught. The rankings in the previous chapters do not break out students as individuals. A basic exam tests the least the children should know, not the most. Scores cannot assess goodness, kindness or wisdom or predict how helpful students will be to society.

There are other legitimate criticisms of probably every test given to California school children. Nonetheless, the tests probably give a fairly accurate picture of how the schools are doing academically. Students who do well in elementary school generally do well in high school and score high on the SAT and go on to succeed in college. With exceptions, the scores correlate with teacher assessments and so on. The exceptions cannot be ignored. A student who does poorly in one educational arrangement may thrive in another. This guide addresses patterns, not individuals.

When your children attend a school with high test scores, they are not assured of success. These schools have their failures. Neither can you be certain that your children will get the best teachers or the right programs. Other schools with lower scores might do better on these points. What you can be certain of is that your children are entering a setting that has proven successful for many students.

The main problem with making sense out of scores concerns what is called socioeconomics, a theory educators love, hate and widely believe.

Socioeconomics

In its crudest form, socioeconomics means rich kids score high, middle-class kids score about the middle and poor kids score low. Not all the time, not predictably by individual. Many children from poor and middle-class homes succeed in school and attend the best colleges. But as a general rule socioeconomics enjoys much statistical support.

Compare the rankings in the preceding chapter with income by cities. Piedmont, rich, high scores; parts of Oakland, poor, low; Union City and San

Scholastic Aptitude Test (SAT) Scores

High School	Enrollment*	% Tested	Verbal	Math
Alameda High	397	70	494	530
Albany High	168	76	551	603
Amador Valley High	484	62	544	576
American High	291	46	489	510
Arroyo High	409	42	466	489
Berkeley High	783	58	544	567
Castlemont Senior High	179	53	356	381
Castro Valley High	539	61	519	553
Dublin High	230	54	518	543
Emery High	59	48	399	397
Encinal High	257	56	445	488
Foothill High	436	69	550	587
Fremont Senior High	231	59	353	400
Granada High	420	53	533	566
Hayward High	392	39	450	482
Irvington High	330	54	498	547
James Logan High	735	64	466	510
Kennedy (John F.) High	303	47	489	550
Livermore High	428	43	528	540
McClymonds Senior High	84	63	336	368
Mission San Jose High	526	91	574	632
Mt. Eden High	455	43	444	469
Newark Memorial High	455	42	474	508
Oakland Senior High	361	66	389	453
Oakland Technical Senior High	258	66	408	443
Piedmont High	214	99	588	604
San Leandro High	419	48	468	517
San Lorenzo High	331	40	424	455
Skyline Senior High	451	59	446	483
Tennyson High	344	44	416	462
Washington High	371	57	502	539

Source: California Department of Education, 2002 tests. SAT scores are greatly influenced by who and how many take the test. The state education department has been pushing schools to have more students take the SAT. A school that has more marginal students taking the test will, by one line of reasoning, be doing a good job, but the scores are likely to be lower. *Senior class enrollment.

Leandro, middle-class towns, middling or middle-plus scores. SAT scores reflect the basic test scores.

Oakland School District has some of the lowest scoring schools in the state and some of the highest. All the teachers are paid the same. All are recruited by the same agency and all, presumably, meet the standards of the district.

Why the difference in scores? The background of the children is different. Montclair and adjoining neighborhoods are home to many professionals and people affiliated with the University of California. Academic culture strong. Scores high.

Oakland flatlands have many poor students, many welfare families. Academic push weak. Scores low.

The flatlands also have many minority children but to define achievement by ethnicity distorts the picture. Many middle-class towns or neighborhoods have high numbers of students from the same ethnic groups. Scores are much higher, sometimes very high.

The difference: probably family stability and a host of other social influences. The same socioeconomic patterns show up around the Bay Area, the country and in other countries.

The federal study, "Japanese Education Today," notes a "solid correlation between poverty and poor school performance...."

Family and Culture

In its refined form, socioeconomics moves away from the buck and toward culture and family influence.

The towns with the highest number of college educated are generally also the towns with the highest scores. If your mom or dad attended college, chances are you will attend college or do well at school because in a thousand ways while you were growing up they and their milieu pushed you in this direction. Emphasis on "chances are." Nothing is certain when dealing with human beings.

What if mom and dad never got beyond the third grade? Or can't even speak English?

Historically, many poor and immigrant children have succeeded at school because their parents badgered, bullied and encouraged them every step of the way and made sacrifices so they would succeed. Asian kids are the latest example of poor kids succeeding but earlier generations could point to the children of peasant Europeans and Blacks risen from slavery.

Does it make a difference if the child is English proficient? Or the parents rich? Individual differences will always count. Immigrant children unfamiliar with English will have more difficulties with literature and language-proficient courses than native-born children. They will need extra or special help in schools.

Nonetheless, the home-school correlation retains much validity: The stronger the educational support the child receives at home, the better he or she will do at school. Simply reading daily to young children supposedly works wonders, studies indicate.

The Socioeconomic flaw

If you carry the logic of socioeconomics too far, you may conclude that schools and teachers and teaching methods don't matter: Students succeed or fail according to their family or societal backgrounds.

National Scholastic Aptitude Test (SAT) Scores

State	*Tested (%)	Verbal	Math
Alabama	9	560	559
Alaska	52	516	519
Arizona	36	520	523
Arkansas	5	560	556
California	**52**	**496**	**517**
Colorado	28	543	548
Connecticut	83	509	509
Delaware	69	502	500
Dist. of Columbia	76	480	473
Florida	57	496	499
Georgia	65	489	491
Hawaii	53	488	520
Idaho	18	539	541
Illinois	11	578	596
Indiana	62	498	503
Iowa	5	591	602
Kansas	9	578	580
Kentucky	12	550	552
Louisiana	8	561	559
Maine	69	503	502
Maryland	67	507	513
Massachusetts	81	512	516
Michigan	11	558	572
Minnesota	10	581	591
Mississippi	4	559	547
Missouri	8	574	580
Montana	23	541	547
Nebraska	8	561	570
Nevada	34	509	518
New Hampshire	73	519	519
New Jersey	82	498	513
New Mexico	14	551	543
New York	79	494	506
North Carolina	67	493	505
North Dakota	4	597	610
Ohio	27	533	540
Oklahoma	8	565	562
Oregon	56	524	528
Pennsylvania	72	498	500
Rhode Island	73	504	503
South Carolina	59	488	493
South Dakota	5	576	586
Tennessee	14	562	555
Texas	55	491	500
Utah	6	563	559
Vermont	69	512	510
Virginia	68	510	506
Washington	54	525	529
West Virginia	18	525	515
Wisconsin	7	583	599
Wyoming	11	531	537
Nationwide	**46**	**504**	**516**

Source: California Dept. of Education, 2002 tests. *Percentage of class taking the test.

Just not the case! No matter how dedicated or well-intentioned the parent, if the teacher is grossly inept the child probably will learn little. If material or textbooks are out-of-date or inaccurate, what the student learns will be useless or damaging. Conversely, if the teacher is dedicated and knowledgeable, if the material is well-presented and appropriate, what the child comes away with will be helpful and, to society, more likely to be beneficial.

The late Albert Shanker, president of the American Federation of Teachers, one of the largest teachers' unions in the nation, argued that U.S. students would improve remarkably if schools refused to tolerate disruptive behavior, if national or state academic standards were adopted, if external agencies (not the schools themselves) tested students and if colleges and employers, in admissions and hiring, rewarded academic achievement and penalized failure. These four reforms do little or nothing to address socioeconomics but many educators believe they have merit.

Admittedly, however, this is a contentious area. Theories abound as to what is wrong with our schools and what should be done to fix them.

Where the Confusion Enters

It's very difficult, if not impossible, to separate the influence of home and schools. To be fair to parents, some experts argue that friends and peer groups exercise greater influence than the home.

When scores go up, often principals or superintendents credit this or that instructional program or extra efforts by teachers.

But the scores may have risen because mom and dad cracked down on excessive TV. Or a city with old and faded low-income housing (low scores) approved a high-end development. The new residents are more middle class, more demographically inclined to push their kids academically.

One last joker-in-the deck, mobility. Johnny is doing great at his school, which has low to middling scores, but programs that seem to be working. And his family is doing better. Mom has a job, Dad a promotion. What does the family do? It moves. Happens all the time in the U.S.A. and this also makes precise interpretation of scores difficult.

Basic Instruction-Ability Grouping

California and American schools attempt to meet the needs of students by providing a good basic education and by addressing individual and subgroup needs by special classes and ability grouping.

In the first six years in an average school, children receive some special help according to ability but for the most part they share the same class experiences and get the same instruction.

About the seventh grade, students are divided into classes for low achievers, middling students and high achievers, or low-middle and advanced —

California College Admissions of Public School Graduates

High School	UC	CSU	CC
Alameda	64	68	214
Albany	48	17	54
Amador (Pleasanton)	51	84	175
American (Fremont)	16	43	113
Arroyo (Livermore)	23	57	131
Berkeley	137	52	240
Castlemont (Oakland)	9	16	78
Castro Valley	77	71	209
Dublin	18	33	108
Emery (Emeryville)	5	11	40
Encinal (Alameda)	21	34	137
Foothill (Pleasanton)	69	70	183
Fremont	15	19	83
Granada (Livermore)	32	70	171
Hayward	14	64	152
Irvington (Fremont)	45	51	105
Kennedy (Fremont)	42	27	144
Livermore	31	35	182
Logan (Union City)	86	152	312
McClymonds (Oakland)	4	15	46
Mission San Jose (Fremont)	199	61	102
Mt. Eden (Hayward)	35	73	107
Newark Mem.	24	59	163
Oakland	48	54	219
Oakland Tech	33	24	130
Piedmont	56	21	30
San Leandro	37	57	168
San Lorenzo	23	68	72
Skyline (Oakland)	68	60	176
Tennyson (Hayward)	20	58	119
Washington (Fremont)	37	76	151

Source: California Department of Education. The chart lists the local public high schools and shows how many students they advanced in the year 2002 into California public colleges and universities. The state does not track graduates enrolling in private or out-of-state colleges. Continuation schools not included. **Key**: UC (University of California system); CSU (Cal State system); CC (Community Colleges).

tracking. Texts, homework and expectations are different for each group. The high achievers are on the college track, the low, the vocational.

Pressured by the state, some schools are curtailing this practice, but many schools retain accelerated English and math classes for advanced seventh- and eighth-graders. Parents can always request a transfer from one group to another (whether they can get it is another matter). The reality often is, however, that remedial and middle children can't keep pace with the high achievers.

In the last 40 years or so, schools introduced into the early grades special programs aimed at low achievers or children with learning difficulties.

Although they vary greatly, these programs typically pull the children out of class for instruction in small groups then return them to the regular class.

Many schools also pull out gifted (high I.Q.) students and a few cluster them in their own classes. Some schools offer "gifted" classes after the regular program.

How Average Schools Succeed

So many local students attend the University of California and California State universities that public and private high schools must of necessity teach classes demanded by these institutions.

Almost all high schools will also offer general education classes in math and English but these will not be as tough as the prep courses and will not be recognized by the state universities. And usually the school will teach some trades so those inclined can secure jobs upon graduation.

Can a school with mediocre or even low basic scores field a successful college prep program? With comprehensive programs, the answer is yes.

College Track

Freshmen attending a California State University, a public community college or a University of California (Berkeley, Los Angeles, San Diego, Davis, Riverside, etc.) are asked to identify their high schools. In this way and others, the state finds out how many students the individual high schools are advancing to college.

The college admissions chart breaks out the high schools in Alameda County and shows how many students from each school went on to the public colleges.

UCs generally restrict themselves to the top 13 percent in the state. CSUs (Cal States) take the top third.

Every school on the chart is graduating kids into college but obviously some are more successful at it than others. Does this mean that the "lesser" schools have awful teachers or misguided programs? We have no idea. It simply may be socioeconomics at work.

Parents with college ambitions for their children should find out as much as possible about prospective schools and their programs and make sure that their kids get into the college-track classes.

Where does the chart mislead?

Students who qualify for a Cal State or even a UC often take their freshman and sophomore years at a community college. It's cheaper and closer to home.

The UCs, to get a more diverse student body, are accepting students who score below the top 13 percent.

But socioeconomics does not sweep the field. Not every student from a high-scoring school goes on to college. Many students from low- and middle-income towns come through.

The chart does not track private colleges. It doesn't tell us how many local students went to Mills College or the University of San Francisco or Stanford or Harvard. Or public colleges out of the state.

Many college students drop out. These numbers are not included.

The chart does confirm the influence of socioeconomics: The rich towns, the educated towns or neighborhoods, send more kids to the UCs than the poorer ones. Berkeley High School and Mission San Jose (affluent neighbhorhood) send the most students to the University of California. Skyline High is located in the well-to-do neighborhoods of Oakland. Piedmont, a small school district, does proportionately quite well.

But socioeconomics does not sweep the field. Not every student from a high-scoring school goes on to college. Many students from low- and middle-income towns come through.

Dissatisfaction

If high schools can deliver on college education and train students for vocations, why are so many people dissatisfied with public schools? These schools can cite other accomplishments: Textbooks and curriculums have been improved, the dropout rate has been decreased and proficiency tests have been adopted to force high school students to meet minimum academic standards.

Yet almost every year or so, some group releases a study showing many California children are scoring below expectations or doing poorly as compared to Japanese or European children.

And the school system is expensive, $42 billion annually just for the state's contribution to K-12 schools. The feds put up another $12 billion.

Comparisons between countries are tricky. If Japanese or European high school students fail or do poorly on their tests, they are often denied admission to college. Those who do well, however, are marked not only for college but the higher-paying jobs. Our system gives second and third chances and allows easy admission to colleges, but bears down on students during college and after they graduate. Then they have to prove themselves at work to get ahead, and this forces many to return to college or get training. Their system pressures teenagers; ours pressures young adults. Some studies suggest that by age 30 the differences even out.

As intriguing as this theory is, many parents and teachers would feel much better if the learning curve showed a sharper rise for the high-school scholars and, of course, our top universities — Cal, Stanford, Harvard — demand top scores for admission.

Registering For School

To get into kindergarten, your child must turn five before Dec. 3 of the year he or she enters the grade.

For first grade, your child must be six before Dec. 3. If he is six on Dec. 4, if she is a mature Jan. 6 birthday girl, speak to the school. There may be some wiggle room. In 2000, the state changed the law to allow schools to admit children who turn six before Sept. 2. But to take advantage of this law, a school must offer pre-kindergarten instruction. Many don't. Talk to the school.

For registration, you are required to show proof of immunization for polio, diphtheria, hepatitis B, tetanus, pertussis (whooping cough), measles, rubella and mumps. If the kid is seven or older, you can skip mumps and whooping cough. New law: continuing students entering the seventh grade must show proof of being immunized against hepatitis B.

Register Early

Just because you enroll your child first does not necessarily mean that you will get your first choice of schools or teachers.

But in some school districts first-come does mean first-served. Enrollment and transfer policies change from year to year in some districts, depending on the number of children enrolled and the space available. When new schools are opened, attendance boundaries are often changed.

Even if the school district says, "There's plenty of time to register," do it as soon as possible. If a dispute arises over attendance — the school might get an unexpected influx of students — early registration might give you a leg up in any negotiations. Persistence sometimes helps in trying for transfers.

Choosing the "Right" School

Almost all public schools have attendance zones, usually the immediate neighborhood. The school comes with the neighborhood; often you have no choice. Your address determines your school.

Always call the school district to find out what school your children will be attending. Sometimes school districts change attendance boundaries and do not inform local Realtors. Sometimes crowding forces kids out of their neighborhood schools. It's always good to go to the first source.

Just say something like, "I'm Mrs. Jones and we're thinking about moving into 1234 Main Street. What school will my six-year-old attend?"

Ask what elementary school your child will attend and what middle school and high school.

Keep in mind that although a district scores high, not all the schools in the district may score high. In some districts, scores vary widely.

Several districts may serve one town, another reason to nail down your school of attendance.

UCs Chosen by Public School Graduates

High School	Berk	Dav	Irv	UCLA	Riv	SD	SB	SC	Total
Alameda	9	22	2	8	1	4	2	16	64
Albany	6	21	0	4	0	9	1	7	48
Amador Valley	4	21	4	3	3	5	3	8	51
American	0	5	2	6	1	0	1	1	16
Arroyo	11	5	0	1	0	2	3	1	23
Berkeley	17	24	3	11	4	9	8	61	137
Castlemont	5	2	0	0	0	0	1	1	9
Castro Valley	17	27	8	2	4	11	2	6	77
Dublin	7	6	0	1	0	1	2	1	18
Emery	4	0	0	0	1	0	0	0	5
Encinal	1	8	0	1	1	3	3	4	21
Foothill	15	16	8	6	4	7	8	5	69
Fremont	6	7	1	0	0	0	1	0	15
Granada	3	4	2	1	2	6	6	8	32
Hayward	3	3	1	2	2	3	0	0	14
Irvington	8	10	6	1	5	8	3	4	45
Kennedy	7	12	4	3	1	6	1	8	42
Livermore	3	10	2	3	3	1	6	3	31
Logan, James	13	27	4	8	3	13	11	7	86
McClymonds	4	0	0	0	0	0	0	0	4
Mission S.J.	31	58	22	25	11	28	11	13	199
Mt. Eden	10	11	3	7	0	1	2	1	35
Newark Mem.	2	5	2	3	0	3	2	7	24
Oakland	20	15	0	5	0	2	2	4	48
Oakland Tech.	14	10	1	3	1	1	1	2	33
Piedmont	8	12	3	8	0	10	5	10	56
San Leandro	9	7	1	1	2	2	9	6	37
San Lorenzo	7	9	2	2	1	1	0	1	23
Skyline	15	28	1	7	2	1	1	13	68
Tennyson	5	8	0	4	0	1	1	1	20
Washington	4	15	1	3	1	4	3	6	37

Source: California Dept. of Education. The chart shows the University of California choices by 2002 local public high school graduates. The state does not track graduates enrolling in private or out-of-state colleges. Continuation schools not included in list. **Key:** Berk (Berkeley), Dav (Davis), Irv (Irvine), Riv (Riverside), SD (San Diego), SB (Santa Barbara), SC (Santa Cruz).

Transfers

If you don't like your neighborhood school, you can request a transfer to another school in the district or to a school outside the district. But the school won't provide transportation.

Transfers to schools inside the district are easier to get than transfers outside the district. New laws supposedly make it easier to transfer children to other districts. In reality, the more popular (high scoring) districts and schools, lacking space, rarely — very rarely — accept "outside" students. This is a changing picture. New federal laws supposedly make it easier to transfer out of schools that do not meet academic standards.

A few parents use the address of a friend or relative to smuggle their child into a high-scoring school or district. Some districts make an effort to ferret out these students and give them the boot.

If your child has a special problem that may demand your attention, speak to the school administrators about a transfer to a school close to your job. If your child's ethnicity adds some diversity to a school or district, it might bend its rules. Never hurts to ask.

Does A Different School Make A Difference?

This may sound like a dumb question but it pays to understand the thinking behind choosing one school or school district over another.

Researching an earlier edition, we contacted a school district (not in this county) that refused to give us test results. This stuff is public information. In so many words, the school administrator said, look, our scores are lousy because our demographics are awful: low income, parents poorly educated, etc. But our programs and staff are great. I'm not giving out the scores because parents will get the wrong idea about our district and keep their kids out of our schools (He later changed his mind and gave us the scores.)

Second story, while working as a reporter, one of our editors covered a large urban school district and heard about a principal who was considered top notch. An interview was set up and the fellow seemed as good as his reputation: friendly, hard working, supportive of his staff, a great role model for his students, many of whom he knew by their first names. But scores at the school were running in the 10th to 20th percentiles, very low.

The reason: the old failing of demographics, weak academic push from home or neighborhood, perhaps indifferent or damaging parents, and so on. This stuff is actually complicated. Some parents do their best but the kid gets diverted by friends or buys into anti-academics.

Although neither person said this, the clear implication was that if the demographics were different, scores would be much higher. And they're probably right. If these schools got an influx of middle- and upper middle-class children, their scores would dramatically increase.

Why don't schools tell this to the public, to parents? Probably because socioeconomics is difficult to explain. Teachers want to work with parents, not alienate them with accusations of neglect. Some educators argue that even with poor socioeconomics, teachers should be able to do an effective job — controversy. Socioeconomics focuses attention on the problems of home and society to the possible detriment of schools (which also need help and funds). School, after all, is a limited activity: about six hours a day, about 180 teaching days a year.

When you strip away the fluff, schools seem to be saying that they are in the business of schools, not in reforming the larger society, and that they should be held accountable only for what they can influence: the children during the school day, on school grounds.

For these reasons — this is our opinion — many teachers and school administrators think that scores mislead and that parents often pay too much attention to scores and not enough to programs and the background and training of personnel. This is not to say that teachers ignore scores and measurements of accomplishment. They would love to see their students succeed. And schools find tests useful to determine whether their programs need changes.

No matter how low the scores, if you, as a parent, go into any school, and ask — can my child get a good education here — you will be told, probably invariably, often enthusiastically, yes. First, there's the obvious reason: if the principal said no, his or her staff and bosses would be upset and angry. Second, by the reasoning common to public schools, "yes" means that the principal believes that the school and its teachers have the knowledge, training and dedication to turn out accomplished students. And the programs. Schools stress programs.

Is all this valid? Yes. Programs and training are important. Many schools with middling scores do turn out students that attend the best universities.

But this approach has its skeptics. Many parents and educators believe that schools must be judged by their scores, that scores are the true test of quality.

Some parents fear that if their child or children are placed in classes with low-achieving or even middle-achieving children they will not try as hard as they would if their friends or classmates were more academic, or that in some situations their children will be enticed into mischief. In some inner-city districts, the children, for misguided reasons, pressure each other not to do well in school.

Some parents do not believe that a school with many low-scoring students can do justice to its few middle- and high-scoring students. To meet the needs of the majority, instruction might have to be slowed for everyone.

Discipline is another problem. Teachers in low-scoring schools might have to spend more time on problem kids than teachers in high-scoring schools.

There's much more but basically it comes down to the belief that schools do not stand alone, that they and their students are influenced by the values of parents, of classmates and of the immediate neighborhood.

To continue this logic, schools and school districts are different from one another and for this reason it pays to move into a neighborhood with high-scoring schools or one with at least middling-plus scores. Or to somehow secure a transfer to one of the schools in these neighborhoods.

To an unknown extent, the marketplace has reinforced this belief. It rewards neighborhoods and towns with high-scoring schools by increasing the value (the price) of their homes.

Woven into all this is the suspicion, held by many in California, that public schools have failed to dismiss incompetent teachers and have become inflexible and unable to address problems. California for decades has been wracked by arguments over the power of the teachers' union, and over testing and teaching methods, and curriculum.

The parents who seem to do best at this business find out as much as possible about the schools, make decisions or compromises based on good information and work with the schools and teachers to advance their children's interests. Each school should be publishing an "accountability report." Ask for it.

Year-Round Schools

Year-round schools are used by many districts, especially in fast-growing towns, as a way to handle rapidly increasing enrollments. Schedules, called "tracks," vary by district but all students attend a full academic year.

Traditional holidays are observed. One group may start in summer, one in late summer and so on. A typical pattern is 12 weeks on, four weeks off. One track is always off, allowing another track to use its class space. Some school districts run a "year-round" program called modified traditional: two months summer vacation, three two-week breaks in the school year.

Families with several children on different tracks are sometimes forced to do quite a bit of juggling for vacation and child care. A new game is being played: how to get the tracks you want. Call your school for information.

Ability Grouping

Ask about the school's advancement or grouping policy or gifted classes.

Without getting into the pros and cons of these practices, schools often tiptoe around them because they upset some parents and frankly because some children have to be slighted. Say the ideal in a middle school is three levels of math: low, middle and high. But funds will allow only two levels. So low is combined with middle or middle with high. If you know the school is making compromises, you might choose to pay for tutoring to bridge the gap.

Miscellaneous

- For much of the 1990s, California, in a tough economy, pulled the purse strings tight against school spending. Teacher salaries fell behind what was paid in other states. Programs were cut. Quality, many believe, suffered. In the late 1990s, the economy came roaring back and pushed billions of extra dollars into the state treasury.

- Teacher salaries were raised, class sizes in the first three grades were lowered (to 20-1), programs were restored.

- Going into 2004, California has burned through its surplus and is saddled with a deficit of $38 billion. We are entering another era of stingy state spending. So far, schools have been spared deep cuts but they may suffer in subsequent budgets. In 2003, Oakland district, perhaps betting on the dotcom economy to supply funding, was forced into bankruptcy. The state loaned the district $100 million and put its own administrator in charge of the district.

- On the positive side, several years ago voters dropped the approval vote for local bonds for school construction from two-thirds of ballots cast to 55 percent. School districts that had lost several bond elections went back to the voters and won approval.

- So while the state is reducing its contribution, local districts have picked up theirs, and rare is the city or suburban district in the state that has not passed a construction bond since 1990.

- In 1998, voters passed a state bond to spend $9.2 billion on school construction and renovation. Of this, $6.7 billion went to K-12 schools, and $2.9 billion to community colleges and universities.

- Private vs. public. A complex battle, it boils down to one side saying public schools are the best and fairest way to educate all children versus the other side saying public education is inefficient and will never reform until it has meaningful competition. The state is allowing up to 350 schools to restructure their programs according to local needs — an effort at eliminating unnecessary rules. These institutions are called charter schools.

- Once tenured, teachers are almost impossible to fire, which opens schools to accusations of coddling incompetents. If your child gets a sour teacher, request a transfer. Better still, become active in the PTA or talk to other parents and try to identify the best teachers. Then ask for them.

- Educational methods. Arguments rage over what will work. In the 1990s, California schools tilted back to phonics to teach reading. A novel approach to teaching math gives students several ways to view problems and to get a "correct" answer. Supporters say it is much more effective than traditional methods. Opponents say that in the guise of boosting self-esteem, the program fails to teach math. Many districts mix the two methods.

- Courts and school districts have sorted out Proposition 227, which curtailed non-English instruction in public schools. Parents can request a waiver, which under certain conditions allows instruction in the native language.

- In well-to-do neighborhoods and rich towns, parents are informally "taxing" themselves to raise money for schools. If you are new to one of these districts, you might be approached by the parents' group — never the school — and asked to contribute $100, $200 or $300 per child to the parents' group. Often the money is used to hire aides for teachers.

- What if you or your neighborhood can't afford voluntary fees? Shop for bargains. Community colleges, in the summer, often run academic programs for children. Local tutors might work with small groups. Specific tutoring, say just in math, might be used to get the student over the rough spots. For information on tutors, look in the Yellow Pages under "Tutoring."

- Busing. School districts can charge and several do. Some low-income and special education kids ride free.

- Uniforms. Schools have the discretion to require uniforms, an effort to discourage gang colors and get the kids to pay more attention to school than to how they look. "Uniforms" are generally interpreted to mean modest dress; for example, dark pants and shirts for boys, plaid skirts and light blouse for girls.

- Closed campus vs. open campus. The former stops the students from leaving at lunch or at any time during the school day. The latter allows the kids to leave. Kids love open, parents love closed.

- Grad night. Not too many years ago, graduating seniors would whoop it up on grad night and some would drink and then drive and get injured or killed. At many high schools now, parents stage a grad night party at the school, load it with games, raffles and prizes, and lock the kids in until dawn. A lot of work but it keeps the darlings healthy.

- T-P. California tradition. Your son or daughter joins a school team and it wins a few games or the cheerleaders win some prize — any excuse will do — and some parent will drive the kids around and they will fling toilet paper over your house, car, trees and shrubs. Damn nuisance but the kids love it.

- The number of teaching days has been increased, from about 172 to 180 but some of these days are coming at the expense of preparation time for teachers.

- Open Houses, Parents Nights. One study, done at Stanford, concluded that if parents will attend these events, the students, or at least some of them, will be impressed enough to pay more attention to school.

- Rather than lug around books, lunches, gym gear, etc., students these days are using rolling suitcases similar to carry-on luggage. "They help your back," said one student. The outfits seem to be particularly popular in schools that have done away with lockers.

- Special education. Sore point in California education. When the feds and the state passed laws requiring schools to meet the special needs of

students, they promised funding that never materialized. This forced school districts to take money from their regular programs and fund the special programs. Arguments and lawsuits followed accusing school districts of shorting special ed kids. The state is now offering more money for these programs.

- More kids are being pushed into algebra, not only in high school but in the seventh and eighth grades. New law requires all students to take algebra before graduating from high school.

- Exit exam. Starting in 2006, students must pass an exit exam to receive a high school diploma. To get the kids prepared, all of them must take the exam by their sophomore year. If they fail, the high school will offer extra help.

- California quietly but steadily has been setting standards as to what students should know at any grade level. If schools and students don't measure up to the standards, they risk, in ways that are still being worked out, the displeasure of the California Department of Education. Tests are being developed to see how thoroughly the students are mastering the required subjects.

- Social promotion, the practice of moving students up to the next grade, even if they have failed the current grade, is being discouraged. Schools are now required to hold back failing students and offer them tutoring and

Community College Transfers

ALTHOUGH PRIMARILY skills and training schools, community colleges are a major source of students for the University of California and for the California State universities.

The students usually take their freshman and sophomore classes at a community college, then transfer to a university.

Community colleges are cheap and often conveniently located. Many community colleges have worked out transfer agreements with local state universities and with the UCs.

The data below show how many students each sector advances.

Tracking All Alameda Co. Students to UCs & CSUs

Student Sector	Graduates	To UC	To CSU
Publ. and Priv. High School	11,791	1,387	1,617
Community Colleges	NA	515	1,281

UC, CSU Transfers by Community College Campus

Community College	To UC	To CSU
College of Alameda	59	101
Chabot College	108	395
Laney College	112	216
Las Positas College	75	173
Merritt College	32	66
Ohlone College	90	277
Vista College	39	53

Source: California Postsecondary Education Commission, Student Profile, 2002. **Note:** Enrolling students counted in 2001-2002 by UCs and CSUs. NA, not available.

special instruction. If schools follow guidelines and the student is still failing, he or she can be held back but parents have right to appeal decision.

• The Calif. Dept. of Education recently named the below schools "Distinguished." This means the state thinks they are well run.

• Will C. Wood Middle School, Alameda
• Albany Middle, Albany
• Berkeley Arts Magnet and Martin Luther King Middle School, Berkeley;
• Independent Elementary, Castro Valley High, Castro Valley Middle, Castro Valley Elementary, Jensen Ranch Elementary, Proctor Elementary, and Stanton Elementary schools, in Castro Valley
• Dublin High and Wells Middle schools, Dublin.
• William Hopkins Junior High, Parkmont Elementary, Forest Park

(Continued on Page 75)

High School Graduates University Choice By County

County	No. of Grads	UC	CSU
Alameda	12,648	13%	14%
Alpine	1	0	0
Amador	422	4	9
Butte	2,048	4	17
Calaveras	446	5	9
Colusa	284	2	18
Contra Costa	9,927	11	11
Del Norte	303	5	10
El Dorado	1,800	5	11
Fresno	9,518	4	13
Glenn	388	4	18
Humboldt	1,440	4	13
Imperial	1,998	4	5
Inyo	278	5	7
Kern	8,501	3	9
Kings	1,294	3	7
Lake	520	4	8
Lassen	331	1	2
Los Angeles	88,471	9	11
Madera	1,243	4	10
Marin	2,290	2	12
Mariposa	180	3	2
Mendocino	1,062	5	8
Merced	3,097	3	9
Modoc	176	2	6
Mono	143	5	6
Monterey	3,761	6	10
Napa	1,347	7	10
Nevada	1,138	6	9
Orange	30,091	9	10
Placer	3,890	5	9
Plumas	276	3	5
Riverside	16,929	6	8
Sacramento	12,707	7	12
San Benito	624	4	11
San Bernardino	19,676	5	9
San Diego	27,757	8	11
San Francisco	5,106	18	17
San Joaquin	6,323	4	9
San Luis Obispo	2,497	6	11
San Mateo	5,951	11	13
Santa Barbara	3,886	8	6
Santa Clara	15,822	13	15
Santa Cruz	2,619	12	9
Shasta	2,053	3	5
Sierra	46	4	22
Siskiyou	527	5	9
Solano	4,351	6	10
Sonoma	4,600	7	10

(Continued on next page)

(Continued from previous page)

High School Graduates Choice of University By County

County	No. of Grads	UC	CSU
Stanislaus	5,562	3	10
Sutter	954	2	8
Tehama	652	2	9
Trinity	185	2	11
Tulare	4,405	3	8
Tuolumne	593	6	8
Ventura	8,447	7	6
Yolo	1,759	16	11
Yuba	780	1	5
Total	344,123	8	11

Source: California Dept. of Education, students graduated in 2002.

(Continued from Page 73)

Elementary, Hirsch Elementary, and Joshua Chadbourne Elementary and Mission San Jose High schools, Fremont
• Eldridge Elementary, Hayward
• Arroyo Mocho Elementary, Christensen Middle,William Mendenhall Middle and Emma C. Smith Elementary schools, Livermore
• James Bunker Elementary, Newark
• Amador Valley High, Foothill High, Harvest Park Middle, Thomas S. Hart Middle, Pleasanton Middle, Alisal Elementary, Fairlands Elementary, Vintage Hills Elementary, Walnut Grove Elementary and Henry P. Mohr Elementary schools, Pleasanton
• Washington Manor Middle School, San Lorenzo
• Pioneer Elementary School, Union City and Thornhill Elementary School, Oakland.

•   In 2002-2003, National Blue Ribbons were awarded to: Amador Valley High, Harvest Park Middle, Pleasanton Middleand Walnut Grove Elementary all in Pleasanton; Hopkins Junior High in Fremont, Eldridge Elementary School in Hayward, Chinese Christian Schools (indpendent) in San Leandro.

SAT Test Scores By County-2002

County	Enroll.	% Tested	Verbal	Math
Alameda	12,604	52	490	527
Alpine	4	0	0	0
Amador	522	27	534	513
Butte	2,604	29	507	520
Calaveras	576	26	505	516
Colusa	360	23	439	446
Contra Costa	10,607	46	526	545
Del Norte	433	24	505	506
El Dorado	2,194	35	530	548
Fresno	10,432	32	461	481
Glenn	417	30	455	456
Humboldt	1,685	30	521	537
Imperial	2,190	29	426	442
Inyo	250	47	504	507
Kern	9,195	26	481	497
Kings	1,516	21	469	469
Lake	700	25	498	509
Lassen	390	33	473	476
Los Angeles	88,352	40	468	497
Madera	1,620	17	481	494
Marin	2,033	59	544	556
Mariposa	214	28	537	545
Mendocino	1,178	33	530	528
Merced	3,625	22	462	475
Modoc	185	18	494	511
Mono	142	43	522	498
Monterey	3,871	35	451	465
Napa	1,388	32	514	524
Nevada	1,055	38	535	536
Orange	30,706	42	515	554
Placer	4,503	33	518	531
Plumas	271	38	513	501
Riverside	19,644	31	471	488
Sacramento	13,817	32	488	512
San Benito	621	38	463	481
San Bernardino	21,934	30	473	491
San Diego	30,465	41	499	519
San Francisco	4,315	60	464	522
San Joaquin	7,827	26	471	494
San Luis Obispo	2,907	32	527	537
San Mateo	5,542	48	501	534
Santa Barbara	4,048	33	516	533
Santa Clara	16,431	49	514	556
Santa Cruz	2,814	36	515	533
Shasta	2,456	23	523	532
Sierra	79	51	490	479
Siskiyou	578	26	497	503
Solano	4,754	32	486	506
Sonoma	4,873	35	529	539

(Continued on next page)

(Continued from previous page)

SAT Test Scores By County-2002

County	Enroll.	% Tested	Verbal	Math
Stanislaus	6,495	22	497	514
Sutter	1,132	24	497	522
Tehama	778	22	498	504
Trinity	190	30	507	513
Tulare	5,573	24	463	479
Tuolumne	596	30	536	536
Ventura	9,257	32	519	538
Yolo	2,004	39	543	564
Yuba	955	15	452	483
Statewide:	365,907	37	490	516

Source: California Dept. of Education, 2002 School year.

School Districts in Alameda County

Albany District
Berkeley District
Piedmont District
Mountain House Elementary District
Emery District
Oakland District
Alameda District
Dublin District
Castro Valley District
San Leandro District
San Lorenzo District
Hayward District
Pleasanton District
Livermore Valley Joint District
Union City
New Haven District
Sunol Glen District
Newark District
Fremont District

Note: Sunol Glen elementary students attend Foothill High School in the Pleasanton District.

School Accountability Report Card

Want more information about a particular school or school district?

Every public school and district in the state is required by law to issue an annual School Accountability Report Card. The everyday name is the SARC report or the SARC card (pronounced SARK). SARCs are supposed to include:

- The ethnic makeup of the school and school district.

- Test results. The results may be presented in several ways but almost without exception the formats follow the presentation methods of the California Dept. of Education.

- Dropout rates for high schools.

- A description of facilities, the curriculum and the programs.

- Description of the teaching staff. How many have teaching credentials. Class sizes, teacher-pupil ratios.

To obtain a SARC, call the school and if the person answering the phone can't help you, ask for the superintendent's secretary or the curriculum department. Some schools want you to pick up the report in person. Many schools have posted their SARCS on their web sites. If you don't know the name of the neighborhood school, start with the school district. Here are the phone numbers of the districts and the towns they serve.

Alameda City Unified School District (510) 337-7060

Albany Unified School District (510) 558-3750

Berkeley Unified School District (510) 644-6147

Castro Valley Unified School District (510) 537-3000

Dublin Unified School District (925) 828-2551

Emery Unified Sch. Dist. (Emeryville) (510) 601-4000

Fremont Unified School District (510) 657-2350

Hayward Unified School District (510) 784-2600

Livermore Valley Joint Unified School District (925) 606-3200

Mountain House Elementary School District (209) 835-2283

New Haven Unified Sch. Dist. (Union City) (510) 471-1100

Newark Unified School District (510) 794-2141

Oakland Unified School District (510) 879-8100

Piedmont City Unified School District (510) 594-2600

Pleasanton Unified School District (925) 462-5500

San Leandro Unified School District (510) 667-3500

San Lorenzo Unified School District (510) 317-4600

Sunol Glen Unified School District (925) 862-2217

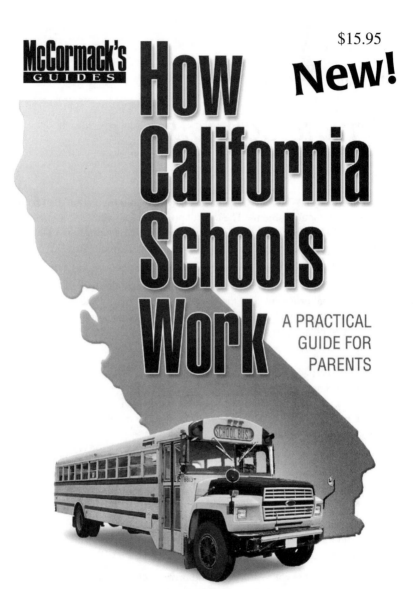

McCormack's GUIDES

How California Schools Work

$15.95

New!

A PRACTICAL GUIDE FOR PARENTS

FROM THE EDITORS OF McCormack's Guides

www.mccormacks.com
1-800-222-3602

Chapter 4

Private Schools

ALTHOUGH PRIVATE SCHOOLS often enjoy a better reputation than public, they are not without problems. The typical private or parochial school is funded way below its public school counterpart. In size, facilities and playing fields, and in programs, public schools usually far outstrip private schools. Private school teachers earn less than public school teachers.

"Typical" has to be emphasized. Some private schools are well-equipped, offer exceptional programs, pay their teachers competitively and limit class sizes to fewer than 15 students. Private schools vary widely in funding. But even when "typical," private schools enjoy certain advantages over public schools.

The Advantages

Public schools must accept all students, have almost no power to dismiss incompetent teachers and are at the mercy of their neighborhoods for the quality of students — the socioeconomic correlation. The unruly often cannot be expelled or effectively disciplined.

Much has been said about the ability of private schools to rid themselves of problem children and screen them out in the first place. But tuition, even when modest, probably does more than anything else to assure private schools quality students.

Parents who pay extra for their child's education and often agree to work closely with the school are, usually, demanding parents. The result: fewer discipline problems, fewer distractions in the class, more of a willingness to learn.

When you place your child in a good private school, you are, to a large extent, buying him or her scholastic classmates. They may not be the smartest children — many private schools accept children of varying ability — but generally they will have someone at home breathing down their necks to succeed in academics.

The same attitude, a reflection of family values, is found in the high-achieving public schools. When a child in one of these schools or a private school turns to his left and right, he will see and later talk to children who read

Since 1954

Engaging Inspiring Enriching

- Small Class Size
- Challenging Academic Program
- Personal Approach to Educating the Whole Child
- 70% of our students score at the 95th percentile or higher in one or more sections in national standardized testing

"Saklan Valley School provides an excellent academic program which includes strong foreign language opportunities in French. My children have fun and take pride in the program."

-Linda Infelise, Parent, Oakland

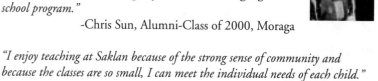

"After graduating from Saklan Valley I moved on to The College Preparatory School in Oakland and have felt very well prepared to meet the challenges of such a demanding high school program."

-Chris Sun, Alumni-Class of 2000, Moraga

"I enjoy teaching at Saklan because of the strong sense of community and because the classes are so small, I can meet the individual needs of each child."

-Carol Schofield, Teacher

"We offer a learning community of students, teachers, and parents united to provide academic excellence with a personal approach to educating and serving the whole child."

-Jonathan Martin, Head of School

PLEASE CALL TO MAKE AN APPOINTMENT FOR A TOUR *TODAY!*

1678 School Street ✪ Moraga ✪ (925)376-7900 ✪ www.saklan.org

California College Admissions of Private School Graduates

High School	UC	CSU	CC
American Heritage	0	NA	3
Arrowsmith	2	23	NA
Bishop O'Dowd	82	51	36
Chinese Christian	16	NA	6
College Prep.	15	1	1
Fremont Christian	8	9	16
Head-Royce	21	1	NA
Holy Names	14	13	11
Maybeck	5	4	7
Moreau	47	84	56
Patten Acad.	0	2	5
Redwood Christian	8	17	12
St. Elizabeth	2	9	22
St. Joseph ND	26	36	34
St. Mary's	39	36	14
Valley Christian	9	1	7

Source: California Dept. of Education. The chart tracks California public colleges or universities, and high school graduates from private schools. It shows how many students from these high schools enrolled as college freshmen in fall 2002. The state does not track graduates enrolling in private colleges or out-of-state colleges. **Note**: Small or family schools not included in list. **Key**: UC (University of California system); CSU (Cal State system); CC (Community Colleges

books and newspapers. A child in a low-achieving school, public or private, will talk to classmates who watch a lot of television and rarely read.

(These are, necessarily, broad generalizations. Much depends on whom the children pick for friends. High-achieving students certainly watch television but, studies show, much less than low-achieving students. Many critics contend that even high-scoring schools are graduating students poorly prepared for college.)

The Quality of Teaching

Do private schools have better teachers than public schools? Impossible to tell. Both sectors sing the praises of their teachers.

Private schools, compared to public, have much more freedom to dismiss teachers but this can be abused. The private schools themselves advise parents to avoid schools with excessive teacher turnover.

Although most can't pay as much as public schools, private institutions claim to attract people fed up with the limitations of public schools, particularly the restrictions on disciplining and ejecting unruly children. Some proponents argue that private schools attract teachers "who really want to teach."

Religion and Private Schools

Some private schools are as secular as any public institution. But many are religion-oriented and talk in depth about religion or ethics, or teach a specific

UCs Chosen by Private School Graduates

School	Berk	Davis	Irv	UCLA	RIV	SD	SB	SC	Total
American Heritage	0	0	0	0	0	0	0	0	0
Arrowsmith	1	0	0	0	0	0	0	1	2
Bishop O'Dowd	11	26	2	6	2	6	4	25	82
Chinese Christian	6	9	0	1	0	0	0	0	16
College Prep.	4	2	0	4	0	1	0	4	15
Fremont Christian	0	3	4	0	1	0	0	0	8
Head-Royce	5	8	0	1	0	2	3	2	21
Holy Names	2	3	1	2	1	1	3	1	14
Maybeck	0	0	0	0	0	0	1	4	5
Moreau	1	19	5	3	2	7	1	9	47
Patten Academy	0	0	0	0	0	0	0	0	0
Redwood Christian	2	2	0	0	1	1	2	0	8
St. Elizabeth	0	0	0	0	0	0	1	1	2
St. Joseph ND	2	5	1	3	7	2	4	2	26
St. Mary's	3	7	5	2	1	3	7	11	39
Valley Christian	3	3	0	0	0	1	1	1	9

Source: California Dept. of Education. The chart shows how many students from these private schools enrolled as UC freshmen in fall 2002. **Key:** Berk (Berkeley), Irv (Irvine), Riv (Riverside), SD (San Diego), SB (Santa Barbara), SC (Santa Cruz).

creed. Or possibly they teach values within a framework of western civilization or some other philosophy.

Public schools teach the history of major religions and touch on the basic tenets of each, and try to inculcate in the children a respect for all religions.

It's hard, if not impossible, however, for public schools to talk about values within a framework of religion or a system of ethics. Often, it's difficult for them to talk about values. Some people argue that this is a major failing.

Many religious schools accept students of different religions or no religion. Some schools offer these students broad courses in religion — less dogma. Ask about the program.

Money

Private-school parents pay taxes for public schools and they pay tuition. Public-school parents pay taxes but not tuition. Big difference.

Ethnic Diversity

Many private schools are integrated and the great majority of private-school principals — the editor knows no exceptions — welcome minorities. Some principals fret over tuition, believing that it keeps many poor students out of private schools. Money, or lack of it, weighs heavily on private schools. Scholarships, however, are awarded, adjustments made, family rates offered.

(Continued on page 87)

Profile of Catholic Schools

THE LARGEST PRIVATE school system in Alameda County,
Catholic schools enroll 12,261 students — 8,582 elementary, 3,679
high school (2002-2003 school year).

The following is based on interviews with Catholic educators and
includes information from the diocese.

- 37 elementary schools, kindergarten through eighth, six high schools,
  one kindergarten (Mission San Jose, Fremont).

- All races, creeds welcome. But where schools are full, preference is
  given to Catholic children from families active in parish, and
  siblings. After that, to active Catholics unable to get into own parish
  schools.

  High schools recruit regionally for students. Admissions tests but
  many accept average students. Standards vary by school.

- School system includes both Alameda and Contra Costa County.
  Contra Costa enrolls 5,699 elementary students, 2,303 secondary.

- Why parents send kids to Catholic schools. Results of survey:
  academics, discipline, religion, safety. Order changes by parish. What
  happens in public schools affects enrollment in Catholic schools, said
  one educator.

  "Parents are looking for safe, positive environment," said another.

- Curriculum. Elementary schools cover same basic subjects as public
  schools but weave in religious-moral viewpoint. "Philosophy based
  in Jesus Christ. Religious values are integral to learning experience."
  State textbooks often used. Each school picks texts.

  High school instruction, although varied, is greatly influenced by
  requirements of University of California.

  Educators advise parents to approach high schools as they would any
  educational institution: ask about grades, what percentage of students
  go on to college, whether school is accredited.

- Non-Catholics. Same instruction as Catholics, including history of
  Church and scripture. Attend Mass but not required to take sacra-
  ments. "We don't try to convert them," said one nun.

- Corporal punishment. Thing of past. Stress positive discipline, name
  on board, detention, probation.

(Continued on page 86)

ST. JOSEPH NOTRE DAME HIGH SCHOOL

Catholic, College Prep Tradition

Since 1881

- *98% College Acceptance*
- *Four Counselors Serving a Student Population of 560*
- *Honors and Advanced Placement Classes*
- *Student Teacher Ratio 14:1*
- *Campus Ministry & Student Leadership*
- *26 Athletic Teams*
- *Fine Arts, Performing Arts, Band & Choral*

1011 Chestnut Street, Alameda, CA 94501 • 510-814-7153 www.sjnd.org

Catholic Schools

(Continued from page 84)

- Few expulsions. Try to work with kid, parents to solve problems. Elementary expulsions usually have to be approved by diocese. Often parents withdraw child before he or she can be expelled.

- Class sizes. Maximum 35, minimum 25. A few higher and lower. Average about 30, somewhat smaller for high schools because of special classes, e.g., French. Would like smaller classes but point out that with well-behaved students, teachers can accomplish a lot. Matter of economics. If parents wanted smaller classes, they would have to pay more.

  "We want to keep affordable prices so all people can choose us, not just rich."

- Tuition assistance often available.

- Schedule. Similar to public schools. 180 teaching days, 8:30 a.m. to 3 p.m.

- Ability grouping. In elementary grades (K-8) not done by class. Some grouping within classes, advanced children working at one level, slow children at another. Tutoring after class.

  All high schools run prep programs, tend to attract prep students, but will accept remedial students if they have remedial instruction. Admission standards vary by high school.

  Scores also vary by school — socioeconomics. Suburban Catholic schools tend to score higher than city schools.

- Report cards. At least four a year, plus results of state tests. Parents are expected to attend conferences, back-to-school nights.

- Teacher quality. Hired for competence and commitment to Catholic educational philosophy. No restriction in hiring non-Catholics but the system tends to attract Catholic teachers. "No trouble in attracting high-quality applicants."

- Uniforms. Yes, generally skirts, blouses for girls, collared shirts, trousers for boys. High schoolers have more sartorial discretion.

- Extended care. Many schools offer before- and after-school care. Ask.

- Drugs. "We're not immune to dangers of the larger society," said one educator. Schools try to work with kids.

Catholic Schools

- Extracurricular activities. Although small, schools try to offer variety of activities, sports, arts, music. At elementary school, much depends on work of parents. "Parents are expected to do a lot."

High schools offer good variety: music, band, arts, intramural sports, many club activities, cycling, golf.

Catholic high schools usually field very competitive football and basketball teams. "They help build school pride."

More information, admissions, call school directly. For list of schools, call education office at diocese, (510) 628-2154. See also directory at end of this chapter.

(Continued from page 83)

What's in Alameda County

Alameda County has hundreds of private schools. Many are one-family schools, mother and father teaching their own children at home. A support network that supplies books and materials has grown up for these people.

Some regular private schools have low teacher-pupil ratios, fewer than 15 students per teacher, occasionally around 10 to 1. Public school classes usually go 25 to 30 per teacher, sometimes higher.

Class sizes in Catholic schools run close to the public-school ratio, and in some schools higher (See Catholic schools profile). Catholic schools, nonetheless, are the most popular, a reflection in part of the high number of Catholics in East Bay. Some Catholic schools have waiting lists.

Private schools in both counties come in great variety, Christian, Jewish, Montessori, Carden (schools with different teaching approaches), prep schools, schools that emphasize language or music, boarding and day schools, schools that allow informal dress, schools that require uniforms.

Choosing a Private School

1. Inspect the grounds, the school's buildings, ask plenty of questions. "I would make myself a real pest," advised one private school official. The good schools welcome this kind of attention.

2. Choose a school with a philosophy congenial to your own and your child's. Carden schools emphasize structure. Montessori schools, while somewhat structured, encourage individual initiative and independence.

Ask whether the school is accredited. Private schools are free to run almost any program they like, to set any standards they like, which may sound enticing but in some aspects might hurt the schools. A few bad ones spoil the reputation of the good.

Many private schools sign up for inspections by independent agencies, such as the Western Association of Schools and Colleges and the California Association of Independent Schools. These agencies try to make sure that schools meet their own goals. Some good schools do not seek accreditation.

3. Get all details about tuition carefully explained. How is it to be paid? Are there extra fees? Book costs? Is there a refund if the student is withdrawn or dropped from the school?

4. Progress reports. Parent conferences. How often are they scheduled?

5. What are the entrance requirements? When must they be met?

    Although many schools use entrance tests, often they are employed to place the child in an academic program, not exclude him from the school.

6. For prep schools, what percentage of the students go on to college and to what colleges?

7. How are discipline problems handled?

8. What are the teacher qualifications? What is the teacher turnover rate?

9. How sound financially is the school? How long has it been in existence? There is nothing wrong per se with new schools. But you want a school that has the wherewithal to do the job.

10. Do parents have to work at functions? Are they required to "volunteer"?

11. Don't choose in haste but don't wait until the last minute. Some schools fill quickly, some fill certain classes quickly. If you can, call the school the year before your child is to enter, early in the year.

12. Don't assume that because your child attends a private school you can expect everything will go all right, that neither the school nor the student needs your attention. The quality of private schools in California varies widely.

Susan Vogel has written "Private High Schools of the San Francisco Bay Area." (1999) Check with bookstores or call (415) 267-5978.

Directory of Private Schools

The directory contains the most current information available at press time.

In California, tuition ranges widely in private schools. Many Catholic elementaries charge from about $2,500 to $3,000 plus. Catholic high schools run $6,500 to $7,500.

Some non-denominational schools with low pupil-teacher ratios charge over $12,000.

Don't let the numbers scare you from calling. Some schools offer scholarships. Discounts are often given for siblings. If strapped, ask about financial help.

Day care costs extra.

Alameda County

Alameda

Alameda Christian, 2226 Pacific Ave., (510) 523-1000, Enroll: 98, K-7th.

Children's Learning Ctr., 1910 Central Ave., (510) 769-7100, Enroll: 47, Ungraded Special Ed.

Peter Pan Acad., 3171 Mecartney Rd., (510) 523-4080, Enroll: 48, K-5th.

Rising Star Montessori Sch., 1421 High St., (510) 865-4536, Enroll: 93, K-5th.

St. Barnabas Elem. Sch., 1400-Sixth St., (510) 521-0595, Enroll: 168, K-8. **See ad page 87.**

St. Joseph Elem. Sch., 1910 San Antonio Ave., (510) 522-4457, Enroll: 307, K-8.

St. Joseph Notre Dame High Sch., 1011 Chestnut St., (510) 523-1526, Enroll: 545, 9th-12th. **See ad page 85.**

St. Philip Neri Elem. Sch., 1335 High St., (510) 521-0787, Enroll: 284, K-8.

Berkeley

Academy, 2722 Benvenue Ave., (510) 549-0605, Enroll: 118, K-8th.

Arrowsmith Acad., 2300 Bancroft Way, (510) 540-0440, Enroll: 107, 9th-12th.

Berkeley Montessori, 2030 Francisco St., (510) 843-8340, Enroll: 207, K-8.

Berkwood-Hedge, 1809 Bancroft Way, (510) 883-6990, Enroll: 100, K-5th.

Black Pine Circle Day Elem., 2027 Seventh St., (510) 845-0876, Enroll: 219, K-8th.

Comm. Sch of the East Bay, 2401 Leconte, (510) 649-0505, Enroll: 41, 7th-8th.

Crowden, 1475 Rose St., (510) 559-6910, Enroll: 78, 4th-8th.

Ecole Bilingue Elem. Sch., 1009 Heinz Ave., (510) 549-3867, Enroll: 445, K-8th.

Maybeck High Sch., 2362 Bancroft Way, (510) 841-8489, Enroll: 101, 9th-12th.

Montessori Family Sch., 1850 Scenic Ave., (510) 848-2322, Enroll: 52, Presch.-6th. **See ad on this page.**

School of the Madeleine, 1225 Milvia St., (510) 526-4744, Enroll: 288, K-8.

Shelton's Primary Ed. Ctr., 3339 Martin Luther King, Jr. Way, (510) 652-6132, Enroll: 84, K-5th.

St. Joseph the Worker Elem. Sch., 2125 Jefferson Ave., (510) 845-6266, Enroll: 106, K-8th.

St. Mary's College High, 1294 Albina Ave. Peralta Park, (510) 559-6237, Enroll: 630, 9th-12th.

Walden Center Elem., 2446 McKinley, (510) 841-7248, Enroll: 93, K-6th.

Castro Valley

Camelot, 2330 Pomar Vista, (510) 481-1304, Enroll: 100, K-6th.

His Acad., 6694 Crow Canyon Rd., (510) 513-3179, Enroll: 117, K-12th.

Our Lady of Grace Sch., 19920 Anita Ave., (510) 581-3155, Enroll: 291, K-8th.

Redwood Christian Elem., 19300 Redwood Rd., (510) 537-4288, Enroll: 433, K-6th.

Redwood Christian Sch. Crossroads Campus, 20600 John Dr., (510) 537-4277, Enroll: 214, K-6th.

Dublin

Quarry Lane Sch., 6363 Tassajara Rd., (925) 829-8000, Enroll: 199, 1st-8th.

St. Philip Lutheran Sch., 8850 Davona Dr., (925) 829-3857, Enroll: 156, K-8.

St. Raymond Sch., 11555 Shannon Ave, (925) 828-4064, Enroll: 300, K-8th.

Valley Christian Elem., 7508 Inspiration Dr., (925) 560-6270, Enroll: 707, K-6.

Valley Christian Jr.-Sr. High, 7500 Inspiration Dr., (925) 560-6250, Enroll: 700, 7th-12th.

Fremont

Annoor Islamic Inst., 33350 Peace Terr., (510) 477-9946 Enroll: 70, K-8th.

Bethel Christian Acad.-Baptist, 36060 Fremont Blvd., (510) 795-1234, Enroll: 82, K-8th.

Christian Community, 39700 Mission Blvd., (510) 651-5437, Enroll: 454, K-8th.

Dominican Kindergarten, 43326 Mission Blvd., (510) 657-2468, Enroll: 32, K.

Fremont Christian Sch., 4760 Thornton Ave., (510) 744-2200, Enroll: 1,176, K-12th.

Holy Spirit Elem. School, 3930 Parish Ave., (510) 793-3553, Enroll: 305, K-8th.

Mission Hills Christian Sch., 225 Driscoll, (510) 490-7709, Enroll: 26, K-8th.

Montessori School of Fremont, 155 Washington Blvd., (510) 490-1993, Enroll: 168, K-6th.

New Horizons Sch., 2550 Peralta Blvd., (510) 791-5683, Enroll: 106, K-6th.

Peace Terrace Acad., 33330 Peace Terrace, (510) 477-9946, Enroll: 52, K-8th.

Prince of Peace Lutheran, 38451 Fremont Blvd., (510) 797-8186, Enroll: 188, K-8th.

Seneca Center, 40950 Chapel Way, (510) 226-6180, Enroll: 53, 1st-12th.

St. Joseph Elem. Sch., 43222 Mission Blvd., (510) 656-6525, Enroll: 287, 1st-8th.

St. Leonard Elem., 3635 St. Leonard's Way, (510) 657-1674, Enroll: 258, K-8th.

Stellar Acad. for Dyslexics, 5301 Curtis St., (510) 687-1490, Enroll: 42, K-8th.

Hayward

All Saints, 22870 Second St., (510) 582-1910, Enroll: 298, K-8th.

American Heritage Christian, 425 Gresel St., (510) 471-1010, Enroll: 180, K-12th.

Cornerstone Christian Acad., 24150 Hesperian Blvd., (510) 786-4281, Enroll: 36, K-12th.

Lea's Christian Sch., 26236 Adrian Ave., (510) 785-2477, Enroll: 73, K-4.

Montessori Children's House, 166 W. Harder Rd., (510) 782-4427, Enroll: 51, K-3rd.

Moreau Catholic High Sch., 27170 Mission Blvd., (510) 881-4300, Enroll: 1,080, 9th-12th.

St. Bede's Elem. Sch., 26910 Patrick Ave., (510) 782-3444, Enroll: 284, K-8th.

St. Clement Sch., 790 Calhoun St., (510) 538-5885, Enroll: 307, K-8th.

St. Joachim's Elem.-Cath., 21250 Hesperian Blvd., (510) 783-3177, Enroll: 312, K-8th.

Woodroe Woods Sch., 22502 Woodroe Ave., (510) 582-3273, Enroll: 40, K-2nd.

Livermore

Celebration Acad., 1135 Bluebell Dr., (925) 277-4313, Enroll: 62, K-12th.

Our Savior's Lutheran, 1385 S. Livermore Ave., (925) 447-2082 Enroll: 363, K-8th.

Sonrise Christian Acad., 164 North L St., (925) 373-2161, Enroll: 69, K-8th.

St. Michael's Elem., 372 Maple St., (925) 447-1888, Enroll: 322, K-8th. **See ad on this page.**

Valley Montessori School, 1273 N. Livermore Ave., (925) 455-8021, Enroll: 155, K-8th.

Newark

American Christian Acad., 36651 Hunyan St., (510) 790-7636, Enroll: 41, 1st-12th.

Challenger, 35487 Dumbarton Ct., (510) 739-0300, Enroll: 533, 1st-8th.

Challenger, 39600 Cedar Blvd., (510) 770-1771, Enroll: 58, K.

St. Edward's Sch., 5788 Thornton Ave., (510) 793-7242, Enroll: 308, K-8th.

Oakland

Acts Full Gospel Christian Acad., 1034 66th Ave., (510) 568-3333, Enroll: 192, K-8th.

GRADES K-8
St. Michael's School
Quality Catholic Education Since 1913

- Positive Christian Atmosphere
- Emphasis on Basic Academic Skills
- Enrichment in Music, Drama, Art
- Motor Development Classes
- Honors Classes in English & Math
- Instruction in Computers
- Departmentalized Classes for Grades 6-8
- Before & After School Care Available

447-1888
372 Maple Street
Livermore

Agnes Mem. Christian Acad., 2372 Int'l Blvd., (510) 533-1101, Enroll: 56, K-12.

Archway, 250 41st St., (510) 547-4747, Enroll: 88, K-8th.

Atherton Academy, 8030 Atherton St., (510) 562-0381, Enroll: 169, K-8th.

Aurora, 40 Dulwich Rd., (510) 428-2606, Enroll: 122, K-5th.

Beacon, 2101 Livingston St., (510) 436-4466 Enroll: 263, K-12th.

Bentley Elem., One Hiller Dr., (510) 843-2512, Enroll: 351, K-8th.

Bishop O'Dowd High, 9500 Stearns Ave., (510) 577-9100, Enroll: 1,145, 9th-12th.

Clara Mohammed, 1652 47th Ave., (510) 436-7755, Enroll: 71, K-8th.

College Prep., 6100 Broadway, (510) 652-0111, Enroll: 320, 9th-12th.

Fred Finch School, 3800 Coolidge Ave., (510) 482-2224 , Enroll: 54, 6th-12th Spec. Ed..

Golden Gate Acad., 3800 Mountain Blvd., (510) 531-0110, Enroll: 115, 1st-12th.

Head-Royce Sch., 4315 Lincoln Ave., (510) 531-1300, Enroll: 751, K-12th.

Herbert Guice Christian Acad., 6925 International Blvd, (510) 729-0330, Enroll: 80, K-4th.

Holy Names High Sch., 4660 Harbord Dr., (510) 450-1110, Enroll: 279, 9-12th.

Ile Omode Elem., 8924 Holly St., (510) 632-8230, Enroll: 32, K-6th.

Julia Morgan Sch. for Girls, 3510 Mountain Blvd., (510) 436-1400, Enroll: 131, 6th-8th.

Lincoln Child Center, 4368 Lincoln Ave., (510) 531-3111, Enroll: 79, K-10th.

Mack Christian Sch., 1279 75th Ave., (510) 382-0965, Enroll: 130, K-12th.

Mills College Children's Sch., 5000 MacArthur Blvd., (510) 430-2118, Enroll: 59, K-5th.

Muhammad University of Islam, 5277 Foothill Blvd., (510) 436-0206, Enroll: 99, K-12th.

Montessori Casa Dei Bambini, 281 Santa Clara Ave., (510) 836-4313, Enroll: 37, K-6th.

Northern Light Sch., 4500 Redwood Rd., (510) 530-9366, Enroll: 107, K-8.

Oakland Hebrew Day Sch., 215 Ridgeway Ave., (510) 652-4324, Enroll: 101, K-7th.

Park Day, Inc., 370 43rd St., (510) 653-0317, Enroll: 234, K-6th.

Patten Acad. of Christian Ed., 2433 Coolidge Ave., (510) 533-8300, Enroll: 176, K-12th.

Pentecostal Way of Truth Acad., 1575 Seventh St., (510) 625-2002, Enroll: 42, K-12th.

Raskob Day, 3520 Mountain Blvd., (510) 436-1275, Enroll: 59, 4th-8th.

Redwood Day Sch., 3245 Sheffield Ave., (510) 534-0800, Enroll: 263, K-8th.

Renaissance Sch., 3668 Diamond Ave., (510) 531-8566, Enroll: 110, 2nd-6th.

Spectrum Ctr. for Ed. & Behavioral Dev., 6325 Camden St., (510) 729-6384, Enroll: 98, Ungraded Special Ed.

St. Andrew Missionary Baptist Private Sch., 2624 West St., (510) 465-8023, Enroll: 192, K-12th.

St. Anthony Year Round Sch., 1500 East 15th St., (510) 534-3334, Enroll: 149, K-8th.

St. Augustine Sch., 410 Alcatraz Ave., (510) 652-6727, Enroll: 112, K-8th.

St. Bernard-Catholic, 1630 62nd Ave., (510) 632-6323, Enroll: 163, K-8th.

Sts. Cyril-Louis Bertrand Elem., 3200 62nd Ave., (510) 638-9445, Enroll: 251, K-8

St. Elizabeth Elem., 1516 33rd Ave., (510) 532-7392, Enroll: 489, K-8th.

St. Elizabeth High Sch., 1530 34th Ave., (510) 532-8947, Enroll: 295, 9th-12th.

St. Jarlath Elem. Sch., 2634 Pleasant St., (510) 532-4387, Enroll: 241, K-8.

St. Lawrence O'Toole Elem., 3695 High St., (510) 530-0266, Enroll: 268, K-8.

St. Leo Elem. Sch., 4238 Howe St., (510) 654-7828, Enroll: 230, K-8th.

St. Martin De Porres, 1630 10th St., (510) 832-1757, Enroll: 45, 6th-8th.

St. Martin De Porres, 675 41st St., (510) 652-2220, Enroll: 124, K-8th.

St. Paschal Baylon Sch., 3710 Dorisa Ave., (510) 635-7922, Enroll: 155, K-8th.

St. Paul's Episcopal Sch., 116 Montecito Ave., (510) 287-9600, Enroll: 281, K-8th.

St. Theresa Elem. Sch., 4850 Clarewood Dr., (510) 547-3146, Enroll: 276, K-8.

St. Vincent's Day Home, 1086 8th St., (510) 832-8324, Enroll: 57, K-6th.

Piedmont

Corpus Christi Elem., One Estates Dr., (510) 530-4056, Enroll: 279, K-8th.

Zion Lutheran Elem. Sch., 5201 Park Blvd., (510) 530-7909, Enroll: 175, K-8th.

Pleasanton

Carden-West, 4466-A Black Ave., (925) 484-6060, Enroll: 109, K-5th.

Hacienda Sch., 3800 Stoneridge Dr., (925) 485-5750, Enroll: 69, 1st-8th.

Quarry Lane, 3750 Boulder St., (925) 846-9400, Enroll: 56, K-1st.

San Leandro

Assumption Elem., 1851 136th Ave., (510) 357-8772, Enroll: 291, K-8th.

Candell's College Prep., 16576 Russell Ct., (510) 632-1110, Enroll: 42, K-12th.

Chinese Christian Sch., 750 Fargo Ave., (510) 351-4957, Enroll: 886, K-12th.

Community Christian, 562 Lewelling Blvd., (510) 351-3684, Enroll: 233, K-12th.

Montessori Sch. of San Leandro, 16292 Foothill Blvd., (510) 278-1115, Enroll: 82, 1st-6th.

Principled Acad., 2305 Washington Ave. #A, (510) 351-6400, Enroll: 94, K-8th.

Seneca Center, 2275 Arlington Dr., (510) 481-1222, Enroll: 101, 1st-12th.

St. Felicitas Elem.-Catholic, 1650 Manor Blvd., (510) 357-2530, Enroll: 268, K-8th.

St. Leander-Catholic, 451 Davis St., (510) 351-4144, Enroll: 265, K-8th.

Stars High, 2050 Fairmont Dr., (510) 678-5591, Enroll: 36, 8th-12th.

San Lorenzo

Calvary Lutheran Elem., 17200 Via Magdalena, (510) 278-2598, Enroll: 184, K-8th.

Lighthouse Christian Acad., 16053 Ashland Ave., (510) 276-9108, Enroll: 84, K-12th.

Redwood Christian Jr./Sr., 1000 Paseo Grande, (510) 317-8990, Enroll: 476, 7th-12th.

St. John Elem.-Catholic, 270 E. Lewelling Blvd., (510) 276-6632, Enroll: 285, K-8th.

Union City

Our Lady of the Rosary Sch., 678 B St., (510) 471-3765, Enroll: 174, K-8th.

Purple Lotus Buddhist, 33615 9th St., (510) 429-8808, Enroll: 36, 1st-12th.

Semore Sch., 4312 Dyer St., (510) 471-1774, Enroll: 90, K-6th.

Union City Christian Acad., 33700 Alvarado-Niles Rd., (510) 489-0394, Enroll: 132, K-12th.

Chapter 5

Infant-Baby Care

FOR LICENSING, California divides child-care facilities into several categories:
- Small family: up to 6 children in the providers' home.
- Large family: 7-12 children in the provider's home.
- Nursery Schools or Child-Care centers.
  A child is considered an infant from birth to age 2.

Individual sitters are not licensed and neither are people whom parents arrange for informally to take care of their children but if a person is clearly in the business of child care from more than one family he or she should be licensed. Each of the three categories has restrictions. For example, the small-family provider with six children cannot have more than three under age 2.

In everyday reality, many of the larger facilities tend to limit enrollments to children over age 2, and some have even higher age limits or a requirement that the child be toilet-trained.

The state and its local umbrella agencies maintain referral lists of local infant-care and day-care providers. All you have to do is call and they will send a list of the licensed providers and suggestions on how to make a wise choice. For a list of family-care providers, call BANANAS at (510) 658-0381 (Oakland) or the 4C's of Alameda County (Southern Alameda) at (510) 582-2182 or Child Care Links (Livermore-Dublin-Pleasanton) at (925) 455-0417.

Here's some advice from one licensing agency:
- Plan ahead. Give yourself one month for searching and screening.
- Contact the appropriate agencies for referrals.
- Once you have identified potential caregivers, phone them to find out about their services and policies. For those that meet your needs, schedule a time to visit while children are present.
- At the site, watch how the children play and interact with one another.
- Contact other parents using the programs. Ask if they are satisfied with the care and if their children are happy and well-cared-for.
- Select the program that best meet your needs. "Trust your feelings and your instincts."

This is a bare-bones approach. The referral centers can supply you with more information. To get you started, we are listing here the names of the infant centers in the county. For older children, see next chapter.

Alameda County

Alameda

Alameda Tiny Tots, 3300 Bridgeview Isle, (510) 521-8025

College of Alameda Children's Ctr., 555 Atlantic Ave., (510) 748-2381

Int'l Child Resource Inst., 2001 Santa Clara Ave., (510) 522-3194

KinderCare, 2155 N. Loop Rd., (510) 521-3227

Little Seeds Children's Ctr., 2055 Santa Clara Ave., (510) 865-5900

Peter Pan Presch., 1510 Encinal Ave., (510) 523-5050

Peter Pan Presch., 2100 Mariner Square Dr., (510) 521-2750

Wee Care Presch. & CC, 2133 Central Ave., (510) 523-7858

Berkeley

Aquatic Park Ctr., 830 Heinz Ave., (510) 843-2273

Berkeley YMCA Early Head Start, 1450 6th St., (510) 558-2110

BUSD-Vera Casey Parent Child, 2246 Martin Luther King, Jr. Way, (510) 644-6954

Cedar Street CC, 2138 Cedar St., (510) 549-3989

Child Ed. Ctr., 1222 University Ave., (510) 528-1414

Cornerstone Children's Ctr., 2407 Dana St., (510) 848-6252

Model Sch. Compre. Humanistic Lrng. Ctr., 2330 Prince St., (510) 549-2711

St. John's CC Prog., 2717 Garber St., (510) 549-9342

UCB-Anna Head Children's Ctr., 2537 Haste St., (510) 642-1960

UCB-Clark Kerr Inf. Ctr., 2601 Warring St., (510) 642-9795

UCB-Inf./ Toddler Ctr., 2340 Durant Ave., (510) 642-1123

Woolly Mammoth CC & Presch., 2314 Bancroft Way, (510) 548-4779

Castro Valley

Camelot Sch., 2330 Pomar Vista, (510) 481-1304

His Growing Grove, 2490 Grove Way, (510) 581-5088

Lil' Sunflowers CDCtr., 20875 Chester St., (510) 881-0378

Dublin

KinderCare, 11925 Amador Valley Ct., (925) 875-0400

La Petite Acad., 5000 Hacienda Ave., (925) 236-7203

My Space To Grow, 7197 Amador Valley Blvd., (925) 829-4063

Resurrection Luth. Inf. Care Ctr., 7557 Amador Valley Blvd., (925) 828-2122

Emeryville

Emeryville CDCtr., 1220 53rd St., (510) 596-4343

Siebel Children's Ctr., 2100 Powell St., (510) 788-4780

Fremont

Children's Galaxy, 34735 Ardenwood Blvd., (510) 793-1696

Kidango-Delaine Eastin CDCtr., 584 Brown Rd., (510) 490-5570

Kidango-Fremont Ad. Sch. Child Dev. Sch., 4700 Calaveras Ave., (510) 494-9601

Kidango-Marie Kaiser Ctr., 4457 Seneca Park Ave., (510) 226-8130

Kidango-Mission Valley ROP CDCtr., 40230 Laiolo Rd., (510) 657-4913

Kidango-Rix Inf. Ctr., 43100 Isle Royal St., (510) 656-3949

Kidango-Washington Hospital, 2000 Mowry Ave., (510) 731-3400

KinderCare, 32710 Falcon Dr., (510) 324-3569

KinderCare, 38700 Paseo Padre Pkwy., (510) 796-0888

Montessori Children's Ctr., 33170 Lake Mead Dr., (510) 489-7511

Hayward

Chabot College Children's Ctr., 25555 Hesperian Blvd., (510) 723-6684

Cherubim's Children's Ctr., 30540 Mission Blvd., (510) 471-7713

Early Childhood Ed. Ctr., 25800 Carlos Bee Blvd., (510) 885-2480

Eden Youth CCCtr., 680 W. Tennyson Rd., (510) 782-6084

ESP-A Special Place CCCtr., 27305 Huntwood Ave., (510) 782-6635

His Kids, 26221 Gading Rd., (510) 786-3641

Li'l Angels at Ruus, 28924 Ruus Rd., (510) 670-9007

S. Alameda Co. Head Start-Eden Youth, 680 W. Tennyson Rd., (510) 782-6207

Kidango-Helen Turner Inf. Dev. Ctr., 23640 Reed Way, (510) 264-0927

YMCA-Eden, 951 Palisade St., (510) 247-8284

YMCA-Y-Kids Eden Self-Sufficiency, 24100 Amador St., (510) 259-2925

Livermore

Cape, Inc.-Jackson Ctr., 560 Jackson Ave., (925) 443-0220

Creative Playschool, 690 N. L St., (925) 294-9955

Kidango-Marylin Inf. Dev. Ctr., 800 Marylin Ave., (925) 371-6376

Kidango-Owl's Landing CDCtr., 860 Hermann Ave., (925) 744-9280

Kidango-Pepper Tree Sch., 714 Junction Ave., (925) 447-0264

KinderCare, 4655 Lassen Rd., (925) 455-1560

Laboratory Employee Children's Ctr., 1401 Almond Ave., (925) 373-0865

New Horizons Nursery Sch.-Inf. Prog., 405 E. Jack London Blvd., (925) 455-6082

Trinity DCCtr., 557 Olivina Ave., (925) 449-5683

Valley Montessori Sch., 1273 N. Livermore Ave., (925) 455-8021

Newark

Kidango-Rushin Inf. Dev. Ctr., 36120 Rushin Blvd., (510) 793-5562

Oakland

AOCS-Brookdale Ctr., 3021 Brookdale Ave., (510) 261-1077

AOCS-Hedco Inf./Toddler Ctr., 2929 Coolidge Ave., (510) 261-1076

Booth Memorial Inf./Toddler Prog., 2794 Garden St., (510) 535-5088

First Step Children's Ctr., 111 Fairmount Ave., (510) 238-0882

Four C's CDCtr., 756 21st St.. (510) 272-0669

Kidango-Chestnut Ctr., 1058 W. Grand Ave., (510) 989-1111

Laney College Children's Ctr., 900 Fallon St., (510) 464-3104

Little Stars Presch., 169 14th St., (510) 286-9800

Merritt College Children's Ctr., 12500 Campus Dr., (510) 531-4911

Mills College Children's Sch., Mills College Campus, (510) 430-2118

PCDCI-Frank G. Mar Ctr., 274 12th St., (510) 835-9236

Alameda County Births — History & Projections

1980s		1990s		2000s	
Year	**Births**	**Year**	**Births**	**Year**	**Births**
1981	17,984	1991	23,252	2001	22,018
1982	18,220	1992	22,678	2002	21,953
1983	18,466	1993	21,919	2003	21,921
1984	19,255	1994	21,387	2004	21,893
1985	19,624	1995	20,941	2005	21,896
1986	20,127	1996	20,668	2006	21,991
1987	20,957	1997	20,766	2007	22,170
1988	21,862	1998	20,933	2008	22,344
1989	22,419	1999	20,547	2009	22,551
1990	23,285	2000	22,164	2010	22,758

Source: California Dept. of Finance, Demographic Research Unit. Projections start in 2001.

Sequoyah Comm. Toddler Ctr., 4292 Keller Ave., (510) 632-3481

Small Trans Depot-Honey Bee, 111 Grand Ave., (510) 286-5130

Spanish Speaking - Foothill Sq. Parent Child Ctr., 10700 MacArthur Blvd., (510) 562-4468

Spanish Speaking-Fruitvale Parent Child Ctr., 1266 26th Ave., (510) 535-6112

Spanish Speaking-Thurgood Marshall Early Headstart, 1117 10th St., (510) 836-0543

Supporting Future Growth #4, 8401 Birch St., (510) 633-3031

Supporting Future Growth #6, 5909 Camden St., (510) 567-8362

Up & Coming Inf. Dev. Ctr., 4143 MacArthur Blvd., (510) 531-9130

YWCA of Oakland-Alice St., 250 17th St., (510) 836-4117

Pleasanton

Hacienda CDCtr., 4671 Chabot Dr., (925) 463-2885

KinderCare, 3760 Brockton Dr., (925) 846-1240

La Petite Acad., 5725 Valley Ave., (925) 277-0626

Quarry Lane Sch., 3750 Boulder St., (925) 846-9400

YMCA-Pleasanton Child Dev. Prog., 4665 Bernal Ave., (510) 451-8039

San Leandro

Davis St. CDCtr., 580 Joaquin Ave., (510) 635-0536

ICRI Early Childhood Ctr., 13305 Doolittle Dr., (510) 357-1588

Union City

Kidango-Decoto Inf. Ctr., 600 G St., (510) 744-9280

Kidango-Logan Inf. Dev. Ctr., 33821 Syracuse Ave., (510) 441-1841

Chapter 6

Day Care

SEE THE PRECEDING chapter on baby care for more information. For insights on how to pick a day-care center or provider, here is some advice offered by a person who runs a day-care center.

- Ask about age restrictions. Many centers and family-care providers will not take care of children under age two or not toilet trained. See previous chapter for infant centers.

- Give the center or home a visual check. Is it clean? In good condition or in need of repairs? Is there a plan for repairs when needed?

- Find out if the person in charge is the owner or a hired manager. Nothing wrong with the latter but you should know who is setting policy and who has the final say on matters.

- Ask about the qualifications of the people who will be working directly with your child. How long have they worked in day care? Training? Education? Many community colleges now offer training in early childhood and after-school care.

- What philosophy or approach does the center use? The Piaget approach believes children move through three stages and by exploring the child will naturally move through them. The job of the teacher is to provide activities appropriate to the right stage. For example, from age 2-7, many children master drawing and language; from 7-11, they begin to think logically. For the younger child art and sorting and language games would be appropriate; multiplication would not.

  Montessori believes that if given the right materials and placed in the right setting, children will learn pretty much by themselves through trial and error. Montessorians employ specific toys for teaching.

  Traditional emphasizes structure and repetition.

  These descriptions are oversimplified and do not do justice to these approaches or others. Our only purpose here is to point out that day-care providers vary in methods and thinking, and in choosing a center, you also choose a distinct philosophy of education.

- For family day-care providers. Some set up a small preschool setting in the home. Often your child will be welcomed into the family as an extended member. Is this what you want?

- Discipline. Johnny throws a snit. How is it handled? Does the provider have a method or a plan? Do you agree with it?

- Tuition. How much? When it is due? Penalty for picking up child late? Penalty for paying late?

- Hours of operation. If you have to be on the road at 5:30 a.m. and the day-care center doesn't open until 6, you may have to look elsewhere or make different arrangements. Some centers limit their hours of operation, e.g., 10 hours.

- Holidays. For family providers, when will the family take a vacation or not be available? For the centers, winter breaks? Summer vacations?

- Communication. Ask how you will be kept informed about progress and problems. Regular meetings? Notes? Calls? Newsletters?

- Classes-Tips for parents. Opportunities to socialize with other parents? Activities for whole family?

- Field trips and classes. Outside activities. Your son and daughter play soccer, an activity outside the day-care center. How will they get to practice? What's offered on site? Gymnastics? Dance?

- Siestas. How much sleep will the children get? When do they nap? Does this fit in with your child's schedule?

- Activities. What are they? How much time on them? Goals?

- Diapers, bottles, cribs, formula, extra clothes. Who supplies what?

- Food, lunches. What does the center serve? What snacks are available?

Remember, day-care centers and providers are in business. The people who staff and manage these facilities and homes may have the best intentions toward the children but if they can't make a profit or meet payrolls, they will fail or be unable to provide quality care. Even "nonprofits" must be run in a businesslike way or they won't survive. Some centers may offer a rich array of services but for fees beyond your budget. You have to decide the trade-offs.

For licensing, the state divides child care into several categories, including infant, licensed family, child-care centers, and school-age centers for older children. The previous chapter lists the infant providers. This chapter will list the large day-care centers, for both preschool and school-age children.

For a list of family-care providers, call BANANAS at (510) 658-0381 (Oakland) or the 4C's of Alameda County (Southern Alameda) at (510) 582-2182 or Child Care Links (Livermore-Dublin-Pleasanton) at (925) 455-0417.

Alameda

ABC Presch., 1525 Bay St., (510) 521-6488

Alameda CCCtr., 2001 Santa Clara Ave., (510) 522-3194

Alameda Head Start-Esperanza, 1901 3rd St., (510) 865-4500

Alameda Head Start-Redwood Ctr., 1700 Santa Clara Ave., (510) 865-4862

Alameda Head Start-Sue Matheson, 1980 3rd St., (510) 865-0108

Alameda Head Start-Washington, 825 Taylor Ave., (510) 748-4007

Alameda Head Start-Woodstock, 1900 3rd St., (510) 748-4012

Alameda Tiny Tots, 3300 Bridgeview Isle, (510) 521-8025

AUSD- Woodstock CDCtr., 190 Singleton, (510) 748-4001

Bayside Montessori Assoc., 1523 Willow St., (510) 865-6255

Child Unique Montessori Sch., 2212 Pacific Ave., (510) 521-1030

Child Unique Montessori Sch., 2226 Encinal Ave., (510) 521-9227

College of Alameda Children's Ctr., 555 Atlantic Ave., (510) 748-2381

Garner Presch. Lrng. Ctr., 2275 N. Loop Rd., (510) 769-5437

Girls Inc.-Bay Farm Activity Ctr., 200 Auginbaugh Way, (510) 769-7426

Girls Inc.-Earhart Activity Ctr., 400 Packet Landing Rd., (510) 769-8545

Girls Inc.-Edison Activity Ctr., 2700 Buena Vista Ave., (510) 769-1975

Girls Inc.-Franklin Activity Ctr., 1433 San Antonio Ave., (510) 521-0121

Girls Inc.-Lum Activity Ctr., 1801 Sandcreek Way., (510) 522-4729

Girls Inc.-Otis Activity Ctr., 3010 Fillmore St., (510) 523-6510

Girls Inc.-Paden Activity Ctr., 444 Central Ave., (510) 523-6977

Golden House CCCtr., 1545 Morton St., (510) 865-3468

Home Sweet Home CCCtr., 2750 Todd St., (510) 748-4314

Kiddie Kampus Coop. Play Sch., 1711 2nd St., (510) 521-1218

KinderCare, 2155 N. Loop Rd., (510) 521-3227

Little Seeds Children's Ctr., 2055 Santa Clara Ave., (510) 865-5900

Montessori of Alameda-Daycare, 1247 Park Ave., (510) 521-2354

Our Children's Cottage, 770 Santa Clara Ave., (510) 865-4536

Peter Pan Presch., 1510 Encinal Ave., (510) 523-5050

Peter Pan Presch., 2100 Mariner Square Dr., (510) 521-2750

Peter Pan Presch. & DC, 3171 McCartney Rd., (510) 523-4080

Rising Star Sch., 1421 High St., (510) 865-4536

Sand Castles Presch., 3189 McCartney Rd., (510) 523-5341

Seedling Child Montessori Sch., 3183 McCartney Rd., (510) 521-5846

Son-Light Presch., 1910 Santa Clara Ave., (510) 865-6367

YMCA-Y-Kids-Haight, 2025 Santa Clara Ave., (510) 522-6526

YMCA-Y-Kids-Washington, 825 Taylor St., (510) 521-6250

Wee Care Presch. & CC, 2133 Central Ave., (510) 523-7858

Albany

Albany Children's Ctr., 1140 9th St., (510) 525-2800

Albany Children's Ctr., 800 Red Oak Ave., (510) 525-5191

Albany Presch., 850 Masonic Ave., (510) 527-6403

Bay Area Kinder Stube, 842 Key Route Blvd., (510) 525-3105

Berkeley Chinese Sch., 720 Jackson St., (510) 525-9666

Bright Star Montessori Sch., 720 Jackson St., (510) 559-6530

City of Albany "Friendship" Club, 1331 Portland Ave., (510) 524-0135

Kid's Club YMCA-Albany Library, 1216 Solano Ave., (510) 524-9737

Kid's Club YMCA-Marin Sch., 1001 Santa Fe Ave., (510) 527-7668

Little Village Presch., 919 Talbot Ave. (510) 528-4401

Wheezles and Sneezles, 1108 San Pablo Ave., (510) 526-7425

Berkeley

ALA/CCCtr. for Dev. Disabled, 1300 Rose St., (510) 527-2550

Aquatic Park Ctr. Presch., 830 Heinz Ave., (510) 843-2273

Bahia Sch. Age Prog., 1718 8th St., (510) 524-7300

Berkeley Hills Nursery Sch., 1161 Sterling Ave., (510) 849-1216

Berkeley Montessori Sch., 2030 Francisco St., (510) 849-8341

Berkeley Youth Alt. Presch. & CD Prog., 1255 Allston Way, (510) 845-9010

Berkeley-Richmond Jewish Comm. Ctr., 1414 Walnut St., (510) 848-0237

BUSD-Columbus Montessori Presch., 920 Allston Way, (510) 644-8812

BUSD- Franklin State Presch., 1460 8th St., (510) 644-6339

BUSD-Hopkins, 1810 Hopkins St., (510) 644-6405

BUSD-King Children's Ctr., 1939 Ward St., (510) 644-6358

Cedar Creek Montessori, 1600 Sacramento St., (510) 525-1377

Cedar Street CCCtr., 2138 Cedar St., (510) 549-3989

Centro Vida Bilingual CCCtr., 1000 Camelia St., (510) 525-1463

Child Ed. Ctr., 1222 University Ave., (510) 528-1414

Children's Comm. Ctr., 1140 Walnut St., (510) 526-9739

Cornerstone Children's Ctr., 2407 Dana St., (510) 848-6252

Claremont Day Nurseries, 2845 Woolsey Ave., (510) 654-2511

Color Me Children Presch., 1141 Bancroft Way, (510) 548-6423

Congregation Beth El, 2301 Vine St., (510) 848-3988

Congregation Beth Israel-Gan Shalom, 2230-32 Jefferson St., (510) 848-3298

Dandelion Nursery Sch., 941 The Alameda, (510) 526-1735

Duck's Nest, 1411 4th St., (510) 527-2331

Ecole Bilingue de Berkeley, 2830 10th St., (510) 549-3867

Ephesian Children's Ctr., 1907 Harmon Ave., (510) 653-2984

Garden Day Montessori, 1332 Parker St., (510) 649-9110

Gay Austin Sch., 1611 Hopkins St., (510) 526-2815

Griffin Nursery Sch., 2410 Prince St., (510) 845-2025

Hearts Leap Presch., 2638 College Ave., (510) 549-1422

Hopkins Street CCCtr., 1910 Hopkins St., (510) 524-1352

I Can Before and After Sch., 2108 Russell St., (510) 644-8204

Jubilee Kids DCCtr., 1125 Allston Way, (510) 540-8111

Kids' Club YMCA-Hillside, 1581 Leroy Ave., (510) 644-3152

Kids' Club YMCA-Le Conte, 2241 Russell St., (510) 867-7834

Kids' Club YMCA-Malcolm X, 1731 Prince St., (510) 867-5315

Kids' Club YMCA-Washington, 2300 Martin Luther King Jr. Way., (510) 812-7365

Kids in Motion, 2955 Claremont Ave., (510) 549-9247

McGee's Farm Presch., 2214 Grant St., (510) 849-3593

Model Sch. Compre. Humanistic Lrng. Ctr., 2330 Prince St., (510) 549-2711

Montessori Family Sch., 1850 Scenic Ave., (510) 848-2322

Monteverde Sch., 2727 College Ave., (510) 848-3313

Mulberry Sch., 207 Alvarado Rd., (510) 540-5778

Mustard Seed Presch., 1640 Hopkins St., (510) 527-6627

New School of Berkeley, 1606 Bonita Ave., (510) 548-9165

New School of Berkeley-Sch. Age, 1924 Cedar St., (510) 548-9165

NIA House Lrng. Ctr., 2234 9th St., (510) 845-6099

Progressive Christian DCCtr., 1728 Alcatraz Ave., (510) 654-6686

Rose Street Comm. CCCtr., 1226 Rose St., (510) 524-4271

Shelton's Primary Ed. Ctr., 3339 Martin Luther King Jr. Way, (510) 652-6132

Snuggery, 2008 McGee Ave., (510) 548-9121

St. John's CCCtr., 2717 Garber St., (510) 549-9342

Step One Sch., 499 Spruce St., (510) 527-9021

UCB-After Sch. Prog., 2601 Warring St., (510) 642-8442

UCB-Anna Head Children's Ctr., 2537 Haste St., (510) 642-3239

UCB-Clark Kerr Campus Children's Ctr., 2900 Dwight Way., (510) 642-5527

UCB-Girton Hall CCCtr., UC Berkeley Central Campus, (510) 642-5677

UCB-Harold E. Jones Child Study Ctr., 2425 Atherton St., (510) 643-5449

Via Nova Children's Sch., 3032 Martin Luther King Jr. Way, (510) 848-6682

Woolly Mammoth CC & Presch., 2314 Bancroft Way, (510) 548-4779

YMCA Head Start, 1227 Bancroft Way, (510) 845-1213

YMCA Head Start-6th St., 1450 6th St., (510) 558-2110

YMCA Head Start-Berkeley Adult Sch., 1222 University Ave., (510) 841-4152

YMCA Head Start-Ocean View, 1422 San Pablo Ave., (510) 559-2090

YMCA Head Start-Sacramento, 3155 Sacramento St., (510) 547-6683

YMCA Head Start-S. YMCA, 2901 California St., (510) 848-9092

YMCA Head Start-W. YMCA 1,2,3,4, 2009 10th St., (510) 848-9092

Castro Valley

Aahl's ABC Presch. & DC, 20135 San Miguel Ave., (510) 581-5577

Adventure Time-Independent, 21201 Independent Sch. Rd., (510) 733-9134

Adventure Time-Jensen Ranch, 20001 Carson Ln., (510) 728-9933

Adventure Time-Vannoy, 5100 Vannoy Ave., (510) 733-0635

Bright World Presch., 20613 Stanton Ave., (510) 581-1580

Camelot Sch.-Valley View Campus, 2330 Pomar Vista, (510) 481-1304

Creative Beginnings Presch., 20121 Santa Maria Ave., (510) 581-5990

CVUSD-Marshall State Presch., 20111 Marshall St., (510) 537-5933

First Baptist Presch.- A Kids Kingdom, 18550 Redwood Rd., (510) 889-8800

Growing Years Day Camp, 20166 Wisteria Ave., (510) 733-0848

Growing Years Presch., 20320 Anita Ave., (510) 581-3731

Happiness Hill Presch., 20600 John Dr., (510) 537-0773

His Growing Grove, 2490 Grove Way, (510) 581-6203

Kids Care Plus-Chabot, 3432 Christensen Ln., (510) 538-7577

Kids Care Plus-Cyn. Mid. Sch., 19600 Cull Canyon Rd., (510) 538-8351

Kids Care Plus-Proctor, 17520 Redwood Rd., (510) 582-0304

Kids Care Plus-Stanton, 2644 Somerset Ave., (510) 733-0775

Lil' Sunflowers CD Prog., 20875 Chester St., (510) 881-0378

Montessori of Castro Valley, 19234 Lake Chabot Rd., (510) 582-9413

Montessori Sch. at Five Canyons, 22781 Canyon Ct., (510) 581-3729

Redwood Forest Presch., 19200 Redwood Rd., (510) 537-0222

Rise 'N Shine Presch., 20104 Center St., (510) 582-9136

R-Kids Ext. Day Ctr., 4779 Heyer Ave., (510) 733-6018

Saybrook Lrng. Ctr., 20375 Wisteria St., (510) 581-2340

YMCA-Y-Kids-Marshall, 20111 Marshall St., (510) 581-4996

YMCA-Y-Kids-Castro Valley, 20185 San Miguel Ave., (510) 881-4458

Dublin

Creative Playschool, 6837 Amador Valley Blvd., (925) 803-4035

Easter Seals Kaleidoscope Ctr., 7425 Larkdale Ave., (925) 828-8857

Extd. Day-Dougherty Elem., 5301 Hibernia St., (925) 803-4154

Extd. Day-Dublin Elem., 7997 Vomac Rd., (925) 846-5519

Extd. Day-Frederiksen, 7243 Tamarack Dr., (925) 833-0127

Extd. Day-Murray, 8435 Davona Dr., (925) 829-4043

Extd. Day-Nielsen, 7500 Amarillo Rd., (925) 829-5443

Fountainhead Montessori Sch., 6901 York Dr., (925) 820-1343

John Knox Coop. Presch., 7421 Amarillo Rd., (925) 828-2887

Joy Presch. & DCCtr., 7421 Amarillo Rd., (925) 829-3233

Kidango-Arroyo Vista Presch., 6700 Dougherty Rd., (925) 560-0669

KinderCare, 11925 Amador Valley Ct., (925) 875-0400

La Petite Acad., 5000 Hacienda Dr., (925) 236-7203

Little Kids Lrng. Ctr., 11760 Dublin Blvd., (925) 828-2081

Love and Care Presch., 8010 Hollanda Ln., (925) 828-1170

Montessori Plus, 7234-40 San Ramon Rd. (925) 829-1321

My Space To Grow, 7197 Amador Valley Blvd., (925) 829-4063

Resurrection Lutheran Presch., 7557-A Amador Valley Blvd., (925) 829-5487

St. Philip Presch., 8850 Davona Dr., (925) 829-3857

Tot's University, 7890 Oxbow Ln., (925) 833-9002

Valley Christian Presch. & DC, 7504 Inspiration Dr., (925) 560-6235

Emeryville

Berkeley YMCA-Head Start, 1220 53rd St., (510) 653-2619

Berkeley YMCA-Head Start, 4727 San Pablo Ave., (510) 655-6936

Emeryville CDCtr., 1220 53rd St., (510) 596-4343

Pacific Rim Int'l. Sch., 5521 Doyle St., (510) 601-1500

Siebel Children's Ctr., 2100 Powell St., (510) 788-4780

Fremont

A Child's Hideaway, 37531 Fremont Blvd., (510) 792-8415

A Child's Hideaway, 45150 Grimmer, (510) 656-3218

Adventure Time-Ardenwood, 33955 Emilia Ln., (510) 797-6280

Adventure Time-Brookvale, 3400 Nicolet Ave., (510) 797-5180

Adventure Time-Glenmoor, 4620 Mattos Dr., (510) 744-0772

Adventure Time-Maloney, 38700 Logan Dr., (510) 797-5373

Adventure Time-Mattos, 37944 Farwell, (510) 713-2158

Adventure Time-Mission San Jose, 43545 Bryant St., (510) 490-7874

Adventure Time-Niles, 37141 2nd St., (510) 797-4806

Adventure Time-Parkmont, 2601 Parkside Dr., (510) 713-2011

Adventure Time-Vallejo Mill, 38569 Canyon Heights Dr., (510) 658-7412

Adventure Time-Warwick, 3375 Warwick Rd., (510) 797-6122

Bay Area CC-Azeveda, 39450 Royal Palm Dr., (510) 651-7041

Bay Area CC-Brier/Glankler, 39201 Sundale Dr., (510) 657-8392

Bay Area CC-Gomes, 577 Lemos Ln., (510) 490-4222

Bay Area CC-Millard, 5200 Valpey Park Dr., (510) 683-8810

Bay Area CC-Olivera, 4180 Alder Ave., (510) 797-8613

Bay Area CC-Patterson, 35521 Cabrillo Dr., (510) 797-9145

Centerville Presby. Nursery Sch., 4360 Central Ave., (510) 797-6757

Children's Galaxy, 34735 Ardenwood Blvd., (510) 793-1696

Christian Comm. Presch., 39700 Mission Blvd., (510) 651-5437

Creative Life School, 40155 Blacow Rd., (510) 656-9955

Evangelical Free Church-Little Lamb Ministries, 505 Driscoll Rd., (510) 656-1359

Fremont Christian Presch., 4760 Thornton Ave., (510) 744-2260

Fremont Christian Presch., 38495 Fremont Blvd., (510) 405-5010

Fremont Congregational Nursery Sch., 38255 Blacow Rd., (510) 793-3999

FUSD-Alvirda Hyman Lrng. Ctr., 4700 Calaveras Ave., (510) 797-0128

FUSD-Blacow State Presch., 40404 Sundale Dr., (510) 353-9728

FUSD-Cabrillo State Presch., 36700 San Pedro Dr., (510) 792-3015

FUSD-Durham Presch., 40292 Leslie St., (510) 656-6360

FUSD-Glankler State Presch., 39207 Sundale Dr., (510) 651-3902

FUSD-Grimmer State Presch., 43030 Newport Dr., (510) 668-1543

Gan Sameach Nursery Sch., 42000 Paseo Padre Pkwy., (510) 651-5833

Happy Bear Forest Children's Lrng. Ctr., 39600 Mission Blvd., (510) 793-2327

Harvest Christian Presch. & DC, 4360 Hansen Ave., (510) 797-0170

Head Start-Conrad Noll, 39600 Sundale Dr., (510) 623-7448

Head Start-Hacienda, 35699 Niles Blvd., (510) 796-9396

Holy Spirit Presch., 3930 Parish Ave., (510) 793-2013

Kidango-Delaine Eastin, 584 Brown Rd., (510) 490-5570

Kidango-Fremont Adult Sch., 4700 Calaveras Ave., (510) 494-9601

Kidango-Grace Draper, 255 H St., (510) 797-2732

Kidango-Mission Valley ROP CDCtr., 40230 Laiolo Rd., (510) 657-4913

Kidango-Ohlone College, 43600 Mission Blvd., (510) 659-6000

Kidango-Peralta Ctr., 1301 Mowry Ave., (510) 797-3724

Kidango-Rix Ctr., 43100 Isle Royal St., (510) 656-3949

Kidango-Washington Hospital, 2000 Mowry Ave., (510) 791-3400

Kiddie Kare, 2450 Durham Rd., (510) 226-7723

Kiddo Land Lrng. Ctr., 46280 Briar Place, (510) 490-7311

Kids Wonderland, 4343 Stevenson Blvd., (510) 651-0515

KinderCare, 32710 Falcon Dr., (510) 324-3569

KinderCare, 38700 Paseo Padre Pkwy., (510) 796-0888

Learning Tree CCCtr., 34050 Paseo Padre Pkwy., (510) 791-6161

Little Mud Puddle's DCCtr., 34072 Fremont Blvd., (510) 791-6158

Mission Playmates, 2367 Jackson St., (510) 656-3722

Monarch Christian Presch., 38895 Mission Blvd., (510) 494-1221

Montessori Children's Ctr., 33170 Lake Mead Dr., (510) 489-7511

Montessori Sch. of Centerville, 4209 Baine Ave., (510) 797-9944

Montessori Sch. of Fremont, 155 Washington Blvd., (510) 490-0919

Montessori Sch. of Fremont Children's House, 1901 Washington Blvd., (510) 490-1727

New Study Sch., 4620 Mattos Dr., (510) 797-0740

One-Two-Three Lrng. Ctr., 46280 Briar Pl., (510) 490-7311

Our Savior Lutheran Presch. & K, 858 Washington Blvd., (510) 657-9269

Parkmont Sch., 4727 Calaveras Ave., (510) 791-2222

Precious Time Christian Presch., 33350 Peace Terr., (510) 429-3990

Rainbow Kids Presch. & Ext. DC, 38000 Camden St., (510) 797-2222

Scribbles Montessori, 38660 Lexington St., (510) 797-9944

Shining Star Montessori, 4047 Alder Ave., (510) 573-2232

Simon's Presch. & DCCtr., 39614 Sundale Dr., (510) 659-0656

Sunshine Kids Presch., 47832 Warm Springs Blvd., (510) 445-0222

YMCA of the East Bay-Blacow, 40404 Sundale Dr., (510) 659-4051

YMCA-Y-Kids-Cabrillo, 36700 San Pedro, (510) 657-5200

YMCA-Y-Kids-Chadbourne, 801 Plymouth Ave., (510) 656-7243

YMCA-Y-Kids-Durham, 40292 Leslie St., (510) 683-9107

YMCA-Y-Kids-Forest Park, 34402 Maybird Cir., (510) 451-8033

YMCA-Y-Kids-Grimmer, 43030 Newport Dr., (510) 651-2457

YMCA-Y-Kids-James Leith, 47100 Fernald St., (510) 683-9147

YMCA-Y-Kids-Mission Valley, 41700 Denise St., (510) 659-9427

YMCA-Y-Kids-Warm Springs, 47370 Warm Springs Blvd., (510) 683-9165

YMCA-Y-Kids-Weibel, 45135 S. Grimmer Blvd., (510) 683-9167

Hayward

ABC Academy, 670 Sunset Blvd., (510) 581-4926

Adventure Time-Lorenzo Manor, 18250 Bengal Ave., (510) 482-0610

Camelot Sch., 21753 Vallejo St., (510) 581-5125

Chabot College Children's Ctr., 25555 Hesperian Blvd., (510) 723-6684

Cherubim's Children's Ctr., 30540 Mission Blvd., (510) 471-7713

Children's Choice Educare, 185 West Harder Rd., (510) 887-3025

Circle Time Nursery Sch., 26555 Gading Rd., (510) 887-1885

CSUH- Early Childhood Ed. Ctr., 25800 Carlos Bee Blvd., (510) 885-2480

Eden Youth Ctr. CCCtr., 680 W. Tennyson Rd., (510) 887-1146

Elmhurst DC & Presch., 380 Elmhurst St., (510) 786-1289

ESP-A Special Place CCCtr., 27305 Huntwood Ave., (510) 782-6635

Fairview Hills Presch., 2841 Ramagnolo Ave., (510) 581-0604

Head Start-Darwin, 2560 Darwin St., (510) 264-9252

Head Start-Eden, 951 Palisade St., (510) 728-4923

Head Start-Glassbrook, 925 Schafer Rd., (510) 732-6628

His Kids, 26221 Gading Rd., (510) 786-3641

HUSD Child Dev.-Bowman, 520 Jefferson, (510) 582-1743

HUSD Child Dev.-Burbank, 353 B St., (510) 582-1675

HUSD Child Dev.-Cherryland, 585 Willow Ave., (510) 582-1737

HUSD Child Dev.- Helen Turner, 23640 Reed Way, (510) 783-3793

HUSD Child Dev.-Muir, 24823 Soto Rd., (510) 582-1792

HUSD Child Dev.-Palma Ceia, 27679 Melbourne Ave., (510) 293-9822

HUSD Child Dev.-Shepherd, 27211 Tyrrell Ave., (510) 783-1182

Kidango-Glen Berry CDCtr., 625 Berry Ave., (510) 728-0649

Kidango-Hillview Crest CDCtr., 31410 Wheelon Ave., (510) 324-3499

Lea's Christian Sch.-CCCtr., 26236 Adrian Ave., (510) 785-2477

Lil' Angels At Ruus, 28924 Ruus Rd., (510) 670-9007

Montessori Children's House, 26236 Adrian Ave., (510) 782-4427

Montessori Children's Sch., 1836 B St., (510) 537-8155

Montessori Sch. of Hayward, 1101 Walpert St., (510) 581-3729

Supporting Future Growth #7, 22584 S. Garden Ave., (510) 780-9120

State Presch. at Royal Sunset, 20450 Royal Ave., (510) 317-4412

Woodroe Woods Sch., 22502 Woodroe Ave., (510) 582-3273

YMCA-Y-Kids-Eden Self Sufficiency, 24100 Amador St., (510) 259-2925

YMCA-Y-Kids-Strobridge, 21400 Bedford Dr., (510) 538-7459

YMCA-Y-Kids and State Presch.-Eden, 951 Palisade St., (510) 247-8284

Livermore

Ark Presch. & CC, 4161 East Ave., (925) 447-8279

Beth Emek Presch., 1886 College Ave., (925) 443-1689

Bess Platt Presch., 543 Sonoma Ave., (925) 443-3434

CAPE-Jackson Ctr., 560 Jackson Ave., (925) 443-0220

CAPE-Wm. Ormand III Early Ed. Ctr., 800 Marylin Ave., (925) 443-3434

CAPE-Leahy Ctr., 3203 Leahy Way, (925) 443-3434

Celebration Lrng. Ctr., 1135 Bluebell Dr., (925) 245-1252

Christian World CCCtr., 3820 East Ave., (925) 455-5551

Comm. Sch. Age Prog., 2200 Arroyo Rd., (925) 447-0227

Creative Playschool, 676-690 N. L St., (925) 294-9955

Happyland CCCtr., 5800 East Ave., #208, (925) 245-9521

Holy Cross Lutheran Nursery Sch., 1020 Mocho St., (925) 447-1864

Kidango-Owl's Landing CDCtr., 860 Hermann Ave., (925) 744-9280

Kidango-Pepper Tree Sch., 714 Junction Ave., (925) 447-0264

KinderCare, 4655 Lassen Rd., (925) 455-1560

Kinderkirk Nursery Sch., 2020 5th St., (925) 455-0793

Laboratory Employee Children's Ctr., 1401 Almond Ave., (925) 373-0865

Little Rascals Lrng. Ctr., 1893 N. Vasco Rd., (925) 373-8988

Livermore Play Sch., 5261 East Ave., (925) 447-6042

LARPD-Almond, 1401 Almond Ave., (925) 373-5045

LARPD-Altamont Creek, 6500 Garaventa Ranch Rd., (925) 373-5715

LARPD-Arroyo Mocho, 1040 Florence Rd., (925) 373-5715

LARPD-Arroyo Seco, 5280 Irene Way, (925) 373-5731

LARPD-Christensen, 5757 Haggin Oaks Ave., (925) 373-5031

LARPD-Croce, 5650 Scenic Ave., (925) 373-5742

LARPD-Jackson, 554 Jackson Ave., (925) 373-5732

LARPD-Marylin, 800 Marylin Ave., (925) 373-5733

LARPD-Michell, 1001 Elaine Ave., (925) 373-5780

LARPD-Portola, 2451 Portola Ave., (925) 373-5734

LARPD-Rancho, 401 Jack London Blvd., (925) 373-5781

LARPD-Smith, 391 Ontario Dr., (925) 373-5735

LARPD-Sunset, 1671 Frankfurt Way, (925) 373-5736

New Horizons Nursery Sch., 405 E. Jack London Blvd., (925) 455-6082

Our Savior Lutheran Early CDCtr., 1385 S. Livermore Ave., (925) 443-0124

Razan's Wonderland, 949 Central Ave., (925) 449-4999

St. Bartholomew's Episcopal CCCtr., 678 Enos Way, (925) 373-9564

Storyland Presch. & CCCtr., 2486 East Ave., (925) 449-1531

Sunset Christian Sch. & Presch., 2200 Arroyo Rd., (925) 443-5594

Trinity DCCtr., 557 Olivina Ave., (925) 449-5683

Valley Montessori Sch., 460 N. Livermore Ave., (925) 455-8021

Wee Care, 359 Jensen St., (925) 443-9977

Newark

Acad. Montessori Int'l., 37815 Birch St., (510) 796-3866

Birch Grove Presch., 6020 Robertson Ave., (510) 792-1759

Challenger Sch., 35487 Dumbarton Ct., (510) 739-0300

Challenger Sch., 39600 Cedar Blvd., (510) 770-1771

Diversity Children's Ctr., 37371 Filbert St., (510) 797-7190

Head Start-Ash, 37365 Ash St., (510) 796-9511

Head Start-Whiteford, 35725 Cedar Blvd., (510) 791-1966

Kidango-Newark, 36120 Ruschin Dr., (510) 794-9186

King's Kids Presch., 38325 Cedar Blvd., (510) 791-8555

Montessori Sch. of Newark, 35660 Cedar Blvd., (510) 792-4546

Newark Comm. Ctr. Annex, 35501 Cedar Blvd., (510) 745-1124

Oakland

24 Hr. Oakland Parent Teacher CC #1, 4700 E. 14th St., (510) 532-0574

24 Hr. Oakland Parent Teacher CC #2, 3500 E. 9th St., (510) 261-0162

ABCs and 123s CDCtr., 2530 90th Ave., (510) 568-5021

ABCs and 123s Presch., 3136 13th Ave., (510) 261-1016

ACTS Full Gospel Christian Acad., 1127 62nd Ave., (510) 638-1978

ACTS Full Gospel Christian Acad., 1034 66th Ave., (510) 568-3333

Advance DCCtr., 2236 International Blvd., (510) 434-9288

Adventure Time-Chabot, 6686 Chabot Rd., (510) 655-8151

Adventure Time-Crocker Highlands, 525 Midcrest Rd., (510) 834-1578

Adventure Time-Glenview Elem. Sch., 4215 Lacresta Ave., (510) 530-6081

Adventure Time-Hillcrest, 30 Marguerite Dr., (510) 482-0610

Adventure Time-Joaquin Miller, 5525 Ascot Dr., (510) 531-7782

Adventure Time-Kaiser, 25 S. Hill Ct., (510) 845-3371

Adventure Time-Montclair, 1757 Mountain Blvd., (510) 482-0610

Adventure Time-Thornhill, 5880 Thornhill Dr., (510) 482-0610

Affordable Acad., 5607 Holway St., (510) 436-0844

Agnes Memorial, 2372 E. 14th St., (510) 533-1101

Ala Costa Ctr., 3400 Malcolm St., (510) 527-2550

Alice St.-Oakland Pub. Sch., 250 17th St., (510) 879-0856

Apple Garden Montessori, 5667 Thornhill Dr., (510) 339-9666

AOCS-Ellen Sherwood, 3021 Brookdale Ave., (510) 261-1077

Arroyo Viejo-Oakland Pub. Sch., 1895 78th Ave., (510) 879-0802

Auntie Carla's CC and Presch., 2421 Kingsland Ave., (510) 534-4545

Beacon Day Sch., 2101 Livingston St., (510) 436-4466

Bernice & Joe Playschool, 7001 Sunkist Dr., (510) 638-3529

Blossom Day Sch., 4701 Market St., (510) 658-5892

Booth Memorial DC, 2794 Garden St., (510) 535-5088

Broadway Children's Sch., 394 Adams St., (510) 763-9337

Building Blocks, 2370 Grande Vista Pl., (510) 434-7990

CCUMC Nursery Sch., 321 8th St., (510) 268-8210

Centro Infantil de la Raza-Oakland Pub. Sch., 2660 E. 16th St., (510) 879-0819

Chatham Sch., 4359 39th Ave., (510) 531-1534

Chinese Comm. Nursery, 321 8th St., (510) 268-8210

Claremont Day Nurseries, 5830 College Ave., (510) 658-5208

Color Me Children, 8115 Fontaine St., (510) 430-1322

Color Me Children Presch., 3625 MacArthur Blvd., (510) 482-7507

Daisy CDCtr., 5016 Daisy St., (510) 531-6426

Deerview Christian Acad., 3780 Mountain Blvd., (510) 531-0415

Dr. Herbert Guice Christian Acad., 6925 International Blvd., (510) 729-0330

Duck Pond, 4426 Park Blvd., (510) 530-0851

Duck's Nest Piedmont, 4498 Piedmont Ave., (510) 428-0901

East Hills Ext. DCCtr., 12000 Campus Dr., (510) 531-6908

Felicia's Giant Step Presch., 3261 Martin Luther King Jr. Way, (510) 652-8110

First Covenant-Treehouse Presch., 4000 Redwood Rd., (510) 531-0320

First Step Children's Ctr., 111 Fairmount Ave., (510) 239-0880

Four C's CDCtr., 756 21st St., (510) 272-0669

Gan Avraham Nursery Sch., 327 MacArthur, (510) 763-7528

Gan Mah Tov Presch., 3778 Park Blvd., (510) 530-2146

Garfield-Oakland Pub. Sch., 1640 22nd Ave., (510) 532-0358

Giggles, 6009 Colby St., (510) 601-6526

Grace Children's Acad., 993 53rd St., (510) 653-1115

Grand Lake Montessori, 466 & 472 Chetwood St., (510) 836-4313

Grand Lake Montessori, 281 Santa Clara Ave., (510) 836-4313

Growing Light Montessori Sch., 4700 Lincoln Ave., (510) 336-9897

Halimah's Presch., 1150 63rd St., (510) 654-7381

Head Start-55th Ave., 1800 55th Ave., (510) 273-3164

Head Start-85th Ave., 8501 International Blvd., (510) 544-3821

Head Start-92nd Ave., 9202 E. 14th St., (510) 568-1406

Head Start-Arroyo Viejo Park, 7701 Krause Ave., (510) 635-4035

Head Start-Brookfield, 9600 Edes Ave., (510) 615-5737

Head Start-Dignity, 690 15th St., (510) 832-5331

Head Start-Eastmont Mall, 7200 Bancroft Ave., (510) 636-1153

Head Start-Fannie Wall, 647 55th St., (510) 658-0960

Head Start-Franklin Ctr., 1010 E. 15th St., (510) 238-1306

Head Start-Frank Mar, 274 12th St., (510) 238-3165

Head Start-Lockhaven, 1327 65th Ave., (510) 615-5798

Head Start-Manzanita, 2701 22nd Ave., (510) 535-5627

Head Start-Maritime Ctr., Oakland Army Base, Bldg. #655, (510) 238-3165

Head Start-San Antonio, 2228 E. 15th St., (510) 535-5639

Head Start-San Antonio Park, 1701 E. 19th St., (510) 535-5737

Head Start-Seminary, 5818 International Blvd., (510) 615-5585

Head Start-Sungate, 2563 E. 14th St., (510) 535-5649

Head Start-Tassafaronga, 975 85th Ave., (510) 639-0580

Head Start-Virginia, 4335 Virginia Ave., (510) 261-1479

Head Start-Willow, 1682 7th St., (510) 238-2268

Horizon Sch., 9520 Mountain Blvd., (510) 635-7470

Ile Omode Sch., 8924 Holly St., (510) 632-8230

Jewish Comm. Svcs., 412 Monte Vista Ave., (510) 658-9222

Kidango-Chestnut, 1058 W. Grand Ave., (510) 989-1111

Kennedy Tract Parent-Child Ctr., 3001 Chapman St., (510) 261-4993

Lake Merritt CCCtr. #1, 12834 Lakeshore Ave., (510) 839-2828

Lake Merritt CCCtr. #2, 301-345 12th St., (510) 834-3399

Lake Sch., 304 Lester Ave., (510) 839-4227

Lakeshore Children's Ctr., 3518-3546 Lakeshore Ave., (510) 893-4048

Lakeview - Oakland Pub. Sch., 746 Grand Ave., (510) 879-0857

Lakeview Presch., 515 Glenview Ave., (510) 444-1725

Laney College Children's Ctr., 900 Fallon St., (510) 839-7875

Laurel CDCtr.-Oakland Pub. Sch., 3825 California St., (510) 879-0820

Little Folks Presch., 360 W. MacArthur Blvd., (510) 653-4650

Little Stars Presch., 169 14th St., (510) 839-9600

Lockwood CDCtr.-Oakland Pub. Sch., 1125 69th Ave., (510) 879-0823

Lockwood PreK-Oakland Pub. Sch., 6701 International Blvd., (510) 879-0827

Longfellow-Oakland Pub. Sch., 880 39th St., (510) 879-1350

Lossieland, 8130 Plymouth St., (510) 569-8150

Manzanita CDCtr.-Oakland Pub. Sch., 2618 Grande Vista Ave., (510) 879-0829

Martin Luther King, Jr. CDCtr.,-Oakland Pub. Sch., 960-A 10th St., (510) 879-0822

Merritt College Children's Ctr., 12500 Campus Dr., (510) 436-2436

Merritt College Presch. Practicum, 12500 Campus Dr., (510) 436-2588

Mills College Children's Sch., Mills College Campus, (510) 430-2118

Monroe's Lrng. Ctr., 3415 Maple Ave., (510) 531-2781

Montclair Comm. Play Ctr., 5815 Thornhill Dr., (510) 339-7213

Mountain Blvd. Presch. Lrng. Ctr., 4432 Mountain Blvd., (510) 482-2850

My Own Montessori Sch., 5723 Oak Grove Ave., (510) 652-5979

New Day Presch. & Lrng. Ctr., 460 W. Grand Ave., (510) 465-8591

Northern Light Sch., 4500 Redwood Rd., (510) 530-9366

Oakland Montessori Sch., 3636 Dimond St., (510) 482-3111

Oakland Progressive DC, 733 Beatie St., (510) 835-0131

Organized Youth Expression, 1086 Alcatraz Ave., (510) 508-1011

OUSD-Bella Vista, 2410 10th Ave., (510) 879-0805

OUSD-Brookfield CDCtr., 401 Jones Ave., (510) 633-0462

OUSD-Cox, 9860 Sunnyside St., (510) 879-0807

OUSD-Emerson CDCtr., 4801 Lawton Ave., (510) 879-0811

OUSD-Fruitvale CDCtr., 3200 Boston Ave., (510) 879-1170

OUSD-Golden Gate, 6232 Herzog St., (510) 879-0814

OUSD-Harriet Tubman, 800 33rd St., (510) 547-1832

OUSD-Hawthorne PreK, 2920 E. 18th. St., (510) 879-1326

OUSD-Highland, 1322 86th Ave., (510) 879-0815

OUSD-Hintil Kuu Ca, 11850 Campus Dr., (510) 879-0840

OUSD-Howard, 8755 Fontaine St., (510) 635-7517

OUSD-International CDCtr., 2825 International Blvd., (510) 879-4236

OUSD-Jefferson, 1975 40th Ave., (510) 436-3700

OUSD-Lafayette, 1700 Market St., (510) 879-1290

OUSD-Piedmont, 86 Echo Ave., (510) 652-5740

OUSD-Prescott, 800 Campbell St., (510) 893-5882

OUSD-Santa Fe, 5380 Adeline St., (510) 879-0837

OUSD-Woodland CDCtr., 1029 81st Ave., (510) 879-0190

OUSD-Yuk Yau, 291 10th St., (510) 893-1659

OUSD-Yuk Yau Annex, 314 E. 10th St., (510) 832-4388

Pacific Coast Montessori Prog., 326 51st St., (510) 653-3129

Parker CDCtr.-Oakland Pub. Sch., 7901 Ney Ave., (510) 879-0828

PCDCI-First Presbyterian, 2619 Broadway, (510) 452-0492

PCDCI-Great Beginnings, 1643 90th Ave., (510) 635-1690

PCDCI-Little Learners, 690 18th St., (510) 451-8459

PCDCI-Sch. Age CDCtr., 1094 56th St., (510) 653-2065

PCDCI-Small Citizens, 6203 Avenal Ave., (510) 562-0777

Peek "A" Boo Dev. CCCtr., 2656 68th Ave., (510) 632-2101

Peter Pan Coop. Nursery Sch.-Maxwell House, 4618 Allendale Ave., (510) 261-5210

Pilgrim's Enrichment & Presch. Prog., 3900 35th Ave., (510) 531-3715

Rainbow Sch., 5918 Taft Ave., (510) 658-2034

Renaissance Sch., 3668 Dimond Ave., (510) 531-8566

Rockridge Montessori, 5610 Broadway, (510) 652-7021

Sequoia Nursery Sch., 2666 Mountain Blvd., (510) 531-8853

Sequoyah Presch., 4292 Keller Ave., (510) 632-3481

Skyline Presch., 12540 Skyline Blvd., (510) 531-8212

Smiles Day Sch., 5621 Thornhill Dr., (510) 339-3830

Smiles Day Sch., 5701 Thornhill Dr., (510) 339-9660

Snow White Presch., 214 W. MacArthur Blvd., (510) 655-8353

Spanish Speaking-De Colores, 1233 38th Ave., (510) 535-6107

Spanish Speaking-Foothill Square Parent Child Ctr., 10700 MacArthur Blvd., (510) 553-9926

Spanish Speaking-Fruitvale Parent Child Ctr., 1266 26th Ave., (510) 535-6112

SSUC-Thurgood Marshall Early Head Start, 1117 10th St., (510) 836-0543

St. Leo's PreK, 4238 Howe St., (510) 654-7828

St. Mary's Ctr. Presch., 635 22nd St., (510) 893-4723

St. Vincent's Day Home, 1086 8th St., (510) 832-8324

Starlite CDCtr., 2354 Telegraph Ave., (510) 482-3213

Starlite CDCtr. II, 246 14th St., (510) 238-8809

Stonehurst CDCtr.-Oakland Pub. Sch., 901 105th Ave., (510) 879-0838

Supporting Future Growth #1, 3208 San Pablo Ave., (510) 658-7606

Supporting Future Growth #2, 860 30th St., (510) 834-5267

Supporting Future Growth #3, 1466 Havenscourt Blvd., (510) 635-9268

Supporting Future Growth #4, 8401 Birch St., (510) 633-3031

Supporting Future Growth #5, 5410 Fleming Ave., (510) 534-4808

Supporting Future Growth #6, 5909 Camden St., (510) 567-8362

Supporting Future Growth #8, 936 32nd St., (510) 834-5267

Temple Sinai Presch., 2808 Summit St., (510) 451-2821

Therapeutic Nursery Sch., 6117 Martin Luther King Jr. Way, (510) 428-3406

Tilden CDCtr.-Oakland Pub. Sch., 4655 Steele St., (510) 879-0841

Washington-Oakland Pub. Sch., 6097 Racine St., (510) 547-1875

Webster Acad.-Oakland Pub. Sch., 7980 Plymouth St., (510) 879-0842

Wee Li'l People Presch., 650 Alma St., (510) 433-0288

YMCA-Y-Kids, 3265 Market St., (510) 654-9622

YMCA-Y-Kids-Hoover, 890 Brockhurst, (510) 428-0749

YMCA-Y-Kids Presch. & CDCtr., 1106 Madison St., (510) 444-6586

YMCA-Y-Kids Presch., 3265 Market St., (510) 654-9622

Piedmont

Highlands Presch., 400 Highland Ave., (510) 547-4242

Linda Beach Presch., 400 Highland Ave., (510) 547-4432

Piedmont Play Sch., 401 Hampton Ave., (510) 654-4371

Piedmont Schoolmates-Beach Sch. , 100 Lake Ave., (510) 420-3077

Piedmont Schoolmates-Havens Sch., 1800 Oakland Ave., (510) 420-3078

Piedmont Schoolmates-Wildwood Sch., 301 Wildwood Ave., (510) 420-3076

Pleasanton

Adventures In Lrng., 3200 Hopyard Rd., (925) 462-7123

CAPE Head Start- Hill N'Dale Presch., 4150 Dorman Rd., (925) 426-8341

Carden-West Sch., 4466 Black Ave., (925) 484-6060

Child Day Schools, 883 Rose Ave., (925) 462-1866

Children's World Lrng. Ctr., 7110 Koll Center Pkwy., (925) 462-2273

Early Years Children's Ctr., 1251 Hopyard Rd., (925) 462-2202

Extd. Day CC-Walnut Grove, 5199 Black Ave., (925) 484-3312

Hacienda CDCtr., 4671 Chabot Dr., (925) 463-2885

KinderCare, 3760 Brockton Dr., (925) 846-1240

Kinderkirk Christian Presch., 4300 Mirador Dr., (925) 846-2465

La Petite Acad., 5725 Valley Ave., (925) 462-7844

Quarry Lane Sch., 3750 Boulder St., (925) 846-9400

Shining Light Presch., 4455 Del Valle Pkwy., (925) 846-6622

Sonshine Enrichment Ctr. Presch., 1225 Hopyard Rd., (925) 417-8411

St. Clare's Christian Presch., 3350 Hopyard Rd., (925) 462-0938

YMCA-Pleasanton CD Prog., 4775 Bernal Ave., (510) 451-8039

YMCA Y-Kids-Fairlands, 4151 W. Las Positas, (925) 426-1992

YMCA Y-Kids-Lydiksen, 7700 Highland Oaks Dr., (925) 426-9784

YMCA Y-Kids-Mohr, 3300 Dennis Dr., (925) 484-9429

San Leandro

Adventure Time-Corvallis, 14790 Corvallis St., (510) 352-5782

Adventure Time-James Madison, 14751 Juniper St., (510) 658-7412

Adventure Time-Jensen Ranch, 20001 Carson Ln., (510) 728-9933

Avenue Presch., 1521-41 159th Ave., (510) 276-1700

Beth Sholom Presch., 642 Dolores Ave., (510) 357-7920

Davis St. CC at Garfield Sch., 13050 Aurora Dr., (510) 567-0322

Davis Street CCCtr., 1190 Davis St., (510) 635-5437

Davis Street CDCtr.-Joaquin, 580 Joaquin Ave., (510) 635-0536

Davis Street Comm. Ctr., 951 Dowling Blvd., (510) 777-9317

Davis Street-Jefferson, 14311 Lark St., (510) 483-3637

Footprints Presch., 14871 Bancroft Ave., (510) 352-8351

Head Start-Jefferson, 14432 Bancroft Ave., (510) 895-5107

Head Start-Madison, 14811 Juniper St., (510) 483-2924

ICRI- Early Childhood Ctr., 13305 Doolittle Dr., (510) 357-1588

Li'l Angels DCCtr., 890 Fargo Ave., (510) 895-8736

Montessori Sch., 16492 Foothill Blvd., (510) 278-1115

Montessori Sch., 14795 Washington Ave., (510) 278-1115

Noah's Ark Presch., 1699 Orchard Ave., (510) 483-8940

Our Future Tots, 963 Manor Blvd., (510) 352-7400

Principled Acad., 2305 Washington Ave., (510) 351-6400

St. James Christian Presch., 993 Estudillo Ave., (510) 895-9590

St. Leander PreK, 451 Davis St., (510) 351-4144

Stepping Stones Growth Ctr., 311 MacArthur Blvd., (510) 568-3331

San Lorenzo

Adventure Time-Bay Sch., 2001 Bockman Rd., (510) 276-5406

Adventure Time-Del Rey, 1510 Via Sonya, (510) 482-0610

Adventure Time-Grant, 879 Grant Ave., (510) 658-7412

Calvary Lutheran Presch., 17200 Via Magdalena, (510) 278-2598

Challenger Sch., 2005 Via Barrett, (510) 481-8690

Comm. Church Presch., 945 Paseo Grande, (510) 276-4808

Lighthouse Kiddie Kingdom, 16053 Ashland Ave., (510) 276-9114

Lollipop Lane Presch., 341 Paseo Grande, (510) 481-2114

Union City

Adventure Montessori Acad. & Sch., 4101 Pleiades Ct., (510) 489-4191

Free to Be Presch., 188 Appian Way, (510) 471-0731

Head Start-Decoto Plaza, 500 E St., (510) 489-8211

Kidango-Alvarado CDCtr., 31100 Fredi St., (510) 675-9326

Kidango-Cabello Presch. Dev. Ctr., 4500 Cabello St., (510) 489-4141

Kidango-Decoto CDCtr., 600 G St., (510) 489-2185

Kidango-Eastin CDCtr., 34901 Eastin Dr., (510) 475-9630

Kidango-Kitayama CDCtr., 1959 Sunsprite Dr., (510) 675-9350

Kidango-Logan Presch., 33809 Syracuse Ave., (510) 487-1689

Kidango-Pioneer Presch., 32737 Bel Aire St., (510) 487-4530

Kidango-Searles CDCtr., 33629 15th St., (510) 471-2772

Little Peoples Presch. & DC, 33700 Alvarado-Niles Rd., (510) 489-8650

Semore Sch., 4312 Dyer St., (510) 471-1774

Chapter 7

Hospitals & Health Care

GOOD HEALTH CARE. You want it. Where, how, do you get it? The question is particularly puzzling these days because so many changes are taking place in medicine and medical insurance.

The "operations" of a few years ago are the "procedures" of today, done in the office, not the surgery, completed in minutes, not hours, requiring home care, not hospitalization.

Large insurance companies, through their health maintenance plans, are setting limits on what doctors and hospitals can charge, and — critics contend — interfering with the ability of doctors to prescribe what they see fit. The companies strongly deny this, arguing they are bringing reforms to a profession long in need of reforming. In 2001, money arguments between insurance firms and hospitals and medical groups forced many people to change HMO plans.

Many hospitals are merging, the better to avoid unnecessary duplication and to save money by purchasing supplies and medicine in larger amounts.

Universal health insurance having failed to clear congress, about 44 million Americans are not covered by any medical plan. Unable to afford medical bills, many ignore ailments and illnesses. Another big issue, the cost of prescriptions, especially for the elderly. In 2004, Congress is supposed to pass some relief. We'll see.

This chapter will give you an overview of Northern California health care and although it won't answer all your questions — too complex a business for that — we hope that it will point you in the right directions.

For most people, health care is twinned with insurance, in systems that are called "managed care." But many individuals, for a variety of reasons, do not have insurance. This is a good place to start: with nothing, all options open. Let's use as our seeker for the best of all health-care worlds — on a tight budget — a young woman, married, one child. Her choices:

No Insurance — Cash Care

The woman is self-employed or works at a small business that does not offer health benefits.

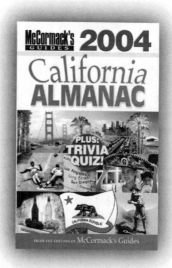

She comes down with the flu. When she goes into the doctor's office, she will be asked by the receptionist, how do you intend to pay? With no insurance, she pays cash (or credit card), usually right there. She takes her prescription, goes to the pharmacy and pays full cost.

If her child or husband gets sick and needs to see a doctor, the same procedure holds. Also the same for treatment of a serious illness, to secure X-rays or hospitalization. It's a cash system.

Medi-Cal

If an illness strikes that impoverishes the family or if the woman, through job loss or simply low wages, cannot afford cash care, the county-state health system will step in.

The woman fills out papers to qualify for Medi-Cal, the name of the system (it's known elsewhere as Medicaid), and tries to find a doctor who will treat Medi-Cal patients.

If unable to find an acceptable doctor, the woman could turn to a county hospital or clinic. There she will be treated free or at very low cost.

Drawbacks-Pluses of Medi-Cal

County hospitals and clinics, in the personal experience of one of the editors — who has relatives who work at or use county facilities — have competent doctors and medical personnel. If you keep appointments promptly, often you will be seen with little wait. If you want immediate treatment for, say, a cold, you register and you wait until an urgent-care doctor is free.

If you need a specialist, often the county facility will have one on staff, or will be able to find one at a teaching hospital or other facility. You don't choose the specialist; the county physician does.

County facilities are underfunded and, often, inconveniently located — a major drawback. Some counties, lacking clinics and hospitals, contract with adjoining counties that are equipped. You have to drive some distance for treatment.

County hospitals and clinics are not 100-percent free. If you have money or an adequate income, you will be billed for service. Some county hospitals run medical plans designed for people who can pay. These people can ask for a "family" doctor and receive a higher (usually more convenient) level of care.

Let's say the woman lacks money but doesn't want to hassle with a long drive and, possibly, a long wait for treatment of a minor ailment. She can sign up for Medi-Cal to cover treatment of serious illnesses, and for the colds, etc., go to a private doctor for treatment and pay in cash, ignoring Medi-Cal.

There are many ways to skin the cat, and much depends on circumstances. For the poor and low-income, Medi-Cal is meant to be a system of last resort.

Medicare — Veterans Hospital

If our woman were elderly, she would be eligible for Medicare, the federal insurance system, which covers 80 percent, with limitations, of medical costs or allowable charges.

Many people purchase supplemental insurance to bring coverage up to 100 percent (long-term illnesses requiring hospitalization may exhaust some benefits.)

If the woman were a military veteran with a service-related illness, she could seek care at a Veteran's Administration clinic or hospital.

Indemnity Care

Usually the most expensive kind of insurance, this approach allows complete freedom of choice. The woman picks the doctor she wants. If her regular doctor recommends a specialist, she can decide which one, and if she needs hospital treatment, she can pick the institution. In reality, the choice of hospital and specialist often will be strongly influenced by her regular doctor but the patient retains control. Many indemnity plans have deductibles and some may limit how much they pay out in a year or lifetime. Paperwork may be annoying.

Managed Care

This divides basically into two systems, Preferred Provider Organizations (PPO) and Health Maintenance Organizations (HMO). Both are popular in California and if your employer provides health insurance, chances are almost 100 percent you will be pointed toward, or given a choice of one or the other.

PPOs and HMOs differ among themselves. It is beyond the scope of this book to detail the differences but you should ask if coverage can be revoked or rates increased in the event of serious illness. Also, what is covered, what is not. Cosmetic surgery might not be covered. Psychiatric visits or care might be limited. Ask how emergency or immediate care is provided. Ask about drug costs.

Preferred Provider

The insurance company approaches certain doctors, clinics, medical facilities and hospitals and tells them: we will send patients to you but you must agree to our prices — a method of controlling costs — and our rules. The young woman chooses her doctor from the list, often extensive, provided by the PPO. The physician will have practicing privileges at certain local hospitals. The young woman's child contracts pneumonia and must be hospitalized. Dr. X is affiliated with XYZ hospital, which is also signed up with the PPO plan. The child is treated at XYZ hospital.

If the woman used an "outside" doctor or hospital, she would pay extra — the amount depending on the nature of the plan. It is important to know the doctor's affiliations because you may want your hospital care at a certain institution.

Hospitals differ. A children's hospital, for instance, will specialize in children's illnesses and load up on children's medical equipment. A general hospital will have a more rounded program. For convenience, you may want the hospital closest to your home.

If you need specialized treatment, you must, to avoid extra costs, use the PPO affiliated specialists. The doctor will often guide your choice.

Besides the basic cost for the policy, PPO insurance might charge fees, co-payments or deductibles. A fee might be $5 or $10 a visit. With co-payments, the bill, say, comes to $100. Insurance pays $80, the woman pays $20.

Deductible example: the woman pays the first $250 or the first $2,000 of any medical costs within a year, and the insurer pays bills above $250 or $2,000. With deductibles, the higher the deductible the lower the cost of the policy. The $2,000 deductible is really a form of catastrophic insurance.

Conversely, the higher the premium the more the policy covers. Some policies cover everything. (Dental care is usually provided through a separate insurer.) The same for prescription medicines. You may pay for all, part, or nothing, depending on the type plan.

The PPO doctor functions as your personal physician. Often the doctor will have his or her own practice and office, conveniently located. Drawback: PPOs restrict choice.

Health Maintenance Organization (HMO)

Very big in California because Kaiser Permanente, one of the most popular medical-hospital groups, is run as an HMO. The insurance company and medical provider are one and the same. All or almost all medical care is given by the HMO. The woman catches the flu. She sees the HMO doctor at the HMO clinic or hospital. If she becomes pregnant, she sees an HMO obstetrician at the HMO hospital or clinic and delivers her baby there.

With HMOs you pay the complete bill if you go outside the system (with obvious exceptions; e.g., emergency care). HMOs encourage you to pick a personal physician. The young woman wants a woman doctor; she picks one from the staff. She wants a pediatrician as her child's personal doctor; the HMO, usually, can provide one.

HMO clinics and hospitals bring many specialists and services together under one roof. You can get your eyes examined, your hearing tested, your prescriptions filled, your X-rays taken within a HMO facility (this varies), and much more.

If you need an operation or treatment beyond the capability of your immediate HMO hospital, the surgery will be done at another HMO hospital within the system or at a hospital under contract with the HMO. Kaiser recently started contracting with other facilities to provide some of the services that it used to do in its own hospitals or clinics. One example: Kaiser contracts with Children's Hospital in Oakland for treatment of some illnesses afflicting children. HMO payment plans vary but many HMO clients pay a monthly fee and a small per visit fee. Often the plan includes low-cost or reduced-cost or free prescriptions.

Drawback: Freedom of choice limited. If HMO facility is not close, the woman will have to drive to another town.

Point of Service (POS)

Essentially, an HMO with the flexibility to use outside doctors and facilities for an extra fee or a higher deductible. POS systems seem to be popular with people who don't feel comfortable limiting themselves to an HMO. They pay extra but possibly not as much as other alternatives.

Tiered Plans

One of the latest wrinkles. Because hospital stays make up a large part of insurance bills, insurers are shifting some of these costs onto employers and consumers. This approach divides hospitals, based on their costs, into three tiers or price levels. When a patient is admitted to a hospital, he or his plan pays extra, the amount depending on the tier rating.

Choices, more information

If you are receiving medical insurance through your employer, you will be limited to the choices offered. In large groups, unions often have a say in what providers are chosen.

Some individuals will base their choice on price, some on convenience of facilities, others on what's covered, and so on.

Many private hospitals offer Physician Referral Services. You call the hospital, ask for the service and get a list of doctors to choose from. The doctors will be affiliated with the hospital providing the referral. Hospitals and doctors will also tell you what insurance plans they accept for payment and will send you brochures describing the services the hospital offers.

For Kaiser and other HMOs, call the local hospital or clinic.

A PPO will give you a list of its member doctors and facilities.

Ask plenty of questions. Shop carefully.

Here's some advice from a pro on picking a health plan: Make a chart with a list of prospective health plans in columns across the top.

Down the left side of the chart, list the services or attributes that you think are important. Review the health plans and check off the "important" services in each plan. Choose or investigate further those plans that have the most check marks.

Common Questions

The young woman is injured in a car accident and is unconscious. Where will she be taken?

Generally, she will be taken to the closest emergency room or trauma center, where her condition will be stabilized. Her doctor will then have her admitted into a hospital. Or she will be transferred to her HMO hospital or, if indigent, to a county facility.

If her injuries are severe, she most likely will be rushed to a regional trauma center. Trauma centers have specialists and special equipment to treat serious injuries. Both PPOs and HMOs offer urgent care and emergency care.

The young woman breaks her leg. Her personal doctor is an internist and does not set fractures. What happens?

The personal doctor refers the case to a specialist. Insurance pays the specialist's fee. In PPO, the woman would generally see a specialist affiliated with the PPO. In an HMO, the specialist would be employed by the HMO.

The young woman signs up for an HMO then contracts a rare disease or suffers an injury that requires treatment beyond the capability of the HMO. Will she be treated?

Often yes, but it pays to read the fine print. The HMO will contract treatment out to a facility that specializes in the needed treatment.

The young woman becomes despondent and takes to drink. Will insurance pay for her rehabilitation?

Depends on her insurance. And often her employer. Some may have drug and alcohol rehab plans. Some plans cover psychiatry.

The woman becomes pregnant. Her doctor, who has delivered many babies, wants her to deliver at X hospital. All the woman's friends say, Y Hospital is much better, nicer, etc. The doctor is not cleared to practice at Y Hospital. Is the woman out of luck?

With a PPO, the woman must deliver at a hospital affiliated with the PPO — or pay the extra cost. If her doctor is not affiliated with that hospital, sometimes a doctor may be given courtesy practicing privileges at a hospital where he or she does not have staff membership. Check with the doctor.

With HMOs, the woman must deliver within the HMO system.

Incidentally, with PPOs and HMOs you should check that the doctors and specialists listed in the organization's booklets can treat you. Some plans may restrict access to certain doctors. Some booklets may be out-of-date and not have an accurate list of doctors.

The young woman goes in for minor surgery, which turns into major surgery when the doctor forgets to remove a sponge before sewing up. Upon reviving, she does what?

Some medical plans require clients to submit complaints to a panel of arbitrators, which decides damages, if any. The courts are starting to take a skeptical look at this requirement. Read the policy.

The woman's child reaches age 18. Is she covered by the family insurance?

All depends on the insurance. Some policies will cover the children while they attend college. (But attendance may be defined in a certain way, full-time as opposed to part-time.) To protect your coverage, you should read the plan thoroughly.

At work, the woman gets her hand caught in a revolving door and is told she will need six months of therapy during which she can't work. Who pays?

Insurance will usually pay for the medical costs. Workers Compensation, a state plan that includes many but not all people, may compensate the woman for time lost off the job and may pay for medical costs. If you injure yourself on the job, your employer must file a report with Workers Comp.

You wake up at 3 a.m. with a sore throat and headache. You feel bad but not bad enough to drive to a hospital or emergency room. You should:

Call the 24-hour advice line of your health plan. This is something you should check on when you sign up for a plan.

While working in her kitchen, the woman slips, bangs her head against the stove, gets a nasty cut and becomes woozy. She should:

Call 9-1-1, which will send an ambulance. 9-1-1 is managed by police dispatch. It's the fastest way to get an ambulance — with one possible exception. Lately in the Bay Area, 9-1-1 calls placed on cellular phones have been running into delays. If you are on the road and in need of emergency help and your cellular phone keeps getting busy signals, try one of the emergency call boxes.

What's the difference between a hospital, a clinic, an urgent-care center and a doctor's office?

The hospital has the most services and equipment. The center or clinic has several services and a fair amount of equipment. The office, usually, has the fewest services and the smallest amount of equipment but in some places "clinic-office" means about the same.

Hospitals have beds. If a person must have a serious operation, she goes to a hospital. Hospitals have coronary-care and intensive-care units, emergency care and other specialized, costly treatment units.

When hospitals are purchased by the same group, usually each hospital is kept open but instead of, say, two hospitals in the same region offering obstetrics, the service might be consolidated in one hospital.

Some hospitals are contracting out certain treatments — for example, neonatal care — to other hospitals that specialize in this type care. In recent years, hammered by rising costs, hospitals have been looking for ways to avoid duplications and cut expenses. Some of their reductions have drawn criticism. Opponents contend they erode the quality of care.

Many hospitals also run clinics for minor ailments and provide the same services as medical centers.

Urgent care or medical centers are sometimes located in neighborhoods, which makes them more convenient for some people. The doctors treat the minor, and often not-so-minor, ailments of patients and send them to hospitals for major surgery and serious sicknesses. Some doctors form themselves into groups to offer the public a variety of services.

Some hospitals have opened neighborhood clinics or centers to attract patients. Kaiser has hospitals in some towns and clinic-offices in other towns.

The doctor in his or her office treats patients for minor ailments and uses the hospital for surgeries, major illnesses. Many illnesses that required hospitalization years ago are now treated in the office or clinic.

Some hospitals offer programs outside the typical doctor-patient relationships. For example, wellness plans — advice on how to stay healthy or control stress or quit smoking.

Major Hospitals in & near Alameda County

Alameda County Medical Center, 1411 E. 31st. St., Oakland, 94602. Ph. (510) 437-4800. Also includes a facility at15400 Foothill Blvd., San Leandro, 94578. Ph. (510) 667-7800. Drop-in clinic, internal medicine, primary care, AIDS, pediatric clinic, specialty clinics, Alzheimer day care services, outpatient rehabilitation services, physical therapy, occupational therapy, speech pathology and audiology, inpatient acute rehabilitation services, skilled nursing facility, 229 beds.

Alameda Hospital, 2070 Clinton Ave., Alameda, 94501. Ph. (510) 522-3700. ICU, CCU, OB-GYN, emergency services, acute care, surgical services, outpatient surgery, physical referral, physical therapy, radiology, sub-acute care, cardial rehabilitation. General acute care hospital.135 beds.

Alta Bates Medical Center, Ashby Campus, 2450 Ashby Ave., Berkeley, 94705. Herrick Campus, 2001 Dwight Way, Berkeley, 94704. Ph. (510) 204-4444. ICU, CCU, OB/GYN, birth center, NICU, women's center, mental health center, heart & vascular center, comprehensive cancer center, burn center, skilled nursing, home health care, orthopedics, neurosciences, emergency services, chest pain emergency center, respiratory services, surgery & surgical subspecialties, health education & support groups. Physician referral and 24-hour audio health library with over 400 recorded health topics: (800) 606-2582. 548 beds.

Alta Bates, Summit Campus, (formerly Merritt Peralta Medical Center and Providence Hospital), 350 Hawthorne Ave., Oakland, 94609. Ph. (510) 655-4000. CCU, ICU, cardiac care, work hardening and cardiac rehabilitation, OB, GYN, perinatology, 24-hour emergency services, alcohol and chemical dependency, orthopedics, physical therapy, physician referral, diagnostic imaging, diabetes treatment center, health access/health screening and wellness program, health resource library, oncology, ophthalmology, outpatient surgery/subacute, sports medicine, surgery, geriatrics, radiology, ambulatory treatment center, skilled nursing facility, adult day health care, lifeline emergency response program, respiratory care. 534 beds.

Children's Hospital Oakland, 747 52nd St., Oakland, 94609. Ph. (510) 428-3000. Only pediatric hospital in Alameda County. Regional pediatric trauma center, pediatric ICU and level 3 intensive care nursery. 30 subspecialties, including pediatric cardiology, sickle-cell center, burn center, pulmonology, neurology, hematology/oncology, gastroenterology and infectious disease, rehabilitation, child development center, prenatal diagnosis and craniofacial. Inpatient/outpatient care. Children's health advice line. 171 beds. Subspecialty services in Fremont, Pleasanton, Brentwood and Walnut Creek.

Eden Medical Center, 20103 Lake Chabot Rd., Castro Valley, 94546. Ph. (510) 537-1234. ICU, CCU, OB, GYN, level II intensive care nursery, trauma center, emergency services, chest pain emergency unit, physical/occupational/speech therapy, hand therapy clinic, acute rehabilitation, skilled nursing facility, women's health services, maternity education, home care, geriatric services, senior housing and transportation, cancer treatment, inpatient and outpatient surgery, laser optics, adult psychiatric services, cardiac catheterization, cardiopulmonary services and rehabilitation, nuclear medicine, radiology, wellness programs, support groups. 275 beds. **See ad page 115.**

Highland General Hospital, 1411 E. 31st St., Oakland, 94602. Ph. (510) 437-4800. ICU, CCU, OB-GYN, trauma center, emergency care, pediatric services, radiology, geriatric services, cancer treatment. Clinics include services for AIDS, allergy, arthritis/rheumatology, cardiac, dermatology, gastroenterology, geriatrics, hematology/oncology, internal medicine/general medicine, endocrinology, neurology, renal. Special services: Rape crisis center, START prenatal care, healthy infant program, community adult day health care, death and dying project, chaplaincy project, triage project, pediatric van services. Acute care hospital. County facility. Division of Alameda County Medical Center. 316 beds.

John Muir Medical Center, 1601 Ygnacio Valley Rd., Walnut Creek, 94598. Ph. (925) 939-3000. Regional Trauma Center, 24-hour emergency services, physician referral, neuroscience ICU, medical/surgical ICU, CCU, Birth Center, OB-GYN, Level III neonatal intensive care nursery, pediatrics, physical medicine and rehabilitation, neurosciences, orthopedics, cardiac services, cancer services, Breast Center and Cancer Resource Library, Diabetes Center, senior services (information and referral), full range of outpatient services. Private, not-for-profit, 321 beds. Part of John Muir/Mt. Diablo Health System.

Kaiser Permanente Medical Center, 27400 Hesperian Blvd., Hayward, 94545. Ph. (510) 784-4000. Typical hospital services, medical social work, pharmacy, optical sales, eye care, OB/GYN, internal medicine, health education. Also emergency care, hospice, chronic pain, postgraduate training program in orthopedic physical therapy. 210 beds.

Kaiser Permanente Medical Center, 280 W. MacArthur Blvd., Oakland, 94611. Ph. (510) 752-1000. Typical hospital services. Also emergency care, HIV services, MRI nuclear medicine, occupational medicine, pediatric intensive care, Sports Injury Clinic, health education services, NICU, home care, hospice, genetic & prenatal counseling, lithotripsy. 235 beds.

Kaiser Permanente Medical Offices-Fremont, 39400 Paseo Padre Pkwy., Fremont, 94538. Ph. (510) 795-3000. Allergy, ambulatory surgery, dermatology, dietary, optometry, ophthalmology, health education, optical sales, general medicine, internal medicine, lab, neurology, OB/GYN, orthopedics, pediatrics, pharmacy, physical therapy, podiatry, psychiatry, radiology, otolaryngology.

Kaiser Permanente Medical Offices-Pleasanton, 7601 Stoneridge Dr., Pleasanton, 94588. Ph. (925) 847-5000. Allergy, ambulatory surgery, dermatology, dietary, optometry, ophthalmology, optical sales, general medicine, internal medicine, laboratory, neurology, OB, GYN, orthopedics, pediatrics, pharmacy, physical therapy, podiatry, psychiatry, radiology, surgery, otolaryngology.

Kaiser Permanente Medical Offices-Union City, 3555 Whipple Rd., Union City. Ph. (510) 784-4000. Sports medicine, psychiatry, pharmacy, radiology, alcohol and drug abuse programs.

Mt. Diablo Medical Center, 2540 East St., Concord, 94520. Ph. (925) 682-8200. 24-hour emergency services, ICU, CCU, Chest Pain Center, The Heart Institute, cardiac catheterization laboratory, Cardiac Emergency Network, cardiac rehabilitation, Regional Cancer Center, respiratory services, pulmonary rehabilitation, Breast Health Center, senior services (information and referral), HIV/AIDS Services, Lymphedema Center, Grief Services, Health and Fitness Institute, wellness programs, Center for Diabetes, in/outpatient physical, occupational and speech therapy; industrial medicine, Diablo Valley Outpatient Surgery Center, physician referral, Laser Technology Center, pharmacy. 254 beds. Part of John Muir/Mt. Diablo Health System.

St. Rose Hospital, 27200 Calaroga Ave., Hayward, 94545. Ph. (510) 264-4000. OB-GYN, family birthing center, ICU, CCU, emergency care, radiology services, occupational health services, physical therapy, hand therapy, cardiopulmonary rehabilitation programs, transitional care, skilled nursing, home health care, cancer treatment, breast-care center. Community Mobile Clinic, Silva Pediatric Clinic. 175 beds.

San Leandro Hospital, 13855 E. 14th St., San Leandro, 94578. Ph. (510) 357-6500. 24-hr. emergency care, in/out patient rehabilitation services, general acute care for inpatients, transitional care unit, ICU, CT, MRI, CCU, in/out patient surgical services, endoscopy/special procedures. 122 beds.

ValleyCare Medical Center, 5555 West Las Positas Blvd., Pleasanton, 94588. Ph. (925) 847-3000. Acute care hospital, a ValleyCare Health System facility. ICU/ CCU, surgery, OB, GYN, birth center, level 2 NICU, pediatrics, outpatient surgery, inpatient & outpatient physical therapy, diagnostic imaging, MRI, radiation therapy, home health agency, outpatient drug & alcohol treatment, sports medicine, occupational health services, wellness programs, community health education programs, health resource library, physicians referral, 24-hr. emergency room, cardiac catheterization lab, cancer care, digestive care services, CAT, nuclear medicine, 141 beds.

Valley Memorial Hospital, 1111 E. Stanley Blvd., Livermore, 94550. Ph. (925) 447-7000. A ValleyCare Health System Facility. Physical therapy, skilled nursing, diagnostic imaging, digestive disorders, geriatric psychiatric services, pulmonary rehabilitation, cardiac rehabilitation, cancer care, physicians referral, home health agency, outpatient drug & alcohol treatment, wellness programs, urgent care center, occupational health services, digestive care services, MRI, CAT, nuclear medicine, acute care hospital. 95 beds.

Vencor Hospital, 2800 Benedict Dr., San Leandro, 94577. Ph. (510) 357-8300. ICU, physical therapy, radiology, extended acute care focused on high acuity ventilator-dependent patients. An intensive care hospital. 100 beds.

Veterans Affairs Medical Center, 4951 Arroyo Rd., Livermore, 94550. Ph. (925) 373-4700. 120-bed nursing home care unit for qualified veterans, long-term care, geriatric care, physical rehabilitation, skilled nursing care, home care, outpatient psychiatry, outpatient surgery. 45 beds.

Washington Hospital Healthcare System, 2000 Mowry Ave., Fremont, 94538-1716. Ph. (510) 797-1111. ICU, CCU, OB, GYN, birthing center, emergency services, psychiatric care, physician referral, pediatric services, alcohol & chemical dependency, walk-in clinics, outpatient surgery, radiology, radiation-oncology, physical therapy, heart institute, free-standing heart outpatient catheterization lab, cardiac surgery, cardiac rehabilitation, mental health, outpatient rehabilitation center, geriatric services, diagnostic labs, health & prenatal education. 337 beds.

Key: ICU, intensive care unit; CCU, coronary care unit; OB, obstetrics; GYN, gynecology; MRI, magnetic resonance imaging; NICU, neonatal intensive care unit; CAT, computerized axial tomography.

New!

McCormack's
GUIDES

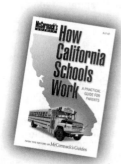

How California Schools Work

A practical
guide for parents . . .

. . . that in plain language provides
information useful in working with schools
and teachers and making decisions about
their children's education

- Advice on choosing a school
- Enrollment procedures
- Curriculum
- Tests and what they mean
- What to do when you have complaints about teachers
- Homework, academic demands
- Gifted, arts, magnet programs
- Tutoring and how to help teachers do their jobs
- Language instruction. Spanish immersion
- Food and nutrition – cafeteria realities
- Charter schools, Montessori, Waldorf
- Special education
- Overview of private schools

At bookstores or order direct **(800) 222-3602**
Order from **www.mccormacks.com**

Chapter 8

Newcomer's Guide

FOR NEWCOMERS to Alameda County here are tips on getting started in your new town and answers to frequently asked questions.

Voter Registration

You must be 18 years and a citizen. Go to the nearest post office and pick up a voter registration postcard. Fill it out and pop it into the mail box. Or pick up the form when you register your vehicle or secure a driver's license.

For more information on voting, call the elections office at (510) 272-6993.

Before every election, the county will mail you a sample ballot with the address of your polling place.

Change of Address — Mail

The change-of-address form can also be picked up at the post office but to assure continuity of service, fill out this form 30 days before you move.

Dog Licensing — Missing Pets

License fees vary by jurisdiction. Animal services often provide low-cost spaying or neutering, disposal of dead animals, and pet adoptions. Dog bites should be reported to animal services.

Typical fees run $10 to $25 a year. The price is reduced if the dog is fixed or the owner is elderly. Bring proof of rabies vaccination. For information on where to register, call your city hall. Phone numbers can be found at the beginning of the white pages in phone directories.

Vehicle Registration

California has the most stringent smog requirements in the country. If your car is a few years old, you may have to spend a couple of hundred dollars to bring it up to code.

You have 20 days from the time you enter the state to register your vehicles. After that you pay a penalty, and face getting a ticket-fine.

(Continued on page 128)

Grocery Prices

Item	Store one	Store two	Average
American Cheese, Kraft, 20 slices	5.39	5.39	5.39
Apple Juice, 1 gal. store brand	4.19	4.79	4.49
Apples, Granny Smith, 1lb.	1.59	1.59	1.59
Apples, Red Delicious, 1 lb.	1.39	1.29	1.34
Aspirin, cheapest, 100 count	4.49	3.99	4.24
Avocado, Hass	1.29	1.79	1.54
Baby Food, Gerber's, Fruit or Veg., 4 oz.	.52	.50	.51
Baby Shampoo, Johnson's, 15 fluid oz.	3.89	3.99	3.94
Bacon, Farmer John Sliced	4.19	4.29	4.24
Bagels, halfa dozen, Sara Lee	3.29	3.59	3.44
Bags, Ziploc, gallon	3.19	3.19	3.19
Bananas, 1 lb.	.69	.79	.74
B-B-Q Sauce, Bull's Eye, 1 lb, 2 oz.	2.69	2.79	2.74
Beans, Green, 1 lb.	2.99	2.49	2.74
Beef, boneless roast, 1 lb.	3.49	3.49	3.49
Beef, ground, 1 lb.	.99	2.99	1.99
Beef, top sirloin steak, 1 lb.	5.99	4.99	5.49
Beer, Budweiser 6-pack bottles	5.79	5.79	5.79
Beer, Coors, 12-pack, cans	9.99	10.19	10.09
Bisquick batter, 2 lbs. 8 oz.	2.99	2.79	2.89
Bleach, Clorox, 1.39 gal	2.49	3.79	3.14
Bok Choy, 1lb.	.69	.69	.69
Bread, sourdough, Colombo, 1.5 lb.	2.39	3.09	2.74
Bread, wheat, cheapest 1.5 lb.	1.99	1.99	1.99
Broccoli, 1 lb.	.99	.99	.99
Butter, Challenge, 1 lb.	4.19	3.99	4.09
Cabbage, 1 lb.	.79	.79	.79
Cantaloupe, 1 lb.	.79	.69	.74
Carrots, fresh, 1 lb.	.49	.59	.54
Cat Food, Friskies, small can	.59	.59	.59
Cereal, Wheaties, 18 oz.	4.69	4.69	4.69
Charcoal, Kingsford, 20 lbs.	8.99	8.99	8.99
Cheese, Cream, Philadelphia, 8 oz.	2.59	2.49	2.54
Cheese, Mild Cheddar, 1 lb.	4.99	4.19	4.59
Chicken breasts, Foster Farms bone/skinless, 1 lb.	5.99	3.99	4.99
Chicken, store brand, whole, 1 lb.	.59	1.39	.99
Chili, Stagg, with beans, 15 oz. can	1.99	1.99	1.99
Cigarettes, Marlboro Lights, carton	40.49	41.49	40.99
Coca Cola, 12-pack, 12 oz. cans	4.99	3.99	4.49
Coffee, Folgers Instant Coffee, 13 oz.	3.99	3.89	3.94
Cookies, Oreo, 20 oz. pkg.	3.89	3.79	3.84
Graham Crackers, 14 oz.	3.59	3.69	3.64
Diapers, Huggies, size 2, (36-pack)	11.29	11.49	11.39
Dishwashing Liquid, Dawn, 25 oz.	3.79	3.79	3.79
Dog Food, Pedigree, 22-oz. can	1.29	1.29	1.29
Eggs, large, Grade AA, 1 doz.	1.89	2.39	2.14
Flour, Gold Medal, 5 lbs.	2.29	2.19	2.24
Flowers, dozen roses	9.99	14.99	12.49
Frozen Dinners, Marie Callendar's Complete	3.99	3.89	3.94
Gin, Gilbeys, 1.75 Ltrs.	17.99	17.99	17.99
Ginger Root, 1 lb.	2.29	1.99	2.14
Granola Bars, 10-bar box	3.29	3.69	3.49
Grapes, Red Seedless, 1 lb.	2.49	1.99	2.24
Ham, boneless, 1 lb.	1.99	1.49	1.74
Ham, sliced, Oscar Meyer, 6 oz.	2.89	2.99	2.94

Grocery Prices

Item	Store one	Store two	Average
Ham, Dubuque, 1.5-lbs., canned	$5.99	$6.99	$6.49
Ice cream, Dreyers, half gal.	5.49	5.99	5.74
Ice cream, Haagen Daz, 1 pint	3.69	3.79	3.74
Jam, Mary Ellen, strawberry, 18 oz.	3.99	4.69	4.34
Kentucky Fried Chicken, 8 pc. family bucket	13.99	13.99	13.99
Ketchup, Heinz, 36 oz.	2.99	2.99	2.99
Kleenex, 160-count box	1.99	1.99	1.99
Kraft Macaroni & Cheese, family size, 14.5 oz	1.99	1.99	1.99
Laundry Detergent, Tide, 87 oz.	8.99	9.19	9.09
Lettuce, Romaine, head	.89	.99	.94
Margarine, I Can't Believe It's Not Butter, 1-lb. tub	1.99	1.99	1.99
Mayonnaise, Best Foods, 1 qt.	3.99	3.99	3.99
Milk, 1% Fat, half gal.	1.99	2.35	2.17
M&M Candies, plain, 14 oz.	2.99	2.99	2.99
Mushrooms, sliced, 0.5 lb.	1.99	2.29	2.14
Olive Oil, cheapest, 17 oz.	3.99	5.69	4.84
Onions, yellow, 1 lb.	.59	.69	.64
Orange Juice, Tropicana, 64-oz., Original Style	4.19	4.29	4.24
Paper Towels, single pack	1.89	1.79	1.84
Pasta Sauce, Prego, 28 oz.	2.99	2.99	2.99
Peanuts, cocktail, Planter's, 12 oz.	3.29	3.79	3.54
Peas, frozen, 16 oz.	1.89	2.39	2.14
Peanut Butter, Jiff, 18 oz.	2.99	3.39	3.19
Popcorn, Orville Reddenbacher, 3-pack	2.99	2.99	2.99
Pork chops, center cut, 1 lb.	3.99	5.29	4.64
Potato Chips, Lays, 12.25 oz.	2.99	2.99	2.99
Potatoes, 10 lbs.	3.19	3.99	3.59
Raisins, 24 oz.	3.69	3.69	3.69
Reese's Peanut Butter Cups, 10 pk.	3.19	3.19	3.19
Rice, cheapest, 5 lbs.	2.99	2.49	2.74
Round Table, large cheese pizza	15.97	15.97	15.97
Salmon, fresh, 1 lb.	5.99	5.99	5.99
Seven-Up, 6-pack, cans	2.99	2.79	2.89
Soap, bar, Zest, 3-pack	2.39	2.49	2.44
Soup, Campbell, Chicken Noodle, 10-oz. can	.99	.99	.99
Soy Sauce, Kikkoman, 10 oz.	1.99	1.99	1.99
Spaghetti, cheapest, 2 lbs.	1.99	1.99	1.99
Sugar, cheapest, 5 lbs.	2.29	2.19	2.24
Tea, Lipton's, 48-bag box	2.99	2.99	2.99
Toilet Tissue, 4-roll pack, cheapest	1.19	1.49	1.34
Tomatoes, on the vine, 1 lb.	1.69	2.99	2.34
Tomatoes, Roma, 1 lb.	.99	1.59	1.29
Toothpaste, Crest, 8.2 oz.	3.99	3.99	3.99
Top Ramen	.33	.33	.33
Tortillas, flour, cheapest, 10-count pack	1.79	2.19	1.99
Tuna, Starkist, Chunk Light, 6 oz.	.99	.99	.99
Turkey, ground, 1 lb.	3.99	2.99	3.49
Vegetable Oil, store brand, 64 oz.	3.49	3.59	3.54
Vegetables, frozen, 16 oz.	1.99	2.39	2.19
Vinegar, apple cider, store brand, 1 pint	1.29	1.39	1.34
Water, 1.5 liters	.89	.79	.84
Whiskey, Seagrams 7 Crown, 750ml.	12.99	12.99	12.99
Wine, White Zinfandel, 750 ml.	5.99	5.99	5.99
Yoplait Original Yogurt, single	.89	.89	.89

(Continued from page 125)

For registration, go to any office of the Department of Motor Vehicles. Bring your smog certificate, your registration card and your license plates.

If you are a California resident, all you need to do is complete a change of address form, which can be obtained by calling the Department of Motor Vehicles at: (800) 777-0133

If going for a driver's license, ask to have the booklet mailed to you or pick it up. Study it. Almost all the questions will be taken from the booklet.

Driver's License

To obtain a driver's license, you must be 16 years old, pass a state-certified Driver's Education (classroom) and Driver's Training (behind-the-wheel) course, and at Department of Motor Vehicles a vision test and written and driving tests.

Once you pass the test, your license is usually renewed by mail. Retesting is rare, unless your driving record is poor. High schools used to offer free driving courses but these have all but disappeared due to state budget cuts. Private driving schools have moved in to fill the gap, at a cost of about $100.

Teenagers older than 15 1/2 years who have completed driver's training can be issued a permit. New law restricts driving hours for young teens to daylight hours and, unless supervised, forbids them for six months to drive other teens. Law also requires more parental training and extends time of provisional license. Purpose is to reduce accidents.

If no driver's education program has been completed, you must be at least 18 years old to apply for a driver's license. Out-of-state applicants must supply proof of "legal presence," which could be a certified copy of a birth certificate. New law allows illegal immigrants to secure driver's licenses and register vehicles.

Turning Rules and Insurance

If signs don't say no, you can turn right on a red light (after making a full stop) and make a U-turn at an intersection.

Stop for pedestrians. Insurance? Must have it to drive and to secure a license.

Earthquakes

They're fun and great topics of conversation, until you get caught in a big one. Then they are not so funny. At the beginning of your phone book is some advice about what to do before, during and after a temblor. It's worth reading.

Garbage Service

The garbage fellows come once a week. Rates vary by city but figure $15 to $25 a month for one can.

Garbage companies, for suburban neighborhoods, use wheeled plastic containers designed to be picked up and emptied by mechanical arms attached to the truck. These carts come in several sizes, the most popular 32 and 64 gallons. Almost every home will receive recycling bins or carts for plastics, glass and cans and garden trimmings. Pickup weekly, usually the same day as garbage.

To get rid of car batteries and motor oils and water-soluble paints, call your garbage firm and ask about disposal sites. Or call city hall. Don't burn garbage in the fireplace or outside. Don't burn leaves. Against law.

Property Taxes

Property taxes are paid in two installments — due by April 10 and December 10. They generally are collected automatically through impound accounts set up when you purchase a home, but check your sale documents carefully. Sometimes homeowners are billed directly.

Property taxes for new buyers vary by taxing jurisdiction but most come in under 1.5 percent of market value at time of purchase. This means generally that the buyer of a $200,000 house will pay property taxes of about $3,000 a year, and the buyer of a $300,000 house will pay $4,500 a year.

After the base rate is established, property tax increases, no matter how high property values soar, are limited to no more than 2 percent a year — unless local voters approve an increase.

Some cities, to fund parks and lights and other amenities in new subdivisions, have installed what is called the Mello-Roos tax. Realtors are required to give you complete information on all taxes. If you buy a resale home in an established neighborhood, Mello-Roos almost never enters the picture.

Sales Tax

In Alameda County, it is 8.25 percent. If you buy something for $1 you will pay $1.08 (8% rounded down) and if the item costs $100, you will pay $108.25. Food is not taxed, except in restaurants.

State Income Taxes

See chart on page 132.

Disclosure Laws

California requires homes sellers to give detailed reports on their offerings, including information on flood, fire and earthquake zones.

Cigarette — Tobacco Tax

Sin tax, passed a few years ago, 50 cents on a pack of cigarettes, plus usual taxes. Many Californians load up on cigarettes in Nevada or Mexico or order over Internet.

Gas and Electricity

Most homes are heated with natural gas. No one, or almost no one, uses heating oil. Up until recently, Pacific Gas and Electric (PG&E) reported that gas bills, year round, averaged about $30 a month, and electric bills $60 a month. The bill for an average three-bedroom home ran $130 to $140 a month.

In 2001, PG&E filed for bankruptcy. California is going through an energy crunch. Rates have been increased but structured to reward conservation. Low consumption will see zero increases, medium 7 percent, medium plus 18 percent, heavy 37 percent. Read your utility bill to see how the system works. The energy crisis is not over; more rate changes may be coming.

Almost never between May and September, and rarely between April and October, will you need to heat your home. Air conditioners are used in the summer but on many days they are not needed.

Cable TV Service — Internet Service

Almost all East Bay homes are served by cable. Rates vary according to channels accessed but a basic rate plus one tier is about $32 a month. Installation is extra. For clear FM radio reception, often a cable connection is required.

High-speed internet service is generally available.

Phone Service

SBC charges $33.01 to run a line to your house. It charges $120 for the first jack and $40 per additional jack. If you're handy, you can do the jack wiring and installation yourself. Many homes will have the jacks in place. The basic monthly charge is $10.69 but with taxes, access to interstate calling, and other miscellaneous items the true cost jumps way up.

Bottled Water

If the direct source for your town's water is the Sierra, then you may not need bottled water. If the source is the Delta or ground water, many people take the bottled.

Love and Society

San Francisco often flaunts its sexuality, hetero, homo and trans. Except in rare instances, the suburbs don't but the cosmopolitan virtues apply. In the Bay Area, consenting adults, in sexual matters, are generally free to do what they want as long as it doesn't harm others.

In Alameda County, same-sex couples attend office parties and social events, and usually no subterfuge is put up to disguise the relationship.

If you act out in the suburbs, if you slobber over your loved one, no matter what the sexual orientation, you won't be stoned but you might be shunned.

If you want the society of men or the society of women or both, numerous groups exist to help to make connections.

Smoking

In public places, increasingly frowned upon and in the workplace forbidden. In 1998 a state law took effect forbidding smoking in saloons, one of the last bastions of smoking. Bars in restaurants comply. Saloons enforce sporadically but many people refrain from smoking and those that do, often hide the cigarette under the table. In San Francisco, people smoke in neighborhood bars but social pressures are curbing the practice.

If visiting socially, you are expected to light up outside.

Dress

For almost all social occasions, even in some circles weddings and funerals, the dress is casual. The person who wears a tie to a restaurant on Friday or Saturday often stands out (depends a little on the town).

Dress formal for dinner in San Francisco and the theater and opera (but even here, many men go in sports coats, no tie; women in slacks).

Age a factor: Older men and women often dress up more than younger. And if your business situation calls for suits, then suits it is. Supposedly, we are entering a more conservative, more serious era where suits might make a comeback. Remains to be seen.

For the coast bring a jacket or sweater. It's often chilly, even during the day.

CALIFORNIA TAX RATE SCHEDULE

Schedule X Single Married Filing Separate Returns

Taxable Income Over	But not over	Computed Tax	On Amount Over
$0	$5,834	$0.00 + 1.0%	0
$5,834	$13,829	$58.34 + 2.0%	$5,834
$13,829	$21,826	$218.24 + 4.0%	$13,829
$21,826	$30,298	$538.12 + 6.0%	$21,826
$30,298	$38,291	$1,046.44 + 8.0%	$30,298
$38,291	AND OVER	$1,685.88 + 9.3%	$38,291

Schedule Y Married Filing Jointly & Qualified Widow(er)s

Taxable Income Over	But not over	Computed Tax	On Amount Over
$0	$11,668	$0.00 + 1.0%	0
$11,668	$27,658	$116.68 + 2.0%	$11,668
$27,658	$43,652	$436.38 + 4.0%	$27,658
$43,652	$60,596	$1,076.24 + 6.0%	$43,652
$60,596	$76,582	$2,092.88 + 8.0%	$60,596
$76,582	AND OVER	$3,371.76 + 9.3%	$76,582

Schedule Z Heads of Households

Taxable Income Over	But not over	Computed Tax	On Amount Over
$0	$11,673	$0.00 + 1.0%	0
$11,673	$27,659	$116.73 + 2.0%	$11,673
$27,659	$35,653	$436.45 + 4.0%	$27,659
$35,653	$44,125	$756.21+ 6.0%	$35,653
$44,125	$52,120	$1,264.53 + 8.0%	$44,125
$52,120	AND OVER	$1,904.13 + 9.3%	$52,120

Example

Richard and Valerie Green are filing a joint return using Form 540. Their taxable income on Form 540, line 19 is $125,000.

Taxable Income	Computed Tax	On Amount Over
Using Schedule Y - $76,582 and over	$3,371.76 + 9.3%	$76,582

They subtract the amount at the beginning of their range from their taxable income.

$125,000
-76,582

$48,418

They multiply the result from Step 2 by the percentage for their range.

$ 48,418
x.093

$ 4,502.87

They round the amount from Step 3 to two decimals (if necessary) and add it to the tax amount for their income range. After rounding the result, they will enter $7,875 on Form 540, line 20.

$3,371.76
+4,502.87
$7,874.63

'03

Chapter 9

Rental Housing

AFTER SEVERAL YEARS of double-digit increases, rents are stabilizing and in some Bay Area counties decreasing.

Local rents are greatly influenced by what happens in Santa Clara County (Silicon Valley) and San Francisco-San Mateo. Between about 1996 and 2001, these counties boomed and added thousands of jobs. But lacking buildable land, they failed to provide housing, both homes and apartments, for the newcomers.

Southern Alameda County, particularly Fremont, Union City and Newark, border or are within a short drive of Santa Clara County. Hayward and San Leandro are just a bridge away from central San Mateo and San Francisco International Airport. Oakland, Emeryville and Berkeley are separated from downtown San Francisco by another bridge, a drive for many of just 10 to 15 miles.

Very quickly people flocked to Alameda County, particularly the mentioned cities, and drove up the rents. Some cities, notably Oakland, rushed into apartment construction to meet demand.

When the dot-coms tanked and the high-tech firms foundered, many jobs disappeared and the apartment shortage evaporated. The Sept. 11 terrorist attack discouraged many from flying and cost jobs at the airport and the hotel-service industry in the City and in San Mateo — further weakening demand.

Berkeley may be the only exception to softening rents. Because of its cultural offerings and the university, the city almost never goes out of style. The university hopes to increase enrollments over the next few years and this should increase demand. For decades Berkeley wrapped itself in rent control and this discouraged residential construction.

The courts forced Berkeley to change its laws to allow market increases when apartments change hands. People who have held apartments for a long time are paying comparatively low rents; people who recently rented or will rent apartments are paying or will pay much higher rents.

Incoming students or newcomers should visit the UC housing office for help and listings. Many students and adults share rentals. Many people housing services or web and newspaper classified ads to find apartments.

The university has thousands of dorms and married-student housing in Albany Village.

Getting back to cheap apartments, many students and adults in Berkeley-Oakland put up in shared rentals. For $500 to $600 a month, you can find something about two miles from the campus.

Older cities with older complexes will offer studios and single apartments for $600 or $700 a month. No pool, no spa, no extras.

If you want the modern apartment with pool and security gates, then you're looking at $1,200 plus. If the apartment complex is located near a BART (commute rail) station, if it's in a safe and nice neighborhood, if it offers extra amenities, the rents will often start over $1,200. Dublin is building many new apartments.

When thinking about rental or temporary housing, apartments come quickly to mind but there are other choices.

For those new to the region and shopping for homes, a hotel might do the trick. Over the last 20 years or so, the major chains have built large and small

Average Rents For Alameda County

City	Studio	1BR,1BTH	2BR,2BTH
Alameda	$991	$1,143	$1,595
Albany	NA	1,128	NA
Castro Valley	800	945	1,210
Dublin	NA	1,274	1,595
Emeryville	1,112	1,371	1,788
Fremont	869	1,048	1,388
Hayward	894	981	1,309
Livermore	NA	980	1,276
Newark	NA	1,078	1,516
Oakland	934	1,212	1,814
Pleasanton	1,050	1,086	1,424
San Leandro	813	938	1,244
Union City	869	1,048	1,391

Source: REALFACTS, Novato, CA. Average rents as of June 2003.

hotels in the suburbs, many of them near freeway exits and a few smack in the middle of residential neighborhoods. Prices range from $80 to well over $100 a night, the higher amount buying more of the extras: pools, game rooms, etc.

Residency hotels offer a slightly different experience. They combine the conveniences of a hotel — maid service, continental breakfast, airport shuttle — with the pleasures of home: a fully-equipped kitchen and a laundry room (coin-operated). They may also have a pool, a spa, a sportscourt, a workout room. Some offer free grocery shopping and in evenings a social hour.

Residency hotels welcome families. Typically, guests remain at least five days and often much longer. At a certain stage, a discount will kick in.

Renting an apartment in California is probably little different from any other place in the country.

You will be asked for a security deposit and for the first month's rent up front. State law limits deposits to a maximum two months rent for an unfurnished apartment and three months for a furnished (This includes the last month's rent.)

If you agree to a year's lease, some places will add an extra month free. If you move out before the lease is up, you pay a penalty.

Some apartments forbid pets, some will accept only cats, some cats and small dogs. Many will ask for a pet deposit (to cover possible damage). Some complexes set aside certain units for people with pets.

To protect themselves, many landlords will ask you to fill out a credit report and to list references.

Rental Sampler from Classified Ads

Alameda
- Apt., 2BR/1BA, balcony, pool, beachfront, $1,200
- Home, 2BR/1BA, big rooms, eat in kitchen, fireplace, $1,800

Berkeley
- Apt., 2BR/1BA, modern, laundry room, $1,150
- Apt.,2BR/1BA, $1,200
- Home, 3BR/2BA, wooded lot, large deck, near transportation, $2,350
- Home, 1BR/1BA, private office, garage, $1,250

Castro Valley
- Apt., 2BR/2BA, gated, storage, $1,395
- Home, 1BR/1BA, excellent condition, includes all appliances, $1,075

Dublin
- Apt., 2BR/2BA, pool/spa, attached garage, fireplace, $1,500
- Home, 3BR/2BA, family room, A/C, new paint, near schools, $1,800
- Apt., 1BR/1BA, near trans., $1,230

Emeryville
- Apt., 2BR/1BA, remodeled, new floor, nice area, $1,100
- Home, 3BR/2.5BA, family room, huge yard, dining room, $2,800
- Apt., 1BR/1BA, high rise, $1,000

Fremont
- Apt., 2BR/1BA, quiet area, $1,035
- Home, 4BR/3BA, fairly new, backyard, two car garage, $2,000
- Apt., 2BR/1BA, pool, sauna, $1,265

Hayward
- Apt., 1BR/1BA, gated community, balcony, laundry facilities, $825
- Home, 3BR/1BA, near trans./schools, $1,350

Livermore
- Apt., 1BR/1BA, garden setting, $850
- Home, 3BR/1BA, fenced yard, $1,300

Newark
- Apt., 2BR/1BA, priv. yard, $1,275
- Home, 3BR/2BA, large yard, $1,550

Oakland
- Apt., 1BR/1BA, carpet, laundry, parking, $825
- Home, 3BR/2BA, office, fully remodeled, near transportation, $2,200
- Apt., 2BR/1BA, fireplace, view, off street parking, $1,200

Pleasanton
- Apt., 2BR/1BA, downtown loc., $880
- Home, 3BR/2BA, upgraded, $1,950
- Apt., 1BR/1BA, 675 sq. ft., $950

San Leandro
- Apt., 1BR/1BA, good location, parking, near transportation, $800
- Home, 4BR/2BA, backyard w/fruit trees, $1,700

San Lorenzo
- Apt., 2BR/1.5BA, garage, $1,175
- Home, 3BR/1.5BA, new paint, $1,800

Union City
- Apt., 1BR/1BA, washer/dryer, $950
- Home, 3BR/2BA, near schools, $1,750

The Fair Housing laws will apply: no discrimination based on race, sex, family status and so on. But some complexes will be designed to welcome one or several kinds of renters. A complex that wants families, for example, might include a tot lot. One that prefers singles or childless couples might throw Friday night parties or feature a large pool and a workout room but no kiddie facilities.

Renters pay for cable service, electricity or gas and phone (in some instances, deposits may be required to start service.)

Some large complexes will offer furnished and unfurnished apartments or corporate setups, a variation of the residency hotel.

If hotels or apartments are not your cup of tea, you might take a look at renting a home. Some homeowners handle the details themselves, others use a professional property manager. In older towns, many of the cottages and smaller homes in the older sections will often be rentals. If you see a "For Sale" sign in front of a home that interests you, inquire whether the place is for rent. You might be pleasantly surprised. Some realty firms double as rental agencies.

What about rates? They vary by town but in a middle-class town you often can rent a three-bedroom home for $2,000 to $2,500 a month. Older, smaller homes in some neighborhoods will go from $1,200 to $1,500.

When you're out scouting for a rental, check out the neighborhood, do a little research, and think about what you really value and enjoy. If you want the convenient commute without the hassle of a car, pick a place near a BART line or bus stop. If it's the active life, scout out the parks, trails and such things as bars and restaurants and community colleges. Say the first thing you want to do when you arrive home is take a long run. Before you rent, get a map of local trails from the city recreation department.

For parents, your address will usually determine what public school your child will attend. If you want a high-scoring school, see the in this book before making a decision. Always call the school before making a renting decision. Because of crowding, some schools are changing attendance zones. You may not be able to get your child into the "neighborhood" school. See chapter on How Public Schools Work.

The same advice applies to day care. Make sure that it is available nearby before signing a lease. Happy hunting!

BUY 10 OR MORE & SAVE!

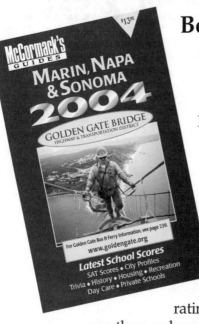

Chapter 10

City & Town Profiles

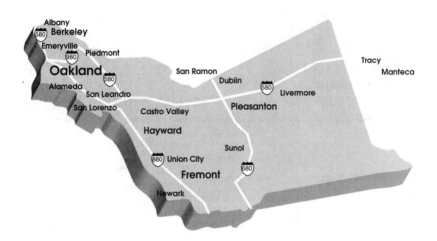

WHERE DO YOU want to live? What can you afford? What are the choices? What is the commute like? The following profiles may help. For more information on local cities, call chambers of commerce.

INDEX TO PROFILES

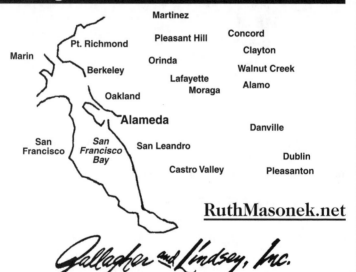

ALAMEDA

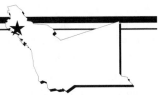

ISLAND-PENINSULA CITY. Located at one of the choicest spots in the Bay Area, population of 74,900. Site of many Victorians and stately homes. Charming. Also many small and modest homes and many apartments. Compared to other towns, a great commute.

School scores middle to high. Crime low suburban average and may decline in the coming years. Alameda is attracting more college educated and more professionals. This should raise schools scores and lower crime.

A town in transition. In 1997, the Navy closed an airfield and naval base and turned over 2,000 acres to the city. Alameda has been debating what to build on the base and over the next 10 years expects to add 5,000 to 10,000 residents to the base and nearby streets. For the immediate, the city hopes to build on the base about 500 homes, one fourth of them with "affordable" subsidized prices.

Alameda is composed of a peninsula and three islands — one tiny, one a Coast Guard base, and the main island two miles wide and seven miles long where most of the housing is located. The main island is separated from Oakland by an estuary. Immediately to the south of the main island is a peninsula called Bay Farm Island. Here is where you'll find some of the newest housing in the city, two 18-hole golf courses, a 9-hole course, a driving range, the training camp for the Oakland Raiders, and a modern, high-tech office park.

The town that tore down all its billboards boasts about 20 parks, seven marinas (over 2,000 berths), a skate park designed by kids and built by volunteers, five yacht clubs, three libraries, model airplane field, trails, many activities (soccer, football, etc.) for kids and adults, and over 100 clubs and service groups. Amenities include a shopping center, first-class restaurants, theater. Annual art and wine festival. Hometown stores that have won the affections of residents, including Tucker's Ice Cream Parlor, Ole's Waffle House, the Boogie Woogie Bagel Boy and Pagano's hardware. Big party and parade on the Fourth of July. Annual sand castle contest.

Jazz and nightclubs nearby, in Jack London Village, Oakland. Movies. The delights of San Francisco are just across the Bay Bridge, a BART ride (from Oakland) of less than a half-hour. Or a drive, assuming traffic moves, of about 20 minutes.

A few miles away, at the Oakland Coliseum, big-time professional sports

(Warriors basketball, Athletics and Raiders). Alameda has what most East Bay cities lack — an open, approachable shore, about six miles of sandy beach, operated as a regional park. Historically, cities have surrendered the shore to industry and the railroad. Water is popular with sailors and windsurfers.

Alameda started out 1900 connected to Oakland. At that time, it was considered a prestige address, attractive to the affluent who built stately homes. Then the-powers-that-be decided to cut a ship-channel and presto, an island came into existence. It is now connected to Oakland by three bridges and two tunnels. As the century progressed, the island gradually was built out with bungalows, apartments, and here and there, more mansions.

Alameda has about 3,500 Victorian and Queen Anne homes, more than San Francisco. Alameda codes protect Victorians and preserve other older buildings and historic shopping districts. Owners love their "Vics" and spend time and money to restore and maintain them. Tours available to visit a few. Streets clean. Graffiti absent. Many small shops. Good town for strolling. Many arguments over quality-of-life issues.

Alameda also has many older homes that are plain and small and some-times run down. It's expensive to upgrade an old home and many owners have just let things slide or done minimal repairs. Some homes have one-car garages. Some garages are converted horse barns.

Thousands of apartments have been built along the shore. After a rush of apartment construction in the 1980s, residents voted to forbid anything bigger than a duplex.

For the fairly new, drive to Harbor Bay, waterfront development on Bay Farm Island. Planned community built around five "villages." Most of the residential growth in the last 25 years has been at Harbor Bay, which also includes the business park, 300 acres. Some neighborhoods — notably Ballena Bay on the main island — feature homes with their own docks.

Housing units in 2003 totaled 31,930, of which 12,931 were single homes, 3,964 single attached, 14,735 multiples, and 300 mobile homes. Outside of the former base, few housing units are being built.

In sum, a real mix of housing and prices across the spectrum.

Traffic is sometimes sluggish on city arterials but the overall commute, compared to other East Bay cities, is good. Buses to Oakland and San Fran-cisco and to BART (commute rail) station in downtown Oakland. Oakland Airport on southern border of Alameda. Commute ferry to Oakland and downtown San Francisco (ferries leave from Bay Farm Island and from main island, near Alameda Point.) Local jobs by the tens of thousands, in Berkeley, downtown Oakland, the Oakland Airport. For many residents, the commute is only a few miles.

Over the next five years or so, the east span of the Bay Bridge is to be replaced. In the best of times, the Bay Bridge is a mess during commute hours. Construction delays will make it worse but Alamedans have choices: the ferries and BART.

Two homicides in 2001, one in 2000, zero in 1999, one in 1998, two in 1997. Counts for previous years are three, zero, one, one, two, six, three, zero, two, and two. Overall crime rate runs to suburban average on low side. Alameda, close to Oakland and San Francisco, gives you the conveniences of the city and the safety of the suburb (but take usual precautions: lock doors, etc.).

Jets take off from Oakland airport. Noise suppression measures have been taken. If purchasing a home or renting a place, spend a few hours listening, or talk to neighbors. Ask about night flights. Oakland airport is to expand its terminals but not its runways. With the expansion, night flights of cargo planes will be restricted.

School rankings middling to 90th percentile, compared to other California schools. Voters in 1989 approved a $48 million bond to repair schools, add classrooms. A few elementary schools are run year-round. In 2002, another tax was approved, this one to fund salaries, enrich programs and decrease class size. Community college adds much to educational life.

Catholic high school. Three Catholic elementary schools. St. Joseph's in 1994 won national Blue Ribbon for academic excellence.

Alameda started the 1990s with 76,459 residents and finished with 72,259 — the drop coming from the base closure. Many people lost their jobs. Stores closed or lost business. Since then, the West End, as the base area is known, has made a comeback. The old residents were blue-collar workers or sailors. The new residents tend to be young professionals. The Coast Guard retained housing for military personnel around the Bay Area.

The military base was one of the most famous in American history. From it, the carrier Hornet sailed in 1942 to venture close to Japan and launch the first bombing raid on that country. The raid shamed the Japanese Navy and influenced its disastrous decision to attack Midway Island, perhaps the decisive naval battle of World War II. In 1998, the city saved from the scrapper's torch the "new" Hornet, commissioned in 1943. The ship, as long as three football fields, was tidied up and turned into a museum.

Put the whole package together — the views, the jobs, the peace, the easy commute, the closeness to San Francisco, Oakland and Berkeley, the charm of the old — Alameda comes across as one of the best addresses in the East Bay. Chamber of commerce (510) 522-0414.

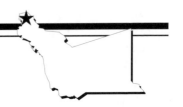

ALBANY

SMALL CITY, STABLE population of 16,800, on the shore, next to and influenced by Berkeley. The university and all it offers — art, music, theater, sports — are within 10 minutes. Quiet. Home to many professionals and married UC students. School rankings high. UC kids make up about 20 percent of school district enrollment. Crime low. Zero homicides from 1997 through 2001. Counts for previous years are, one, one, zero, one, zero, zero, one, zero, one.

Housing rises from Bay to hills with great views. Built out. Many homes are old and small, one and two bedrooms, yet command good prices. High-rise condos near freeway. UC has renovated its housing for students with children. In 2003, the state counted in Albany 7,287 residential units: 3,779 single homes, 181 single attached, 3,321 apartments, 6 mobile homes.

About 50 restaurants, 40 antique stores, many of them on Solano Avenue, loads of charm. From affordable to upscale, eateries offer international cuisines, gourmet hamburgers and more. Evenings full of amblers. The avenue has bookstores and two movie theaters, one leaning toward art-house. Annual "Solano Stroll" street fair draws 100,000. Golden Gate Fields offers trotters, thoroughbreds, satellite betting. Seniors center. Community center. New library. Teen center. Town pool. Soccer, Little League, many activities

Academic rankings among top 15 percent in state, at high school, top 5 percent. Strong school support, what's expected from a university town. Five public schools enroll about 3,000 kids, many in walking distance. In 1993, voters approved a bond to renovate schools, get rid of asbestos, upgrade science labs and library. More funds approved in 1994. Parcel tax passed in 1999 to add math, science and art classes, hire librarians and counselors and improve technology. In 1999, district opened rebuilt elementary and middle schools. High school demolished; earthquake concerns. New state-of-the-art high school. Despite this, schools run into money problems; parents want more than school district can afford. Constant fund raising. Many private schools in Berkeley-El Cerrito. Albany Middle School named a Distinguished School in 2003. Every year about two dozen schools in California crack the 600 mark in the math SAT. In 2003, Albany High hit 603.

Ten minutes to Oakland, 20 minutes to San Fran. Freeway and Bay Bridge congested but an endurable commute. BART stations in Berkeley and El Cerrito. Buses to City and throughout East Bay. Chamber (510) 525-1771.

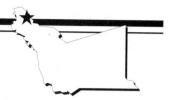

BERKELEY

ONE OF THE MOST famous cities in the world. Intellectually intense, charming and scenic. Hill homes look over the Bay and Golden Gate. Always encouraging the new and innovative but not dynamic in a corporate way. Population 104,600.

Too little land and Berkeley is suspicious of big business and Big Biz reciprocates. This said, the city near its waterfront has many small firms and some bio-tech firms, including a large Bayer facility.

About half of Berkeley's housing stock predates World War II, about 40 percent was built between 1940 and 1970. In the 1990s, Berkeley added just 1,200 housing units, according to 2000 census. Many students and people working at the university live in nearby towns.

A city of contrasts. On the south side of the university, People's Park and Telegraph Avenue, magnets for teenagers and the down and out (but new shops and restaurants are pushing this section a little up the scale). On the north, Holy Hill, a congregation of religious schools, and a quieter neighborhood.

Anchored by Spengers restaurant and fish market, Berkeley's newest flourishing commercial area spreads a few blocks south down Fourth Street. Boutiques offer shoppers European antiques, cafe-quality cappuccino machines, high-fashion shoes and clothing, imported curios and doggie beds fit for a well-to-do human. Artists rent space to work on their craft in the Art Gym, a studio open to the curious and the shopping. Cody's bookstore and a Peet's coffee shop keep the street connected to its Berkeley roots.

Also flourishing: an arts district in the downtown, along Shattuck Avenue. Opened in 2001 in this neighborhood, a new home for the Berkeley Repertory, 600 seats, the Aurora Theater, 160 seats, and Jazz school, 600 students. Moving north, Shattuck becomes more upscale, but the concentration of exotic, varied and inexpensive restaurants has earned the area the moniker: "Gourmet Ghetto." Alice Waters invented "California cuisine" at Chez Panisse, located on the north. Berkeley also sustains butchers and bakeries, an upscale supermarket, Andronico's, and large markets that specialize in organic food, including the Berkeley Bowl and Whole Foods. There's also a farmers' market, very popular. Not all have succumbed to gourmet dining. Berkeley High kids, offered a tasty and nourishing menu, preferred french fries and fat.

A town that enjoys conversation and ideas. Berkeley is staunchly Democratic and liberal and if you followed the town solely through newspaper headlines, it would come across as extremely liberal.

Berkeley school district was one of the first in the nation to integrate its schools through mandated busing. Voters down through the years have passed funding measures to rebuild or overhaul every school in the district and to avoid cuts in academics and extra curricular activities.

Yet many parents send their children to private schools; one study put the number about 23 percent. Arguments abound over education and how the school district deals with problems, particularly at the high school. Berkeley mixes kids of diverse backgrounds. Scores vary by group. Many kids are struggling or doing so-so, many succeeding.

School district has revised attendance policies and boundaries to reduce busing and leave more children in their neighborhood schools but this is a situation where not everyone can be satisfied.

In state comparisons, even the low-scoring Berkeley schools do fairly well, rankings in the 30th and 40th percentiles. Oakland would love to have these scores in many of its schools. For many Berkeley parents, however, these scores are not acceptable. They have high academic ambitions for their children — UC Berkeley, Harvard, Yale, Stanford, etc. On the high end, the school district generally delivers. Berkeley High School usually places second in Alameda County in moving students up to California public colleges, including the University of California. But parents remain critical and wary, and this, combined with the complexity of programs, has taken a toll on teachers and administrators. Berkeley district has a reputation of being tough to govern.

Although residents support education, many have little direct contact with the schools. Berkeley district enrolls about 9,300 students, 9 percent of the town's population. By contrast, Antioch, a bedroom town in neighboring Contra Costa County, has about 22 percent of its population enrolled in its local schools.

These numbers reflect another side of Berkeley: it is to a large extent a singles town, a renters' town. The state tally in 2003 showed 47,027 residential units: 20,131 single homes, 1,756 single attached, 25,081 apartments, 59 mobile homes.

Civic leaders and council members are always talking about laying out the welcome mat for businesses. But when the projects are big, the arguments are fierce. Berkeley council meetings are notorious for droning on and on. Everyone wants to "share." This style has its fans. Berkeley believes in bringing its citizens along through talk and cooperation.

Some streets, particularly Telegraph Avenue near the campus, seem frozen in time and in problems that don't budge.

But in other neighborhoods, notably Shattuck and Fourth Street, the city has been innovative and has made improvements. The town has a good employment base, foremost the university, about 12,000 local jobs.

Cultural-culinary mecca. Berkeley has loads of bookstores, restaurants, coffee shops, clubs, dance halls, art galleries and specialty stores. The university is brimming with activities, many of them open to the public — recitals, symphonies, dance, exhibits, plays, a great variety of classes (extension program), sporting events, notably basketball and football. Berkeley has a night life, for young people and for mature adults.

Many activities for kids. Lawrence Hall of Science. Fishing pier. Boating. Marina. Merry-Go-Round, trails, golf course, botanical garden, playing fields at Tilden Park, which borders Berkeley. City hall sponsors many activities.

Residents fix up their homes and fight for neighborhood quality. To stop speeders and curtail traffic through residential neighborhoods, the city blocked many streets with concrete pylons. Berkeley has its rundown streets near the water but even these will often have homes or apartments that show good care. The Berkeley hills command one of the prettiest vistas on the West Coast — the Golden Gate. Spectacular sunsets.

Berkeley nourishes its neighborhoods, which many will find charming and in character, almost European. In the flatlands, you are never far from a coffee shop or bakery. In 2000, voters approved spending $5 million to renovate the town's libraries. Much of the work was done in 2001 and 2002. In its treatment of the disabled, Berkeley is miles ahead of many municipalities.

Good commute town. Interstate 80 runs along the shore. Highways 13 and 24 run through the hills and along the east side. BART (commute rail) has three stations in town; trains to Oakland and San Francisco. AC Transit runs buses throughout Alameda County and West Contra Costa. Berkeley is only five miles from the Bay Bridge. On the down side, internal traffic is a bear and Berkeley is notoriously short of parking.

Near campus, many students and young people live in old homes divided into small apartments. The university community years ago spread into Kensington, Oakland, Richmond, El Cerrito, Albany. UC Berkeley has rebuilt its married-student housing, located in Albany. Cal students looking for housing should call university housing and dining services. Phone (510) 642-2456.

Being opposite the Golden Gate, Berkeley gets the ocean breezes and sometimes the summer fog. It has its hot days and its cold but the general temperature is pleasantly cool. If you want to swim outdoors you can (at Lake Temescal or Lake Anza in Tilden Park) but many people head for the indoor pools around the city. In autumn, hot and dry Diablos blow into Bay Area. In 1991, a big chunk of the Berkeley-Oakland hills burned; 2,500 homes and apartments lost, 25 dead. If you buy in hills, clear away brush.

In recent years, homicides have dropped but always take care. Difficult to generalize about crime: many neighborhoods, flats and hills, have low crime. Seven homicides in 2002 (preliminary figures), one in 2001, four in 2000, three in 1999, two in 1998. The counts for the previous years are 11, 8, 10, 8, 8, 12, 14, 11, 11, 14, 11. The university has its own police force. Miscellaneous:

• New foot-bike bridge crossing Interstate 80 to the water.

• City hall powers 200 of its vehicles with biodiesel fuel. Costs more than regular gas but burns cleaner.

• Gloomy state budget is forcing cutbacks on UC enrollments.

• Piece by piece, park lovers and government agencies are putting together a trail-park system that one day, they hope, will run from the Bay Bridge to the Delta.

• Good place for gossip and meeting people: the YMCA, which has possibly the best gym-exercise club in town

• Campus is always adding or remodeling buildings. In 2003, Stanley Hall, biomedical research, was under construction, $162 million.

• Why Berkeley is fun. Male sexuality class did some off-campus research with lap dancers. When media broke story, university said it was shocked, shocked and kicked in some changes.

• Chamber of commerce (510) 549-7003.

CASTRO VALLEY

BEDROOM TOWN WITH COUNTRY ATMOSPHERE in hills east of San Leandro and Hayward. Many lovely homes, not opulent, but often large and well cared for. Some homes have great views of Bay and sunset and this has pushed town up market. In the canyons and on the outskirts, horse ranches. Castro Valley also has many ordinary tract homes.

School scores high, top 20 percent in state. Many professionals move into Castro Valley for its schools. A large state university just about borders Castro Valley and boosts education values. Also nearby, a community college. School and community boundaries differ. Call school district for boundaries, (510) 537-3000. Residents passed school bonds in 1998 and 2002. High school has added classrooms, expanded its gym, library and cafeteria and constructed science and math buildings. Canyon Middle School named a Distinguished School in 2003. Also in 2003, science labs added at all elementary schools.

Unincorporated, which means Castro Valley is governed from Oakland by the county board of supervisors. In reality, much local control has devolved to community groups. Many new homes are going up east of Castro Valley and at times it looks like suburbia will extend uninterrupted all the way over the hills to Pleasanton. In recent years, the town has done a good job of sprucing up its downtown. Major medical center, Eden, in downtown.

Castro Valley is part of the Hayward Area Recreation District. Many activities: soccer, baseball, tennis, little theater, dance, community center, art and exercise classes, to name a few. Castro Valley is within a few minutes' drive of large regional parks, including Lake Chabot. Public golf course. Fall arts festival. Annual rodeo. Archery range. Many university classes open to public.

The FBI doesn't track unincorporated towns but communities with Castro Valley's demographics are usually low in crime.

Fast shot to Oakland, Berkeley, Pleasanton by Interstate 580. Buses. BART, which has stations in Hayward and San Leandro, extended its line to Dublin and built a station in Castro Valley. This helps commute. Complaints about traffic along Crow Canyon Road, a short cut to Contra Costa suburbs.

The great strength of Castro Valley is in its neighborhoods: well-maintained, nice looking, stable, and in its residents, highly supportive of schools. Chamber of commerce (510) 537-5300.

DUBLIN

BEDROOM TOWN that started millennium with high hopes of roaring into high tech, then got a blast of new market reality. Nonetheless, if premature, the hopes will probably be fulfilled. Location, location, location. Good town if you are in the market for a new home or apartment.

Population 35,550. School scores high, crime low, commute easy if you have a local job, amusements and shopping plentiful and getting better. A modern and in many ways a progressive town.

In 2002, the job that had residents stewing for years was completed: a new interchange for interstates 580 and 680. Traffic flows smoother now.

At the start of 2001, Cisco, Commerce One and Oracle were committed to building giant complexes in "Digital Dublin." Then the economy tanked and the three, in one way or another, bailed out.

On the plus side, Sybase (software) moved its headquarters and 900 employees from Emeryville to Dublin. Signs of the (modern) times: the Sybase facility includes a day-care center for employees' kids (also a gourmet cafeteria, a fitness center, a children's playground and a jogging track.) Sybase is located in a business park on the east side of Dublin.

Dublin is located at the junction of Interstates 680 and 580 in a bowl called the Amador Valley. Pleasanton, which borders Dublin to the south, and Livermore, to the east, are also located in the Amador Valley. Immediately north of Dublin another valley, the San Ramon, begins. It takes in the Contra Costa County towns of San Ramon, Danville, Alamo and Blackhawk. The region is often referred to as the I-680 corridor.

Danville, Alamo and Blackhawk are upscale to rich. San Ramon, Dublin, Pleasanton and Livermore are middle class plus, high-tech, bedroom towns. San Ramon has Bishop Ranch, 350 firms employing 30,000; major tenants include SBC Pac Bell and ChevronTexaco. Pleasanton has Hacienda Business Park; major tenants, PeopleSoft, AT&T, Safeway headquarters. Livermore has the Lawrence Livermore Lab, a large weapons and nuclear research facility run by the University of California, Berkeley.

In all of these towns, school scores are generally high, crime low. Many residents are college educated, some are brilliant.

The setting is pretty. Hills and valleys, Mt. Diablo to the northeast. Green in spring and winter, gold in summer and fall. The less enlightened might call

David Dufresne, Broker/Owner
Realty World/Real Estate Solutions
11620 Regio Court
Dublin CA 94568
(925) 855-8444 Direct
www.Solutions4realestate.com
David@solutions4realestate.com
Log on for direct listing or
email me today

+ *Over 38 years experience and 1500+ successful closed transactions*

+ *Representing both Buyers and Sellers*

+ *Covering the entire Bay Area with specialization in the East Bay*

+ *Serving all your real estate and financial needs with direct wholesale pricing on all clients' purchases*

+ *Log on to our websites for all of the up-to-date homes for sale, VA, FHA-HUD foreclosures, school information, community news and more!*

John Trowbridge, Broker/Owner
Realty World/Professional Brokers
2211 San Ramon Valley Blvd., Suite D
San Ramon CA 94583
1-800-456-6544 Direct
www.Johntrowbridge.com
Johntrow@earthlink.net
Log on for direct listing or
email me today

the gold "dried-out grass" but no matter, the region cast its charms. Wineries dot the east side of the Amador Valley, cachet by the vat.

Over the past 25 years or so the region has been jelling as a high-tech haven, in large measure because it has brains but to a greater extent because it has land and good freeways. Both Silicon Valley, about 30 miles to the south, and San Francisco, 30 miles to the west, are short of land. In the 1990s, BART (commute rail) was extended to Dublin-Livermore.

Dublin, named by Irish pioneers, lagged behind San Ramon and Pleasanton. Up until about 1960, the town was no more than a farm hamlet under the jurisdiction of the county government.

When the housing came, it followed a plan but residents soon became dissatisfied. The county had one vision, the residents another — an old story in California. In 1982, Dublin incorporated as a legal city and took control of its own planning. It revised its general plan and focused its energy on securing a diverse economy with a good base of high-tech and retail.

The initial housing followed middle-class tract lines, nothing fancy. As the prosperity of the region increased, homes stepped up in quality and size. The oldest housing, much of it spruced up and remodeled, is found on the valley floor near the freeway. As you move west into the hills, the homes become newer, wood-shake roofs give way to terra cotta or tile and at a certain point utility lines are placed underground. Some hill homes command great views of the valley and the Diablo hills.

In the 1990s, Dublin approved a plan to build thousands of homes and apartments on its east side — Dublin Ranch. This section, close to the BART station, set aside large parcels for high-tech firms, hotels and modern retail stores in a large mall.

Much of this work is under way. The mall, called Hacienda Crossings, is up — Barnes and Noble bookstore, Pier I, Old Navy, Bed, Bath and Beyond, restaurants, etc. Safeway has built a giant store here and another in downtown Dublin. Wells Fargo has opened a banking complex. Target, Mervyn's, Ross, Marshalls can be found in the downtown. Stoneridge Mall, with a Macys and Nordstrom, is located a few miles to the south. There's a Costco and a Wal-Mart a few miles to the east. If you like to shop, Dublin and environs have much to offer. IKEA, the furniture store, is scheduled to open one of its giant stores in Dublin in 2004. Pleasanton has a Trader Joe's.

New apartments are available for rent, new homes (at Dublin Ranch) are being sold. The hammers are still flying, homes and apartments. And, finally, the internal roads in East Dublin have come together; for several years, detours and deadends grated the nerves.

In the 1990s, Dublin schools split from Pleasanton and formed their own district. Scores follow demographics: in state rankings, Dublin is scoring in the

80th and 90th percentiles. A bond was passed to add classrooms and other amenities. The new housing is being taxed, often indirectly, to provide schools as the tracts are built. The east side added an elementary in 2000; another elementary and a middle school are to be built by 2004. Dublin High and Wells Middle schools named Distinguished Schools in 2003.

Dublin and Pleasanton subscribe to the belief that if you pay teachers more, you will get better teachers. The two districts pay some of the highest salaries in the East Bay.

Many activities for children. Tennis courts, bowling center, ice-skating rink, six parks, a swim center and a library. Summer water carnival. Movie complex with 20 screens and an IMAX (giant) screen. Soccer thrives. Nearby San Ramon has a roller-skating rink. Golf course coming with development. Seniors center and community center. Adult schools offer variety of classes, many vocational or hobby oriented. Little theater. Heritage center. SPCA recently opened a large center that encourages adoptions. It puts the dogs through obedience training. Among new parks: Emerald Glen on east side: lighted tennis and basketball courts, baseball and softball diamonds, soccer fields, skate park. Fairgrounds in Pleasanton; many events, including — hoot mon! — the annual Scottish Festival.

New, large library in the civic center complex. Old library to be converted to a senior center.

About 230 cities and towns in this great nation allow the sale of fireworks for the Fourth of July. Dublin is one. For safety, Dublin directs the buyers to certain local parks where they can fire away without setting the countryside ablaze.

If you have a local job, the commute is a snap. If you toil in Oakland or Berkeley, your nerves will grate but your sanity should remain intact. If you're heading for San Francisco and driving ... good luck. You're going to need it. The Bay Bridge is being rebuilt; chaos. In a few years, another BART station will open in Dublin. Interstate 680 to San Jose was widened in 2002; this will help this often miserable trek.

One homicide each in 2001 and 2000, zero in 1999, two in 1998, zero in 1997, 1996 and 1995, one in 1994, zero in 1993 and in 1992, two in 1991, zero in 1990, 1989, 1988, 1987. Police officer killed in 1998 during a restaurant stickup. Suspects arrested and convicted.

Just east of town, two jails, one run by county, one by feds. The locals don't like them. The fed place is noted for its alumni, who include Patricia Hearst and Theodore Kaczynski, Unabomber. Dublin's population includes about 5,000 inmates. County wanted to build a juvenile detention center near county jail but residents said, forget it, and killed project. Also on the east side, Camp Parks, training ground for Army reservists.

In 1989, Dublin opened a civic center, a building that gives more substance to the idea of a downtown and heart of town. But Dublin still wrestles with the criticism that it lacks an "identity." Its response: mild regret to indifference. Downtown being spruced up and public art encouraged. City has hired an enforcer to crack down on code violations. The state tally in 2003 showed 11,939 residential units: 7,128 single homes, 1,301 single attached, 3,483 apartments or condos, 27 mobile homes. Miscellaneous:

• Altamont Commute Express runs trains from Manteca to San Jose with a stop in Pleasanton. Popular.

• Dublin has zoned the land around the BART station and the freeways for business and apartments and mixed uses (retail stores and housing). Four-lane arterials to the new subdivisions move traffic quickly to freeway. More development is coming on the east side.

• Thousands of homes are going up in the hills and valleys north of Dublin. Dougherty Road, which runs through Dublin, is being widened to handle the traffic from these master-planned communities.

• 2003 saw the opening of the BART line to San Francisco International Airport. The Dublin-Pleasanton line is the only one that goes directly to SFO. No transferring necessary.

Chamber of commerce (925) 828-6200.

Population by Age Groups in Alameda County

City or Area	Under 5	5-19	20-34	35-54	55+
Alameda	4,057	12,923	14,725	24,579	15,975
Albany	988	3,069	3,737	5,627	3,023
Berkeley	4,109	15,984	34,939	28,635	19,076
Castro Valley	3,266	11,603	9,586	19,424	13,413
Dublin	1,758	5,297	8,434	11,090	3,394
Emeryville	257	636	2,525	2,170	1,294
Fremont	15,137	41,823	46,463	67,437	32,553
Hayward	11,011	30,494	35,761	38,831	23,933
Livermore	5,650	16,622	14,461	25,178	11,434
Newark	3,062	9,736	9,806	12,998	6,869
Oakland	28,292	81,300	101,273	117,175	71,444
Piedmont	582	2,936	731	3,979	2,724
Pleasanton	4,359	14,821	10,262	23,738	10,474
San Leandro	5,032	14,332	16,580	24,191	19,317
San Lorenzo	1,336	4,741	3,909	6,712	5,200
Union City	4,870	15,644	15,283	20,416	10,656
County Total	98,378	293,865	341,818	449,224	260,456

Source: 2000 Census.

EMERYVILLE

SMALL BUT DYNAMIC. On the Bay near the Bay Bridge. One of the best commutes in the East Bay. Loaded with shops, restaurants. Many apartments and condos. Favorite town of young professionals and empty nesters. Population 7,550.

In 2001 and 2002, after years of success upon success, Emeryville took a few hits. Sybase, the large software firm, relocated to Dublin. When dot-coms flourished, many called Emeryville home. The world and Emeryville have far fewer dot-coms now.

On the other hand, Chiron (bio-tech) expanded, adding labs and offices and a garage with 1,000 spaces. Pixar is adding three buildings and a garage.

In 2002, the first phase of "Bay Street" opened: stores, restaurants, a movie complex of 16 screens, Barnes & Noble book store. When finished, this project will include 65 stores, nine restaurants, 363 housing units and a luxury hotel. The town already has several.

The state tally in 2003 showed 4,615 residential units: 270 single homes, 329 single attached, 3,979 apartments or condos, 37 mobile homes. Over the next few years, the city intends to bring its housing total up to about 6,000 units. Most of the new units will be condos.

In recent years, Emeryville has won the headquarters of Pixar Animation Studios, run by Steve Jobs of Apple fame. Other recent additions: an office tower, 16 stories, west of Interstate 80; two hotels, each 11 stories, and an IKEA, a giant furniture that draws mobs on weekends.

Emeryville has an Amtrak station and a freeway, Interstate 80, that bisects the town.

Emeryville was born 104 years ago when residents, fed up with the sluggishness of the county government, voted to incorporate themselves into a city. For income, the new city went in for heavy industry and later trucking, and fun, notably horse racing, minor league baseball and gambling. When Prohibition came, Emeryville blissfully ignored the law of the land and won the wrath of Earl Warren, then district attorney of Alameda County (later California governor and chief justice of the U.S. Supreme Court). Warren raided and fulminated and castigated, all apparently to little avail. World War II came and went, the race track closed but for decades after Emeryville was known as a good place for a shot and a beer and a card game.

Alameda County Single-Family Home Prices

City	Sales	Lowest	Highest	Median	Average
Alameda	144	$37,000	$1,525,000	$485,000	$515,044
Albany	41	161,500	732,000	487,500	476,438
Berkeley	210	46,000	1,885,000	561,000	594,002
Castro Valley	214	30,000	1,080,000	430,000	444,331
Dublin	143	115,000	960,000	503,000	516,295
Emeryville	46	46,000	450,000	282,000	274,156
Fremont	623	48,500	3,000,000	453,000	499,401
Hayward	519	35,000	1,990,000	363,000	370,697
Livermore	371	76,500	1,275,000	420,000	455,824
Newark	129	41,000	780,000	407,500	388,401
Oakland	1,061	25,000	3,675,000	340,000	441,461
Pleasanton	274	33,364	2,100,000	569,000	650,616
San Leandro	288	42,000	764,273	360,000	346,267
San Lorenzo	114	90,000	495,000	362,500	340,057
Union City	184	25,000	957,000	450,000	443,046

Source: DataQuick Information Systems, Inc., La Jolla, Calif. **Key:** Resale single-family detached housing sales from May 1, 2003 to July 31, 2003.

The forces of change, however, were at work. The Bay Bridge, built in the 1930s, and the freeways, built in the 1950s, elevated the value of Emeryville's location. Came the day when the city council approved the construction of Watergate, an apartment-condo complex that brought in the educated middle class. Within a few years, they voted out the Old Crowd and began to fix up Emeryville.

In the 1980s, high-tech and biotech discovered the town. Emeryville draws many of its brains from the UC-Berkeley crowd.

In the 1980s and 1990s, Emeryville reoriented its retail and amusements to its younger audience. Restaurants, a Trader Joe's and a Borders bookstore were opened. Waterfront trails were spruced up, bike lane added. Hotels were built, bringing in more restaurants. The new apartment complexes came with pools, workout rooms and saunas. The town has a marina — sailing, fishing, boating.

Emeryville sits almost opposite the Golden Gate. Many residents and hotel guests have great views of San Francisco and the Bay. San Francisco is within 10 minutes, Berkeley and Oakland are next door. All three are loaded with things to do.

Served by Emery Unified School District, one elementary school, one middle, one high. Enrollment about 900. School rankings bounce all over but many land in the 30th to 50th percentile. Bond passed in 1995 to spend $8 million to improve the schools and buy them computers.

Superintendent resigned after it was discovered that district was spending more than it had. According to newspaper, the district had a reserve of $1.5 million when he took over and a $1.8 million debt when he left. Only a small number of residents have kids in the schools but the headlines and the screwups embarrassed the town and more attention is now being paid the schools. In 2003, residents passed a parcel tax to fund educational needs.

Overall crime rate is way above what's found in almost any city in the Bay Area but not as bad as it sounds. General and auto theft account for almost 85 percent of the reported crimes. Emeryville has many stores and this to some extent accounts for many thefts. The high rate, however, gives the impression that if it's not nailed down in this town, kiss it goodbye!

As for serious crime, it's there and you always have to be wary but it may not be as bad as found in other metropolitan cities. Three homicides in 2001, zero in 2000 and 1999, three in 1998, zero in 1997 and 1996, one in 1995, two in 1994.

Why doesn't crime ruin Emeryville as upper middle-class address? Because much of the crime hits visitors. The main housing complexes have hired security guards and installed devices and procedures to protect their residents. Emeryville has more officers per 1,000 residents than many other suburban cities and the small size of the town, 1.5 square miles, makes for a rapid response. Miscellaneous:

• Many of Emeryville's residential units can be found in just three complexes: Watergate, 1,247 condos, Pacific Park Plaza, 30 stories with 583 condos, and Emery Bay, 684 apartments.

• City has a small artists colony residing in live-work lofts.

• City runs free buses around town and to BART stations. Popular service, over 700,000 passengers a year.

• Summer fogs cool the air, winter fogs decrease visibility.

• Many industrial buildings remain but they are steadily being pushed out by sleek and modern buildings.

Chamber of commerce (510) 652-5223.

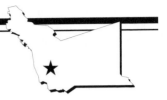

FREMONT

BEDROOM HIGH-TECH CITY in south county. Population 209,000. School scores high. Almost every school is scoring above the 50th percentile and some are scoring in the 90th percentile, among the tops in the state. In 2002, passed a $157 million bond to renovate its schools.

Overall crime rate low. Zero homicides in 2001, three in 2000, one in 1999. The counts for previous years, 9, 4, 3, 2, 6, 4, 6, 2, 2, 2, 2, 1. Bicycle patrols in some neighborhoods. New police headquarters.

Fremont rises from the Bay to the hills, which to a large extent have been spared housing. In winter, the hills turn green and snow sometimes caps Mission Peak. Streets clean. Homes kept in good repair. Trees plentiful, softening the lines of the housing. Fremont has been honored for planting many trees. The town has also done a good job on the little touches that at first you might miss then you notice: for example, the median strip along Mission Boulevard planted with shrubs, flowers and small trees.

Temperate climate. Breezes from the Bay yet warm enough for many homes to use solar heat.

Hard work and intelligent planning have helped Fremont but the city owes much of its good fortune to timing and fate.

First came the Indians, called Ohlones, then the Spanish, who built the mission in 1797 and passed on diseases that killed just about all the Indians. Fremont has a large Indian cemetery a short distance from the mission, which has been restored.

Then came the Americans who farmed and welcomed the railroad. In the early 20th century, Charlie Chaplin shot some silent films in the Niles neighborhood, which now celebrates a June festival of silent movies.

As the century progressed, five hamlets blossomed and in 1956, seeing development coming, they incorporated themselves into the City of Fremont, population 22,443. A big city. Fremont, in square miles, is almost double the size of San Francisco. Left as five villages, "Fremont" would have grown up disjointed and difficult to administer. Also by this time, planning for suburban cities was shedding its diapers and becoming more of a force. New cities are often more cleverly designed than old ones. Fremont officials established zones for homes, for apartments, for light industry, for shops and malls.

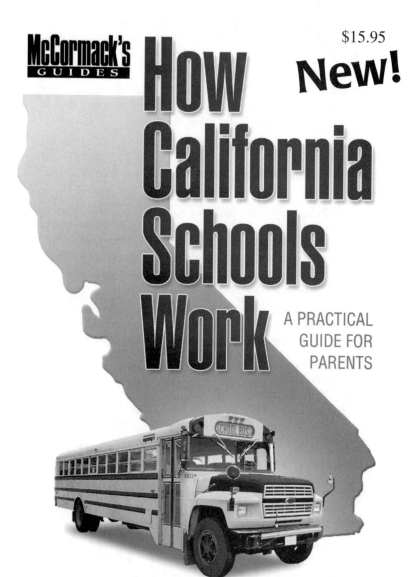

McCormack's GUIDES

$15.95

New!

How California Schools Work

A PRACTICAL GUIDE FOR PARENTS

FROM THE EDITORS OF McCormack's Guides

www.mccormacks.com
1-800-222-3602

Meanwhile, across the Bay, reachable over the Dumbarton Bridge and Highway 237, Silicon Valley was coming to life and home prices on the Peninsula were rising. Many families looked east to Fremont.

By 1960, the population had jumped to 43,790 and then it soared, reaching 100,869 by 1970. In the 1970s, Fremont added about 32,000 residents and in the 1980s, about 41,000. By this time, the city was running out of land. In the 1990s, Fremont increased its population by 30,000.

In the 1960s and 1970s, housing tastes were changing. Garages went from one stall to two and three, bedrooms from three to four and five, stories from one to two. Lots shrunk. With both parents working, low-maintenance landscaping found favor over lawns.

Fremont has its very old housing, built around the original towns. And it has its old suburban tracts, built just after World War II. But having built so many units after 1960, the city comes across as "new," particularly in the hills, along and above Mission Boulevard, and down near Interstate 880. The state in 2003 counted 70,289 residential units: single homes 41,988, single attached 7,136, multiples 20,409, mobile homes 756.

The old Fremont used to be considered blue-collar. It had a large auto plant that employed thousands. The plant is still there, General Motors-Toyota NUMMI, and it is still the city's largest employer, about 5,100 workers.

By and by, Silicon Valley also ran out space for plants and research facilities. Up to Fremont it came and built hundreds of high-tech firms, and later bio-tech firms. This wiped out the blue-collar image and turned Fremont into a Silicon Valley town. Needing highly skilled and educated workers, the new firms pushed the demographics further up the scale, which explains in part the high academic rankings.

In SATs, among Alameda County high schools, Mission San Jose High usually places first or second in math and among the top five in verbal. Every year only about two dozen California high schools crack the 600 mark in the math SAT. Mission San Jose High School is always in this elite group. Parents in this neighborhood, the richest in the city, are prickly about education.

When the board tried to change attendance boundaries of the schools serving the Mission San Jose neighborhood, parents said, no way, hired lawyers and petitioned to form their own school district. In 2001, the state rejected the petition and, meanwhile, the school board softened its reorganization plan.

Fremont also has a large community college, Ohlone, a big plus. Community colleges are loaded with activities and classes open to the public. In 2002, Ohlone won approval of a bond to build a campus in Newark and to renovate its Fremont facilities and add a student services building. In 2002, William Hopkins Middle School won National Blue Ribbon for academic excellence. Mission San Jose High School named a Distinguished School in 2003.

Activities plentiful. About 40 parks and playgrounds. Lake in middle of town. Large library, small neighborhood libraries. Symphony orchestra. Trails, bay wildlife refuge, historic farm. Annual arts festival draws about 350,000. Mission Days Festival. Festival of India. Celtic Festival. Performing arts center at Ohlone features touring shows. Ice-skating rink, in part a tribute to local girl who made good: Kristi Yamaguchi, winner of Olympic gold in figure skating. Skate park. City sponsors dozens of activities and classes, gymnastics, dance, cooking, singing, kiddie and toddler get togethers, jazzercize, etc. Usual kid sports, soccer, softball, football. New nine-hole golf course. Lagoon is being converted into a water recreation park. East Bay Regional Park District opened a swimming beach at its 450-acre Quarry Lakes Park, which has been stocked with fish.

Ohlone College runs summer programs for young children — sports, arts, drama, English, math, chess, computers and more.

University of California at Berkeley offers extension classes in town. Many of the classes are aimed at working professionals. Several other schools — Silicon Valley College, Northwestern Polytechnic — also offer courses for working adults.

Fremont promotes ethnic harmony and throws a Heritage Festival. Churches and schools help with the getting along. Many residents are professionals who came in the immigration wave that started in the 1970s.

Commute better than most. Buses, BART (commute rail), freeways, bridge to Silicon Valley. Boulevards, almost all four-lane, crisscross the city and end usually at a freeway. Two freeways: Interstate 680 and Interstate 880. The latter used to be a real dog, always congested, but in recent years it has been widened and overpasses and exits have been added or renovated. The result: still a mutt. More people, more cars ... can't win.

If you're taking BART to Oakland or San Francisco, you have to rise about a half hour earlier than Berkeley residents and make the station by 7 a.m. On the plus side, Fremont being the beginning of the BART line, you're assured of a seat. The Altamont Commuter Express, trains from Stockton to San Jose, makes stops in Fremont and Santa Clara.

In 2000, Santa Clara County voters approved a sales tax increase that will raise money to extend BART to San Jose, and possibly beyond. When completed, the BART extension will make life easier for many commuters but the job is going to take years. In the same year, Alameda voters extended a half-cent sales tax for transit projects.

Miscellaneous:

• After years of arguing, Wal-Mart won permission to build a store at Osgood Road and Auto Mall Parkway. Another recent addition: a Target.

• Mountain lions occasionally spotted in the hills. Shy animals. No one attacked. Also spotted: the helmeted hang glider. The ridges seem ideal for this pursuit.

• The original towns were Niles, Centerville, Irvington, Mission San Jose and Warm Springs. As a way of building neighborhood cohesiveness, the city is restoring these old towns as business centers and gathering places (restaurants, cafes, a movie house or a theater).

• Where the commercial action is: Pacific Commons, a large new business park near the Bay. In 2000, Cisco announced it was building in the park a giant research-office that would employ 10,000. Came the reality of 2001 (and 2002 and 2003) and the project was put on "hold." In 2002, city revamped Pacific Commons to allow construction of a shopping center that might include a Costco. More land was also allotted to selling cars. The Costco would replace a smaller store in Fremont

• Attention red-light runners. Fremont employs camera and sensors at some intersections to nail motorists who run red light. Camera takes a picture of car and driver, ticket in the mail.

• Washington Medical Center is located near BART station.

• Fremont has an ordinance discouraging home construction in the hills.

• The largest undeveloped parcel in town, 427 acres, straddles Ardenwood Boulevard at the Paseo Padre Parkway, near Highway 84. Initial plans ask permission to build 1,800 homes but much negotiating and political massaging remains.

• Bumps to lumps. The first, planted on busy residential streets, were forcing emergency vehicles to slow down — too slow. The city in 2002 replaced them with lumps that allow easier passage.

Chamber of commerce (510) 795-2244.

HAYWARD

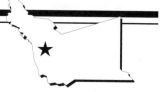

EAST SHORE BEDROOM city, suburban, third-most populous in Alameda County, 144,700 residents. Good commute. Recently renovated many of its schools. Educational offerings include a community college and a California State University, both of which wave the flag for academics.

Following World War II, thousands of GIs, having sampled California sunshine on their way to the Pacific, migrated to the West Coast. Hayward and countless other suburbs were built for them. Practical and unpretentious, these towns were oriented around home, school, recreation and reasonable proximity to jobs. Home designs favored the three-bedroom, two-bath model.

Almost half the city's housing units were built between 1950 and 1970. The great majority of the homes and apartments were constructed on the flat or gently sloping land to the west of Mission and Foothill, two of the main boulevards.

Hayward ascends gradually from the Bay to the hills and east of Mission Boulevard soars into elevations that command sweeping views of San Francisco Bay. After 1970, Hayward, in its hills neighborhoods and near the university, moved upmarket with 4-6 bedroom homes. For the best of what Hayward offers, take a spin up Skyline Drive.

Hayward also has older, smaller housing around its downtown.

All this means a good housing mix with prices across the spectrum. Many people coming in at the low end are buying their first homes.

The state in 2003 counted 46,757 housing units, of which 23,237 were single homes, 3,396 single attached, 17,825 apartments and 2,299 mobile homes.

Job under construction: a 100-acre high-tech business park, 578 homes, 25-acre sports park with lights for night games, baseball, soccer, softball. The project is located near the Bay.

Around the downtown BART station and the civic center, the city has been encouraging "smart growth," in this instance townhouses, live-work lofts and condos. "Smart growth" tries to place people near transit centers and favors apartments and multiple units over single homes.

Amtrak has a station just west of the downtown. In recent years, Amtrak has started a commute schedule called the Capitol Corridor, trains from Silicon

Valley to Sacramento.

Hayward has a second BART station near Mission Boulevard on the south side. BART also has a station in Castro Valley, within a short drive of North Hayward.

About 17 miles to Bay Bridge on Interstate 880, recently widened. About 10 miles to Peninsula via the Hayward-San Mateo Bridge, which in 2002 added a second span (it ties into the first at the San Mateo side.)

Quick shot to Livermore-Pleasanton over Interstate 580. About 15 miles to San Jose. AC Transit buses.

In the 1990s, the school district won money from the state to remove asbestos and remodel many of its schools and equip them for high tech. Local voters in 1997 gave the OK to continue a tax that paid for school landscaping, maintenance of playing fields and graffiti removal. Hayward runs several year-round schools. Academic rankings bounce all over the place.

Several private schools, including a Catholic High School (Moreau).

Shopping malls follow freeways. The Southland Mall came to life with the construction of Interstate 880 and weakened Hayward's old town, about two miles to the east. The city and merchants have been tinkering for years to rejuvenate the downtown and have come up with antique stores, restaurants and shops. One of the two BART stations borders the downtown and this helps attract shoppers. New city hall and fire station. Old city hall sat astride the Hayward Fault. The building was abandoned.

The city is headquarters for Mervyn's Stores and has a small airport, warehouses and light industry down near Interstate 880. These businesses create local jobs, the ideal commute.

Ten homicides in 2001, nine in 2000, eleven in 1999. The counts for the previous years are five, seven, twelve, twelve, twelve, eight, five, ten, four, six, eight, three, five. The hill sections have far fewer incidents of crime than the flatlands and some flatland sections are safer than others.

Many activities. Plays and events at the colleges, baseball, basketball, soccer, tennis, arts and crafts. Bowling alley. Big indoor swimming pool, called the Hayward Plunge. Neighborhood and regional parks. Shoreline preserve. Lake Chabot. Japanese Gardens. Roller-skating rink. Libraries. Movies. Annual zucchini festival. Nine-hole golf course. Many classes at Chabot Community College and Cal State are open to public.

The university and especially the college work with the locals to improve education and give businesses and the community a boost.

Chamber of commerce (510) 537-2424.

LIVERMORE

BEDROOM, HIGH-TECH TOWN, population 78,000, that also grows grapes and fights development, often successfully, but still accepts a fair amount of change and new construction.

Home to Lawrence Livermore Lab, which has helped make the town a brainy place.

School rankings bounce around a bit but many are in the 80 and 90th percentile. The school district mixes parents across a diverse social spectrum, rural to suburban, low income to highly educated. The latter tend to produce high-scoring kids.

In 1999, in partnership with the city government, the school district passed a $150 million bond to renovate schools and make civic improvements. In 2001, the district opened another elementary on the east side, north of the freeway. As enrollment increases, more schools will be built. William Mendenhall Middle School named a Distinguished School in 2003.

Crime low. Zero homicides in 2001 and 2000, two in 1999 and 1998, zero in 1997 and 1996. Counts for previous years are two, one, one, zero, two, two and one.

Commute not as bad as might be thought because the region is loaded with jobs.

In and about Livermore are located 23 wineries, Wente the best known. Residents call Livermore the "Alameda Wine Country." Livermore is situated in a bowl called the Amador Valley. The city is frequently mentioned in connection to its western neighbors, Dublin and Pleasanton, and to a lesser extent, San Ramon.

The town was named after Robert Livermore, an English sailor who married into a Spanish-Mexican family and secured a grant of 44,000 acres. For much of its early history, Livermore crushed the grape and rounded up the cattle. It produced one celebrity, boxer Max Baer, who in 1934 won the heavyweight crown. He was called "the Livermore Larruper."

In 1952, as the Cold War was swinging into high gear, Dr. Edward Teller, father of the H-Bomb, persuaded the U.S. government to build the Lawrence Livermore Lab to do research on nuclear weapons and other defense-related projects. The town at that time had a population of about 7,000.

Homes followed to house the people who worked at the lab and its spinoffs. The freeway, Interstate 580, was gradually extended, making the commute from Livermore to the Bay Area much easier and tying Livermore into the regional economy. Many of its residents now work in other towns.

In the 1960s, Livermore built about 6,400 housing units, in the 1970s, about 6,000 units and in the 1980s, about 4,000 units. In the 1990s, housing starts rose to about 5,700 units (census 2000).

By any standards, this is good amount of housing in a fairly short time. Nonetheless, Livermore about 1970s and 1980s picked up a reputation for being anti-growth.

The Lawrence Lab is run by the University of California at Berkeley. Yes ... that Berkeley! The leader in free speech, environmentalism and a few other causes. The Livermore locals initially saw the lab as this bonanza that would boom the local economy and build homes over the valley and into the hills.

The UC people saw the vineyards and the open hills and the small-town qualities and said, no, no, no, NO! to the development plans. Basic cultural clash, the kind that happens when people from different galaxies meet.

But even without the Berkeley connection, the fights would have come. In the 1980s and 1990s, the whole region, including San Ramon, Dublin and Pleasanton, went high-tech and up-market, bringing in thousands of professionals with upscale ideas of slowing growth and protecting the countryside. The same fights that show up in Livermore broke out in the other towns, the main difference being intensity. Livermore tops the scale in this category.

The big job, fought over for decades, is the equivalent of a new city, on Livermore's north border: 12,500 homes, condos and apartments. How all this will play out is anyone's guess. In 2000, residents passed a measure restricting growth in the area but this will not be the last shot fired in the battle.

Down through the years, however, the pro and anti groups learned somewhat to work together to the benefit of the town. Instead of ripping out the vineyards, ways were devised to protect them and blend in the housing. Much of the new housing and retail stores were built near Interstate 580. Livermore is forever trying to revive its downtown. It has had some success but removed from the freeway, the neighborhood will never be the vibrant center it once was. In some quarters this amounts to the end of the world, in others ... no big deal. And it's by no means a dead downtown. It has movies, restaurants, shops, a regional hospital, and a certain old-fashioned charm. Every day the flag goes up at a tall pole at the top of Livermore Avenue, the main street. And the horse-tackle store wheels out a life-size plastic horse. And predictably every once in a while the kids will throw soap in the town fountain near the flag pole.

Like most towns, Livermore built to the demands of the times. When the times called for middle-class housing, that's what it built, standard three-bedroom tract models, especially around its downtown. In the 1980s, many people were taking the equity in their first homes and moving into something bigger and better.

Livermore went in this direction. Many of the new homes run to four-bedrooms, with walk-in closets in the master bedroom, large or gourmet kitchens, plenty of windows and natural light, living rooms oriented toward the television or entertainment center and modern wiring.

In the overall picture, there's a good amount of variety. This includes custom homes, some built near the downtown, others in the country. And it includes in the downtown, cottages and bungalows erected before 1950. On many of the older streets the trees have matured into leafy umbrellas that cast pleasing shadows for the hotter days.

The state in 2003 counted 27,854 residential units, of which 20,409 were detached single homes, 2,271 attached homes, 4,743 apartments or condos and 431 mobile homes.

Many new homes sell for $600,000 plus and some soar over $1 million. The resale market offers old homes for less but Livermore is no longer the affordable town it used to be. See profiles on Dublin and Pleasanton.

In 2002, the Lawrence Lab, which employs about 8,000, celebrated its 50th anniversary. With the end of the Cold War, there was talk of closing the Lab but after cutbacks, it won a contract to build a super laser, cost about $2 billion. Besides research into nuclear weapons (computer testing and modeling) and disposal of aging bombs, the lab does research on cancer detection, fusion energy and mapping the genetic code, developing stronger materials and stopping bio-terrorism. After Sept. 11, Americans took national security more seriously and if anything this only underscored the importance of the lab.

A study done about six years ago disclosed that about 46 percent of the lab's regular employees live in Livermore and that the lab and its employees pump about $16 million a month into the town's economy. Across the street is the Sandia National Lab, different outfit, approximately same mission, about 1,000 employees. Years ago, a newspaper reported that Livermore had one of the highest — if not the highest — concentrations of Ph.Ds in the world. This boast is hard to prove but the labs are crawling with scientists.

Lawrence Lab and Las Positas Community College run special programs for the kids. Lab also trains teachers. Las Positas, which attracts many adults, in 1996 opened a science-technology center.

Of the $150 million approved in the 1999 bond, $20 million went for a new library, $20 million for a seniors center, a teen center, and a swim center, and $110 million for schools. The school district is also getting building funds from the state. The civic projects, including the swim center and library, are scheduled to be finished in 2003 and 2004. The town also has two branch libraries.

Livermore is attracting many professionals with young families. The school bond reflects the town's high interest in education. But this said, arguments about school funding are many and in 2003 the district had its fingers slapped for not putting enough in reserve.

BART station was opened in 1997 in nearby Dublin, a comfort to commuters, especially those traveling to San Francisco. Local buses and express buses to Silicon Valley job sites.

In 2002, two big jobs were completed that really will help the commute. In the first, the rebuilding of the interchange of Interstates 580 and 680 at Pleasanton was finished. For years, this interchange jammed traffic. In the second, Interstate 680 was widened south of Pleasanton, easing the commute for people working in Silicon Valley.

Altamont Commuter Express started service in 1998 — trains from Stockton to San Jose with stops in Livermore and Pleasanton. This is removing a little traffic from Interstate 680. Some residents are bothered by the train horns.

Even with these improvements, however, if you have a long commute, you will often find it a time-consuming drive. The Bay Bridge, the main route to San Francisco, is almost always backed up at commute hours. Many people now commute from the Central Valley and this is congesting Interstate 580.

Nonetheless, many Livermore residents have a short commute because they have local jobs. Besides the Lawrence Lab and Sandia, the region has attracted such high-tech or office firms as: Pac Bell, AT&T, ChevronTexaco, Hewlett-Packard, PeopleSoft and Sybase.

Located on the east side of the coastal range, Livermore is warmer and drier than the shore cities of Alameda County but not as hot as the Central Valley, which is separated from Livermore by the Diablo range. Livermore and Pleasanton occasionally trap some of the smog that blows around the Bay Area but air quality in the region has been improving. Just east of Livermore is the Altamont Pass, site of a notorious rock concert of the 1970s. (Rolling Stones hired Hell's Angels for security; bedlam meets mayhem.) Windy. About 5,000 windmills, power generators. Many dislike windmills, eye-insulting bird killers. Plans afoot to tear down many of the small ones and replace them with fewer but larger and more powerful ones that supposedly will kill fewer birds.

To elaborate on the appearance, Livermore is suburban nice with a strong country presence. Empty or almost empty hills still surround the city. Mt. Diablo rises to the northwest and in the winter takes on a mantle of snow. The homes are generally well-maintained, the streets clean, graffiti rare to the point of escaping notice. New police station, city hall renovated.

The freeway stores include a Costco, a Target, a Mervyn's, Home Depot, a Lowe's and a Wal-Mart. New homes are going up behind the Costco, north of the freeway. Dublin is to open an Ikea, giant furniture, in 2004.

Usual recreation — baseball, soccer, activity classes, softball — probably better than you'll find in any suburban city. About 40 parks or play facilities. Three golf courses. Bowling alley. Annual rodeo. Large state park, Del Valle, which has camping, boating, windsurfing and swimming. Equestrian events are popular. Thoroughbred ranches in hills. Plenty of horse and hiking trails. Camelot amusement center: video games, miniature golf, go-carts. Wine-country social life, of sorts, with an intellectual underpinning (the lab people). Livermore throws a harvest festival, a wine and honey festival and an arts festival. Wine museum. Skate park.

Dublin has a movie complex, 20 screens and an IMAX (giant) screen and a large bookstore. Pleasanton also has its big bookstore and a downtown popular with the restaurant crowd. And a giant mall with a Nordstroms and a Macys. Other goodies, a Trader Joe's.

In the 1950s, when the Lab arrived, Livermore and the region really were hicksville. Television, movies, small markets and a few greasy spoon restaurants — and that was it. Now ... a much different picture, not only for Livermore but for affluent suburbia. The giant supermarkets routinely field bakeries, delis, fish markets, pharmacies and banks. For the harried commuter and soccer parents all this means more convenient shopping. Starbucks and other coffee shops.

Local groups are not only staging plays but operas, a demanding art. The more ambitious productions draw on talent from the Bay Region.

• BART in 2003 started direct service from Dublin to San Francisco International Airport. Another BART station is to be built in Dublin — which is to say, right on the Livermore border.

• For local medical attention, Valley Memorial Hospital and Kaiser clinics.

• Livermore runs many of its recreation programs through a park and recreation district, an agency separate from city hall. For information and a schedule of activities, (925) 373-5700.

  • Livermore Airport, located to west of downtown. If moving near airport, check out noise, especially at night. Airport is home to about 580 planes.

  • For Yosemite and the mountains and snow slopes, Livermore offers a quick getaway — three or four hours.

  • Dr. Teller, a brilliant and unusual man, died in 2003. On one occasion, at a general meeting of lab personnel, he opened by playing a piano sonata. And a controversial man. The lab was built to fight the Cold War — now over and won. Book upon book has been written about the Atomic Age and its implications.

Chamber of commerce (925) 447-1606.

MOUNTAIN HOUSE CENTRAL VALLEY

NEW TOWN to be built from scratch on border of Alameda County, near Tracy. The first homes were put on sale in 2003.

Mountain House is coming in as a master-planned community. Before anything is built, the whole design, in some detail, will be laid out, with special attention paid to moving traffic quickly to the freeways.

Plans calls for 16,000 housing units for up to 44,000 people, with buildout over 20 to 40 years. The project also includes shops, schools, and parks, recreational facilities and commercial space.

Alameda County is divided roughly by two hill-mountain ranges. The first separates the shore cities, such as Oakland and Hayward, from the central county cities of Livermore and Pleasanton (Amador Valley). The second, reached through the Altamont Pass, separates the Amador Valley from the Central Valley (Tracy, Modesto, Stockton, etc.).

Over the last 20 years, as home prices have soared in the Bay Area, developers have built in the Central Valley thousands of homes priced $100,000 to sometimes $500,000 cheaper than their counterparts in the Bay Area. The result: the Central Valley's population soared, the commute became longer for many people, the freeways, particularly Interstate 580, became congested. Some towns, however, fared better than others. Tracy, the first town over the Altamont, is considered a more desirable commute than, say, Modesto.

Mountain House, coming just before Tracy, should be well received by people who work in the East Bay or even Silicon Valley because of its, by today's standards, endurable commute.

Some maps will show Mountain House in Alameda County — that's how close it is to the county line. To reach the new project, take Interstate 580 to Interstate 205 and as you cross the line into San Joaquin County look for the signs. Mountain House is forming north of the freeway, past the cows. The town will be served by the Lammersville School District, which now has about 300 students. Teens will attend high schools in Tracy.

For more information, see McCormack's Guide to Greater Sacramento and the Central Valley. Order blank at end of guide.

NEWARK

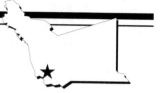

SHORT OF LAND FOR HOMES, plants and business facilities, Silicon Valley has reached out to embrace cities that missed out on the initial waves of high-tech development.

Newark, population 43,950, was one of the last cities to join the Silicon family. In 1999, Sun Microsystems opened a complex of about 1 million square feet for offices, manufacturing and research. Hewlett-Packard and other firms had already set up plants in the town, spurring the construction of homes, condos and apartments.

The result: a city that blends the old with the new and fairly new, pays more attention to appearances, and offers housing that is attracting more high-tech professionals.

Served by Newark Unified School District, which passed an improvement bond in 1990 and a second one, for $66 million, in 1997. The money was spent to upgrade and repair the schools and equip them for high tech. In 2002, the high school opened a tech center and a new cafeteria. Among California schools, Newark schools historically have landed about the middle but as the city changes these numbers may rise. Scores often follow demographics; Newark, in many parts, is ascending into middle-class plus.

Ohlone Community College leases space for classes in Newark and in 2002 won a voter approval of a bond to build a large, well equipped campus, cost $100 million. To be located on Boyle Road near Mowry Avenue, the place will open about 2007. The City of Newark will help fund the college library on condition that it also serve the public. Washington Hospital, to train its medical students, will open a clinic at the new campus.

Zero homicides in 2001, three in 2000, zero in 1999 and 1998, two in 1997, five in 1996. The counts for the previous years are two, zero, zero, four, one, five, zero, zero. Overall crime rate low-medium.

In commuting, Newark falls into the category of, "not bad." The town borders I-880, one of the main freeways to San Jose and Silicon Valley. The Dumbarton Bridge, located just northwest of the city, leads directly to North Santa Clara County and, not coincidentally, to the large Sun Microsystems complex in Menlo Park. BART stations in nearby Fremont and Union City.

As for appearance, Newark, especially in its northeast section, has built neighborhoods and many homes that would fit very nicely into any upscale town. One development is built around a lake ringed by open space and trail.

The city has planted trees (about 15,000 of them) all over the place. Graffiti absent, homes and lawns generally well-maintained. In some sections, industry and housing live side by side, which some people may not like. The town works with the older industries to buffer them from residential areas.

Ten parks. City adjoins a large (29,000 acres) shore refuge and just over city limits is a regional park with historic farm. Newark is developing 28 acres into a sports complex. Fields have been laid and work completed on facility that includes teen center, gym and rooms for aerobics and day care. Town also has a seniors center. City hall runs activities for kids and adults. Fireworks sold locally on the Fourth of July. Farmers market.

Scheduled to open in late 2003 or early 2004, a large indoor swimming complex that will include a lap pool, two water slides, a spa and a wheelchair-friendly pool.

In 1956, Fremont, seeing growth coming, incorporated itself as a legal city. What is now Newark was included in the original "Fremont" but a dispute arose over how "Fremont" would develop "Newark." The locals pulled out of the proposal and pushed through their own cityhood drive. Newark's suburban boom began about this time. About 1,500 housing units were built in the 1950s and 4,000 in the 1960s.

In the postwar era, the East Bay economy was built around large industrial plants, General Motors, Ford, Caterpillar Tractors, Peterbilt Trucks, and around San Francisco International Airport, easily reached by the Dumbarton or San Mateo bridges. Newark's initial housing was priced and designed to serve this blue-collar market, the standard three-bedroom home forming the backbone of the units built.

In the following years, many of the industrial plants were closed or reduced in size and a new type of job appeared: computer, high tech. Newark still has many residents working blue-collar jobs, and many outsiders probably still hold the image of Newark as a blue-collar town. But with the influx of white-collar workers and professionals, the housing and social mix has become more varied and the town has moved up the scale.

The state in 2003 counted 13,404 residential units, of which 9,197 were single detached homes, 1,238 single attached, 2,910 apartments and 59 mobile homes.

Large plants of the old type remain. But, as Sun demonstrates, the new technology has found a home. And so have auto dealerships and a large mall with a Macys, a Sears, and Penneys (tax revenue for civic amenities). Another hotel opened in 2002. The state is buying many of the salt ponds and returning them to marsh.

If you want to meet the town's business and civic leaders, break out the tie

Home Price Sampler from Classified Ads

Alameda
•3BR/2BA, modern kitchen, $515,000
•3BR/2BA, orig.wood floors, $799,000

Berkeley
•2BR/1BA, private garden, $399,000
•4BR/2BA, close to marina, $529,000
•3BR/1BA, attic & basement, $645,000

Castro Valley
•3BR/3BA, many upgrades, $659,000
•5BR/4BA, near schools, $799,000

Dublin
•5BR/4.5BA, lg. master ste.,$899,000
•4BR/3BA, near transport., $688,950
•3BR/1.5BA, remodeled, $405,000

Fremont
•3BR/2BA, extra lg. dining, $409,000
•2BR/2BA, new paint/carpet, $275,888
•3BR/2BA, family-room, $399,888

Hayward
•3BR/1BA, landscaped, $375,000
•4BR/2.5BA, extra large lot, $487,500

Livermore
•3BR/3BA, 100-acre prop., $1,959,000
•3BR/1.5BA, updated, $429,950
•3BR/2BA, 1,344 sq. ft., $360,000

Newark
•4BR/2BA, spacious backyard, $469,000
•3BR/2BA, corner lot, $446,000

Oakland
•4BR/2BA, separate office, $599,000
•4BR/2.5BA, canyon views, $699,000
•3BR/2BA, 2-story, lg. yrd., $425,000
•2BR/2BA, many amenities, $285,000

Pleasanton
•2BR/2.5BA, priv. backyard, $379,000
•5BR/3.5BA, pool, spa, $1,150,000
•4BR/2BA, newer roof, $495,000

San Leandro
•3BR/2BA, newly re-built, $399,000
•3BR/1.5BA, breakfast nook, $409,000

San Lorenzo
•3BR/1BA, hardwood floors, $353,000
•3BR/1BA, good location, $375,000

Union City
•4BR/2.5BA, vault. ceilings, $619,000
•4BR/2.5BA, 7 years old, $585,000
•4BR/2.5BA, remodeled, $415,000

and tails or the flowing gown. Every September residents and business people celebrate Newark Days with a fair, a parade and a grand ball.

In Dumbarton, Scotland, stands a castle named Newark. Pioneering developer came from Scotland and remembered the old castle. Hence, Newark.

Chamber of commerce (510) 744-1000.

OAKLAND

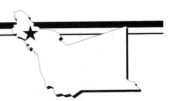

LARGEST AND MOST POPULOUS (412,200 residents) city in county. Great commute. Many jobs. Dynamic and lively downtown. International airport. Largest shipping port in Northern Cal. Big-time sports.

Crime high in some neighborhoods. Scores low at many schools. School district went bankrupt and had to borrow $100 million from state.

In other words, a mixed bag. Many pluses, some minuses.

In 2003, after voters passed three bonds to renovate the schools and a new superintendent was brought in and class sizes were lowered and Oakland district seemed to be making progress, the people in charge forgot to keep tabs on what they were spending and were forced to declare bankruptcy. Superintendent was fired and the state installed an experienced money person to run the show. Many fingers were pointed, many sighs heaved and it will take a while to sort things out.

On the slightly bright side, many of the schools have been overhauled and some of the program improvements will remain. As for academics, many schools do score low but a fair number score at the middle and at the top.

It should also be noted that Oakland in effect runs two school systems: the public and the private, in the form of many private schools in Oakland and nearby communities. One study estimated that about 22 percent of the school-age children attend private schools.

In 1999, homicides fell to their lowest number in 32 years but then began to rise and by 2002 and 2003 had people shaking their heads.

Despite this, Oakland continues to add residents and many people will find it a pleasing home. Oakland is like many a big city. It has serious problems but people adjust to them and it has neighborhoods with low crime and fairly high scores.

The state in 2003 counted 160,089 residential units, of which 71,868 were single homes, 6,645 single-homes attached, 81,120 apartments or condos, 456 mobile homes.

Founded in 1852, Oakland grew quickly and by 1900 was the second biggest city in the Bay Area and the civic and business leader of the East Bay. In 1910, Oakland counted 150,000 residents; in 1950, it counted 385,000. After 1950, Oakland lost residents to the suburbs, then gradually came back and in some ways surpassed its crossbay rival, San Francisco. That city is built on a peninsula; expensive and time consuming to reach by train and truck. Oakland put together a containerized port that shut down the San Francisco docks.

Being an old city, Oakland has plenty of old housing, ideal for immigrants and people starting up the housing ladder. Oakland also has a good deal of middle and upper-income housing.

The city starts at the bay on flatlands then ascends into low and steep hills. Many homes have views of the bay and Golden Gate. In situations like this, often the cheaper housing is in the flatlands (next to the downtown) and the expensive housing in the hills. This generalization holds for Oakland but there are exceptions. Some low-income neighborhoods are built over hills and have great views. Some high-income neighborhoods were erected in the flatlands (around Lake Merritt).

Oakland borders Berkeley on its north side and in this section — Montclair, Hiller Highlands, Claremont, Rockridge — has become part of the university community. The Oakland hills, running the length of the city, favor upscale housing. The views are sweeping; the homes back up to regional parks; the crime is low.

Moving toward the flatlands, housing values, with exceptions, decline then rise at the waterfront where live-work lofts are being built. Many homes on the south side were built just after World War II for the veterans; here the three-bedroom home is favored.

Oakland is the government seat of Alameda County and the headquarters for the University of California system. Downtown has large federal complex (twin buildings, 18 stories). In recent years, the downtown has added two hotels and several office buildings, including a 20-story tower, and made efforts to land high-tech.

Moving down the shore to Hegenberger Road, Oakland has erected a sports complex that hosts the Athletics (baseball), the Warriors (basketball) and the Raiders (football). The Warriors have not won anything of note for decades but the A's almost always make the playoffs and in 2002 the Raiders made the Super Bowl (but lost).

Just across the freeway from the sports complex is Oakland International Airport, which specializes in cheap flights. Among its carriers, Southwest and Jet Blue (and more). The airport has improved its access roads and is expanding its terminals and is considered a success, about 12.8 million passengers a year. Many East Bay residents prefer to take off from Oakland than from San Fran.

Among Oakland's cultural and recreational ornaments are a first-class museum specializing in California history, concerts, plays, ballets, a symphony orchestra, about five dozen parks, first-class restaurants, hotels, zoo, a convention center, marinas, ice skating rink. Concerts and shows in restored Paramount Theater or at the Coliseum. Victorian neighborhood preserved in downtown. Night life thrives around Jack London Village, which has one of best jazz clubs in the Bay Area, a giant bookstore, movies, restaurants and shops.

Large lake and park in downtown. At almost any time during the day, residents and workers can be found walking and jogging or skating around lake. All the usual activities for kids and adults: softball, football, Little League, etc. Many enrichment classes offered through schools. Libraries. Several community colleges and four-year private colleges, including Mills, the women's college. Fairyland, popular amusement park for kids, recently renovated. In 1999, after years of work and fund-raising, the Chabot Space and Science Center was reopened in the hills — state-of-art planetarium and large telescope (see cover). Berkeley and San Francisco and all they offer are within a few minutes drive or a BART ride.

Homicides numbered 108 in 2002 (preliminary figures), 84 in 2001 and 80 in 2000. The counts for the previous years are 60, 72, 99, 93, 138, 140, 154, 165, 149, 146, 129, 112, and 114.

Almost all the homicides take place in flatlands in the low-income neighborhoods. Many are drug related and this has called attention to failed drug prevention and prison efforts.

If the figures were broken out, many of the hill neighborhoods — Montclair, Claremont, Hiller Highlands, Rockridge, the homes near the Oakland Zoo — probably would show low-crime rates.

For suburban average, the neighborhoods above or east of Lake Merritt, including Trestle Glen, Temescal, the Dimond District would probably fall in this grouping.

These are generalizations. If you drive the poorer neighborhoods, you will see many homes with security doors and window bars but you will also find sections where the homes are well kept, the streets clean, the security devices less-frequently employed. In the poor neighborhoods, the law abiding are many, the criminal are few but unfortunately damaging. Oakland is a diverse and changing city; the demographics, the social chemistry, are always in flux. Whatever the neighborhood, however, the rules of big-city life apply: take care.

Excellent commute for many residents, with the exception of the Bay Bridge, which during peak hours tries everyone's nerves. Damaged in the 1989 quake, the east span of the bridge is to be replaced over the next five years. Traffic congestion may worsen. BART, which has stations all around Oakland, offers a convenient alternative to the bridge. Amtrak stations. Buses. Ferries to San Francisco.

Improvements costing about $1.4 billion are being made to the Oakland airport. Terminals and gates are to be added, cargo space expanded, garage built to more than double parking spaces, access roads improved. On the last job, the roads, it is much easier now to get to and from the freeway.

City also intends to build a monorail to carry people from BART station to airport. Another big job: overhaul of the port, new rail yard, deeper channels, new berths.

About $100 million is being spent to turn the land around the Fruitvale BART station into a "transit village" that will include housing, offices, a senior center, a child-care center, a library and a larger parking lot. Other BART station neighborhoods are also being improved.

A city Mother Nature smiles on — lovely weather — and afflicts. The 1989 earthquake collapsed a double-deck stretch of Interstate 880, called the Cypress section, and a portion of the Bay Bridge, and seriously damaged many buildings in the downtown. Two years later, fueled by hot winds called Diablos, a fire killed 25 in the hills and destroyed over 2,500 homes and apartments. Oakland bounced back. The Cypress was rebuilt to modern earthquake standards. The apartments and homes destroyed in the fire have been rebuilt.

Opposite the Golden Gate, Oakland catches the Pacific breezes and fogs and enjoys cool and balmy weather almost year round. The cool air discourages outdoor pools. Annual rain: flatlands, 18 inches; hills, 27. Miscellaneous:

• Oakland has some high-rise condo housing and senior housing around Lake Merritt.

• Oakland has distinctive neighborhoods, some set off by freeways, some by housing and personal styles. Montclair is built over hills and ravines and is heavily wooded. It has its own shopping "downtown," a library, churches and community buildings. Highway 13 defines one border, Highway 24 another and two regional parks mark the other boundaries. The result: a sense of being a separate village and strong feeling of community. Lake Merritt is ringed with luxury apartment and retirement buildings. The Temescal and Rockridge section have cafes, restaurants, upscale shops. The Fruitvale neighborhood draws many immigrants. Many Asians have settled in and around downtown Oakland and this section is winning renown for its restaurants — Chinese, Vietnamese, Burmese, Korean, Cambodian, Thai and Indian.

• Oakland schools run diverse arrangements: some are magnet with special programs. One school, Lazear, operates under a charter that gives parents and teachers a great deal of influence. Another charter school follows a military regimen. Oakland district also runs some year-round schools.

For many poor immigrants and poor people in general, the flatlands are an inviting, comfortable place with affordable homes and apartments. For the middle class and rich, for people who can afford better housing, drive the hills and upper-income neighborhoods. You'll find much that is pleasing and scenic.

Chamber of commerce (510) 874-4800.

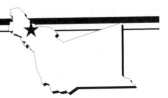

PIEDMONT

ONE OF THE WEALTHIEST and prettiest cities in the East Bay, Piedmont from its beginnings has attracted the boss, the broker, the heir, the heiress and the professional. But some things do change. Piedmont used to be a bastion of the Republican party but these days most voters call themselves Democrats.

Crime low, scores high, remodelings many, new homes few. Piedmont is surrounded by Oakland; no room to grow. In 1960, the census counted 11,150 residents. In 2002, the state put the population, 11,150. Piedmont does build new homes but very few — according to the 2000 census, zero in the 1990s and only 31 in the 1980s.

Served by the Piedmont Unified School District, enrollment about 2,725. Academic rankings in the 90s, one of the highest scoring districts in the state. Piedmont High is one of the few Bay Area schools that every year scores over 600 in the math SAT. In the 1990s, Piedmont voters raised their taxes several times to improve and retain academic programs and renovate and add buildings. In 2001, voters renewed parcel taxes to pay for class aides and sports, music and fine arts. In a town that prizes the old, the schools present the most modern face. Piedmont High graduates students into the most prestigious universities in the U.S. Several private and parochial schools in Oakland and Berkeley round out the educational offerings.

Every year the teens stage a bird-calling contest. Winners are often invited on late-night shows (David Letterman) to sound off. In 2002, a group of choir students, many from Piedmont, visited Cuba where they found themselves feted by Fidel himself. The students said he was friendly and talkative, denounced the American media and praised Popeye, because he encouraged children to eat their vegetables. At that, one student broke into "I'm Popeye the sailor man ...." and others joined in, including the Cuban minister of culture.

One of lowest crime rates in East Bay. Zero homicides in 2001 and 2000, one in 1999 and zero between at least 1985 through 1998. Piedmont has its own police department and many homes subscribe to private security services. In the 1999 homicide, wife was slain, husband arrested.

Commute generally very good. Short drives to freeways that lead to the Bay Bridge, which on many days is congested. AC Transit buses to San Francisco and to East Bay cities. BART stations nearby. If you work in Oakland or Berkeley, the commute comes down to 10 to 15 minutes.

Piedmont, located almost opposite the Golden Gate, catches some of the fog that blows through the Gate. Not a place for outdoor pools. Here and there around town some impressive redwoods have taken hold, testament to the nourishing fog. But weakened by distance and sunlight, the fog lacks the thickness of the billows blowing into the western neighborhoods of San Francisco. By midday, Piedmont usually emerges into sunlight.

Lovely town. One park greets visitors with an edifice decorated by what looks like a Grecian urn. As symbolism goes, this kind of sums up Piedmont. Elegant. For the lucky residents, views of the Bay and Golden Gate. Homes exceptionally well-maintained. The kind of place where residents varnish the garage door. Variety of home styles, fair number of custom homes that allowed architects to show their stuff. Trees galore.

Lots to do, if not in town then nearby. Before-and-after school programs for kids, including computers, dance, music, camps. Soccer, basketball, flag football, etc. City and school district offer over 150 programs and activities for adults, from aerobics to flower arranging to yoga. Two golf courses nearby. All that Berkeley and Oakland have to offer. Theater, foreign movies, jazz clubs, first-class cuisine. San Francisco on most evenings can be reached within 20 minutes. Three universities nearby: Berkeley, Holy Names, Mills.

When the businessmen and their families of the 1800s tired of the bustle and grime and probably fog of San Francisco, their eyes drifted across the Bay to the farms and wooded hills of the East Bay. Gradually they purchased lots and built sometimes magnificent homes and by the turn of the century, Piedmont had about 1,000 residents. Cable cars, connecting the hills to the rail station, spurred development, The Great Earthquake of 1906 also helped, people fleeing for what was thought to be safer ground. About this time, the town became embroiled with Oakland in arguments over taxes, school construction, municipal services. Oakland probably could have smoothed some ruffled feathers but it ignored complaints and moved quickly to annex Piedmont. Some residents said, let's form our own city and did. Quickly Piedmont grew to its borders: by 1910, residents numbered 1,719, by 1920 the count went to 4,282, by 1930, to 9,333, close to what it is today.

Although opulent homes stand out, many smaller homes were also constructed, mostly on the west side. In the 1990 census, the three-bedroom home showed itself to be the most popular (36 percent of all units) followed by the four-bedroom (33 percent). The state in 2003 counted 3,861 residential units, of which 3,784 or 98 percent were single detached homes, 69 were multiples and 8 mobiles. Piedmont has maybe two dozen businesses and depends on Oakland, particularly Rockridge and Montclair neighborhoods, for food, stores, restaurants, services and a library.

Old towns, old laws, Piedmont prohibits keeping of lions, tigers, bears and rhinos. You can't wash your clothes on a public street. In modern times, laws were enacted to spare trees on sidewalks, ban gasoline leaf blowers and pooper-scoop the dogs. No chamber of commerce. City hall (510) 420-3040.

PLEASANTON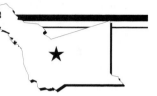

HIGH-TECH SUBURB located at the junction of two freeways. Crime low, school scores high, jobs plentiful. Home to many tech professionals. Well-kept town with many parks and amusements. Population 67,000.

Its name inspired by a Civil War general, Pleasanton for most of its modern history slumbered in rural obscurity serving as a general store for local farmers and a refreshment station for travelers. After World War II, the nation and the state began constructing wide highways and these, combined with a large migration into California, created the suburbs. Being somewhat removed from the old cities, Pleasanton did not boom until the 1960s when Interstates 580 and 680 were built and intersected at Pleasanton. In 1960, the town counted about 1,200 homes and apartments and 4,200 residents.

About this time, several forces were at work that benefitted Pleasanton. In the 1950s, the University of California opened a large research lab at Livermore, the neighboring city, bringing in thousands of highly-educated people. The old cities were running out of space; the large firms began to move operations to the suburbs. Silicon Valley started to boom with the new technology.

Here was Pleasanton (and its neighboring towns): freeways, plenty of cheap land for housing and commerce, high-tech core of residents, educated population. And, credit where credit is due, a savvy city hall and civic leaders. By 1970, the population had risen to 18,328 and by 1980 to 35,160. This number increased to 50,553 by 1990. The 2000 census counted 63,654 residents. Pleasanton is running out of land and in recent years residents have voted to preserve open space and slow development.

By 1960, planners had a much better idea of how to build suburbia and buffer residential streets from traffic. In the 1960s and 1970s, many homeowners were taking their equity and buying up, creating demand for larger homes, two-story instead of one, four bedrooms instead of three. Pleasanton flowered in this market. It is an old town, incorporated in 1894, but a new suburb, filled with new or fairly new homes, many of them up-market.

Pleasanton channeled its high-tech and offices into a modern business park called Hacienda, which is situated near the freeway interchange. The place is loaded with firms, including PeopleSoft, Hewlett Packard. SBC. Also, service firms and miscellaneous clean industries, including Safeway headquarters, the kind that cities do handstands for. Another business park is located on the south side of town. Hotels followed the businesses.

Also near the interchange is a regional mall called Stoneridge (Macys, Nordstrom). Near by are a Costco, a Wal-Mart and a Trader Joe's, the merchants of modern suburbia.

In the 1990s, BART (commuter rail) extended service to the Amador Valley and built a station at Dublin-Pleasanton, which made the town even more attractive to big business.

The result: a nice-looking suburb, attentive to and supportive of its schools, loaded with jobs, housing well-tended, ranging from old and small (pre 1960) to middle-class stalwart (three- and four-bedroom) to knockout, the gated Ruby Hill neighborhood. The lawns are mowed, the homes and apartments are in good repair, graffiti absent, streets clean. Some homes rise into the hills, affording views of countryside. Mt. Diablo to north. Still a good deal of open space at city's edge. Main Street, removed somewhat from the freeways, nonetheless appears to be thriving. The city has spruced up the street with trees and brick sidewalks and helped create a setting that nourishes restaurants, delis, bakeries, cafes and small shops. The old Pleasanton Hotel, now a restaurant, anchors one end of the restaurant row; a library and a park, the other end. County fairgrounds and office complex help the downtown with visitors and noon shoppers.

Served by Pleasanton Unified School District, which in two elections over the last 15 years has passed bonds worth $155 million and used the money to equip, build and renovate schools. The school board in 2000 raised fees on developers to help pay for the renovation and expansion of the town's two high schools, Foothill and Amador Valley. In 2002, Amador High built a library-media center and more classrooms. Foothill High built a pool and added classrooms.

Compared to other California schools, scores are running in the top 10 percent. SAT scores come in well above national and state averages. Community college in Livermore. UC Berkeley and Cal State Hayward and other universities offer classes in nearby towns. Pleasanton teachers are among the highest paid in Alameda County. Dublin, which recently raised salaries, also pays high. The point both are making — we're willing to pay for quality.

In 2002, national Blue Ribbons for academic excellence, a rare award, were won by three Pleasanton schools: Amador Valley High, Harvest Park Middle and Pleasanton Middle. Thomas S. Hart Middle School was named a Distinguished School in 2003.

Overall crime rate low. Zero homicides in 2001. One homicide in 2000, zero in 1999 and 1998, one in 1997, two in 1996. The counts for previous years are two, zero, zero, zero, one, two, two, two, zero, zero, zero.

Good to horrible commute, depending on destination and choice of vehicle. Local jobs are a snap. Freeways and wide arterials move traffic along. For about six years — it seemed forever — the state was rebuilding the interchange of freeways 580 and 680. In 2002, the job was finished. Hallelujah! Altamont Commuter Express (ACE), which began service in 1998, dispatches commute trains from Stockton to San Jose with stops in Tracy, Manteca, Livermore, Pleasanton, Fremont and Santa Clara. ACE recently added another train.

In 2003, BART extended its service to San Francisco International. One perk for Dublin-Pleasanton; its line goes directly to SFO; no transferring.

Trouble spots: Interstate 680. If you are commuting to San Jose and Silicon Valley, this freeway often grinds to halt near Fremont. The good news: another lane was added in 2002. Second spot: the Bay Bridge, which is now rebuilding its east span. This bridge, which leads to downtown San Francisco, simply carries too much traffic and at peak hours often backs up for more than a mile.

In 2000, Alameda County voters extended a sales tax for transportation and Santa Clara County passed one to bring BART to San Jose and make general improvements. Both taxes will fund a variety of projects throughout the two counties and bring some relief to commuters. But more people are coming in, bringing more cars, and inciting residents to vote against developments. The arguments and ballot battles have been going on for decades. See Livermore.

With all its stores and businesses, Pleasanton has a strong tax base. It has used a lot of this money to fund parks and recreation programs for kids and adults. Swim complex with four pools. Regional park with lake. Other regional parks nearby. One of the largest sports parks in Northern Cal: 24 multipurpose fields, basketball and volleyball courts, three play areas for kids, trails. Usual sports, soccer for kids perhaps the most popular. Soccer season kicks off with a parade down Main Street. There's also adult soccer.

About 30 neighborhood parks, teen dances and concerts, ice skating rink in Dublin. Roller rink in nearby San Ramon. In 2000, two high schools were fitted out stadiums with a new type of artificial turf, supposedly very close to real thing. In 2001, the city added another park, 24 acres, three soccer fields, roller hockey rink, climbing wall, water-play areas, garden. A middle school, located in Hacienda Business Park, shares its gym with the community. Trails galore. Skateboard park. Pasta Festival. Pleasanton hosts the county fair, an annual celebration with horse racing and games and many events. The fairgrounds stay open year round and attract a variety of amusements, including Scottish games, dog shows, Octoberfest and hot-rod show. In 2002, the Women's United Soccer Assn. named two Contra Costa women the best soccer moms in the U.S. Interviewed by a reporter, both women said that Pleasanton had some of the best soccer fields in the region.

First-class shopping at Stoneridge Mall. Good mix of restaurants, from fast food to tablecloth. Livermore and Pleasanton have two dozen wineries that down through the years have figured out ways to blend in with housing tracts.

The wineries have encouraged residents to pay attention to wines and tastings and fine dining. Wente, the biggest vintner, sponsors musical events at its winery, which is bordered by a golf course.

Livermore-Pleasanton without the wineries would be attractive suburban towns. With the wineries they have become classy, attractive suburban towns. And a little more interesting and a little more fun.

Library. Senior Center. Driving range. Nine-holes of golf at fairgrounds, two private courses (one at Ruby Hill). Tennis park. Private exercise clubs. Borders Book store located near, in Dublin, a Barnes and Noble bookstore. Dublin has also opened large discount stores and a movie complex, 21 screens, including giant IMAX screen. On the way in 2005, an Ikea, the giant furniture store.

If you like swimming, this is the right side of Alameda County. West of the hills, the waterfront cities catch the cooling, sometimes cold, breezes coming through the Golden Gate On the east side, the hills block or tame the breezes, giving the Amador Valley a warmer climate but the valley bowl sometimes impedes circulation of the air, raising pollutant and pollen counts. Overall, however, mild and balmy and similar to what's found in Napa.

Kaiser clinics and ValleyCare Medical Center provide health care. In 2000, ValleyCare added a wing with 30 beds. The hospital contracts with Lucille Packard Children's Hospital to provide neonatal care.

If shopping for housing, start with the old downtown. As you move out, the homes will get newer and bigger. At Ruby Hill, which is gated, they jump way up the scale but for the most part modern Pleasanton was built for the middle and upper middle class. The state in 2003 counted 24,851 residential units: 16,172 single detached homes, 2,704 single attached, 5,519 multiples and 456 mobiles. Chamber of commerce (925) 846-5858. Miscellaneous:

• Local bus agency, called WHEELS has expanded routes and hours of service along some routes.

• In 2003, Larry Ellison of Oracle made a hostile bid for PeopleSoft, which employs about 3,500 in the Pleasanton area. Had Ellison been Genghis Khan or the merely the big bad wolf wanting to date your daughter, he might have received a warmer reception. PeopleSoft and its lawyers so far are holding Ellison at bay.

• In 2001, Charles Schwab, the stock trading firm, erected three office buildings in Pleasanton and was just about to occupy them when the stock market fell off a cliff. Cease, halt, stop, said Schwab to the builders and let the structures sit idle. In mid 2003, a firm stepped forward and leased one of the three. One swallow or one lease doth not a summer or prosperity make. But maybe things are starting to turn around.

• BART to add another station just east of the existing one.

SAN LEANDRO

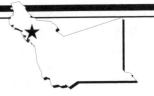

LOCATED JUST SOUTH of Oakland, on the BART (commute rail) line, served by two freeways, one of the better suburban commutes in Alameda County. Population 81,400.

Viewed as a good town to move up to. Good mix of housing and prices. Many of the residents work in Silicon Valley. First-class marina and waterfront with restaurants. School rankings low to middle to fairly high. In 1997, residents passed a $54 million bond to renovate all schools.

In the 1990s, San Leandro increased its housing stock by about 1,100 units and its population by 8,000.

San Leandro rises from the Bay to the hills and has many older neighborhoods, built just after World War II, two- and three-bedroom units. In the flatlands, near Interstate 880, the homes border industrial areas. Although San Leandro retains many blue-collar jobs, the town for some time has been moving into white-collar territory.

In the Sixties and Seventies, several industries pulled out of San Leandro, leaving large empty plants. The city rallied, sought new businesses and took care to keep up appearances and morale.

When the downtown was crippled by bypassing freeways and shopping plazas, the city pulled together and pumped money and planning into the section. The result: The downtown looks nice, attracts shoppers and gives the city a strong center. In recent years, this section and the east side have been landing restaurants.

When people describe San Leandro, two words frequently pop out: stable neighborhoods. The homes are old and plain but the paint is fresh, the lawns neat, the shrubs clipped. Drive the east side to see San Leandro at its best. Drive the west side to see some of the largest suburban lots of any city in the Bay Area. For a final perspective, drive the flatland thoroughfare of International Boulevard-14th Street-Hesperian through several towns. Even the old streets of San Leandro come across as clean and presentable. Graffiti painted over as soon as possible. City staffers are assigned to discourage blight, get people to clean up yards, get rid of junk cars.

State in 2003 counted 31,609 housing units: single homes, 19,182, single attached 2,028, multiples 9,495, mobile homes 904.

Near Interstate 880, large stores have opened, including a Costco and a

Sportmart. Another mall has attracted clothing outlets, including a Nordstroms Rack.

Nice waterfront: parks, a marina, two golf courses, new , restaurants. On sunny weekends, the waterfront attracts strollers, families, golfers, ball players, boaters — a lot of people. Well-stocked library. About 18 parks. Plenty of sports and activities for kids: baseball, soccer, swimming, day camp. Boys and Girls Club. Annual Cherry Festival celebrates local history.

California State University, Hayward, and Chabot Community College are within 10-15 minutes.

One homicide in 2001, five in 2000, three in 1999 and four in 1998. In previous years: 5, 6, 4, 4, 5, 6, 4, 1, 2, 2 5, 1.

Good commute. Besides BART and the freeways, AC Transit buses carry people to San Francisco and East Bay cities. Near Oakland Airport but few noise problems (but check for self). Close to San Mateo and Bay bridges. Interstate 880, which partially collapsed in the 1989 earthquake, was recon-nected in 1997 to the Bay Bridge. This has helped the drive commute but the bridge itself often jams. BART and I-580 are handy alternatives. I-880 recently widened in San Leandro and Hayward. In 2002, the San Mateo Bridge added, in effect, a second bridge. This helps people commuting to jobs around San Francisco International Airport.

Suburban cities inevitably grow old and grow in need of rejuvenation. San Leandro, to its credit, aggressively has tackled its problems and moved the city ahead. City Hall aggressive about finding and keeping businesses (and jobs and tax revenues). Good choice for young families who want to get in the housing market at a reasonable price (relative to rest of Bay Area.) Miscellaneous:

• San Leandro fields over 40,000 jobs. Among the major employers: Kraft General Foods, Incandescent, Albertson's, stores at Bay Fair Mall. City has a technology center and is trying to attract high-tech firms.

• Target moved into Bay Fair Mall, taking over a store vacated by Mont-gomery Wards (bankrupt). The mall also has a Macys and a movie complex, 16 screens.

• Auto mall at Marina Square. Generates about $1 million a year in tax revenue for city.

• On its northwest side, San Leandro just about butts up against Oakland Airport. City hopes to build a business park in this area and serve firms — possibly FedEx — using the airport.

Chamber of commerce (510) 351-1481.

SAN LORENZO

UNINCORPORATED NEIGHBORHOOD between San Leandro and Hayward west of Interstate 880. A member of the Hayward Park and Recreation District. Many activities. Park with lake, golf course. Playground-park at Del Rey School. Community swim center. Homeowners association works to keep appearances up.

Many well-kept lawns, an indication of community pride. Older residences. San Lorenzo got its great spurt just after World War II, when 1,300 homes were built. Many were later remodeled and expanded.

Some new homes are being added but San Lorenzo is fairly stable. Lost 558 residents in 1980s, added 1,911 in the 1990s. The 2000 census counted 21,898 residents.

Served by San Lorenzo Unified School District, enrollment about 10,000. In 2001, the district won a grant to equip just about every student in grades four to 12 with a lap top. San Lorenzo is within 10 to 15 minutes of Chabot Community College and Hayward State University.

Like other towns, becoming more ethnically diverse, many immigrants among the newcomers.

San Lorenzo is governed from Oakland by board of supervisors. Lacking its own city council, San Lorenzo rarely makes headlines and, indeed, the average East Bay resident would probably have difficulty locating the town. Still, it offers much in the way of affordable housing.

Good commute city. Short drive to Oakland and to Bay Bridge. BART stations in nearby San Leandro. Many jobs around Oakland airport.

Hayward airport borders San Lorenzo. Check out plane noise.

Chamber of Commerce (510) 351-1481

UNION CITY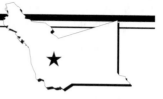

BEDROOM TOWN in south county. Won All-American City Award in 1999, one of ten awarded in the nation. Basically, this says that the city is well-run and innovative in solving problems and is moving forward.

Population 70,300. Many new homes, especially near Mission Boulevard in the hills and along Union City Boulevard in the flatlands near the shore. In the 1990s, the city built about 3,100 homes and apartments.

Many children. Schools enjoy strong community support. Three school bonds, for total $101 million, passed in last 15 or so years, the most recent in 1996. It paid for technological upgrades, improvements to facilities and a new school. Served by New Haven Unified School District.

Academic rankings, on statewide comparisons, land above and below the 50th percentile but elementary schools and Logan High have a reputation for hard work and close attention to academics. Logan sends many kids to top universities and boasts one of the top athletic programs in the state.

Logan, which has probably the largest enrollment of any high school in Northern Cal (about 4,300 students), has innovative student-union building. Place for kids to go after school, keep out of trouble: jukebox, video games, snack bar. School also stages an annual high-tech fair. New swimming pool, which is open to the community in summer months.

School board is wrestling with problem of enrollment at Logan High. Some members favor moving ninth graders to their own school. Other alternative: try for a bond to build a new high school. Or see if the state would put up the money. This would reduce Logan's enrollment to about 3,000.

Guy Emanuele, who retired in 1997, had been superintendent of the school district seemingly forever. He was one of the best schmoozers and administrators in education (top-down style, forceful; he made a lot of the decisions), close to parents and business and civic leaders. It's rare for a school district to win three bonds in short period. And at that time, bonds needed two-thirds approval; now they need 55 percent. Emanuele deserves some of the credit. He's also credited with saving art and science programs at a time when many districts were eliminating them. When he retired, the district named a school after him.Chabot College offers evening classes at Logan High.

Much argument over how many homes should be allowed in the hills. Voters in 1996 passed resolution to restrict development in the hills. Housing units number 19,559— single homes 12,481, single attached 2,367, multiples 3,788, mobile homes 923 (State tally, 2003).

Three homicides in 2001. The counts for previous years are, 2, 2, 0, 0, 0, 3, 3, 1, 2, 1, 0. Overall crime rate about low-suburban average. Curfew for kids. If under 18, with reasonable exceptions, they have to be in by 10 p.m.

About 17 parks. Many sports, soccer, baseball, football, boxing club, softball. Seniors center. Every year the school district stages "Marching On," a dance-musical that gives about 2,000 kids a chance to show their stuff.

BART (commute rail) station. Union City is close to one freeway and bisected by another, the congested I-880, which has been widened in recent years but on many mornings and evenings just crawls along. If commuting to San Francisco, BART might be the best bet. One of these years, thanks to the recent approval of a tax increase in Santa Clara County, BART will be extended to San Jose. Union City is talking about creating a transit hub around its BART station. Around the hub: apartments, high-tech, shops; buses, Amtrak, Altamont Commuter Express.

The other freeway, I-680, is faster and on many days does a better job moving motorists. But in recent years it has become more traveled and is running into traffic snarls. Also nearby, the Dumbarton Bridge, which leads to Silicon Valley and Peninsula. AC Transit buses serve neighborhoods.

About 100 small manufacturing plants in Union City. Kaiser Permanente medical center. Many warehouses. City is trying to attract high-tech firms and is using redevelopment to boost Dyer business section, near I-880 and Alvarado-Niles Road. Dyer Triangle, also known as Union Landing, has a giant supermarket, Office Max, Wal-Mart, movie complex. Also, Borders Books, Lowe's Home Improvement Store, Michael's (Crafts), Kinkos Copies, Krispy Kreme Donuts and In 'N Out Burger.

In early 1990s, to save money, Union City joined Fremont in firefighting. In 2000, Union City split from Fremont and reconstituted its fire department.

Ethnic mix diverse and becoming more diverse. Schools and city are making efforts to help everyone get along. Another part of the mix: Union City is building middle and upper middle housing close to its low-income neighborhoods, one of the more effective and benevolent forms of integration. It brings kids of varied backgrounds together at an early age.

Gladioli used to grow row on row in Union City. The town song starts, "Meet me at the Union City station...."

A town with a little bang. City council voted to outlaw sale of fireworks. Residents voted to bring them back and back they are, for the Fourth of July. Local civic groups, to raise funds, sell the fireworks — supposedly safe.

Chamber of commerce: (510) 471-3115.

Chapter 11

New Housing

SHOPPING FOR A NEW home? This chapter gives an overview of new housing underway in Alameda and nearby counties. Smaller projects are generally ignored. If you know where you want to live, drive that town or ask the local planning department, what's new in housing.

Prices change. Incidentals such as landscaping fees may not be included. In the 1980s, to pay for services, cities increased fees on home construction. Usually, these fees are included in the home prices but in what is known as Mello-Roos districts, the fees are often assessed like tax payments (in addition to house payments).

Nothing secret. By law, developers are required to disclose all fees and, in fact, California has some of the toughest disclosure laws in the country. But the prices listed below may not include some fees..

This information covers what's available at time of publication. For latest information, call the developers for brochures.

If you have never shopped for a new home, you probably will enjoy the experience. In the larger developments, the builders will decorate models showing the housing styles and sizes offered.

You enter through one home, pick up the sales literature, then move to the other homes or condos. Every room is usually tastefully and imaginatively decorated — and enticing.

An agent or agents will be on hand to answer questions or discuss financing or any other aspect you're interested in. Generally, all this is done low-key. On Saturdays and Sundays, thousands of people can be found visiting developments around the Bay Area and Northern California.

Developers call attention to their models by flags. When you pass what appears to be a new development and flags are flying, it generally means that units are available for sale.

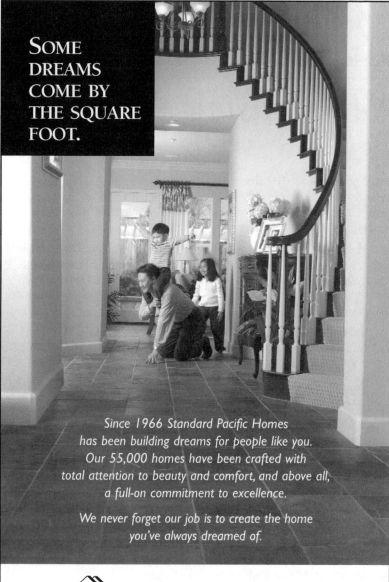

SOME DREAMS COME BY THE SQUARE FOOT.

*Since 1966 Standard Pacific Homes
has been building dreams for people like you.
Our 55,000 homes have been crafted with
total attention to beauty and comfort, and above all,
a full-on commitment to excellence.*

*We never forget our job is to create the home
you've always dreamed of.*

STANDARD PACIFIC HOMES
Signature of Excellence

1-877-STNDPAC (786-3722)
www.standardpacifichomes.com

Home Loans Provided by FAMILY LENDING

ALAMEDA COUNTY

Dublin

Eleven80, Castle Co., (925) 803-9399, Dublin Blvd. at Scarlett Place, from $400,000.

Rainsong, Greenbriar Homes, (925) 829-7330, Camino Tassajara at Lawrence Oakgate Dr., mid $600,000.

Riva, Greenbriar Homes, (925) 829-7330, Camino Tassajara at Lawrence Oakgate Dr., from mid $500,000.

Emeryville

Liquid Sugar, Pulte Homes, (510) 678-7018. Hollis, between 67th and 65th St., from high $300,000.

Fremont

Foothill Terrace, Mission Peak Co., call for location, (510) 490-7712, from $1.2 mil.

Mission Garden, Mission Peak Co., call for location and prices, (888) 754-4000.

Hayward

Eden Shores, Standard Pacific Homes, Union City Blvd. at W. Tennyson, (510) 732-2648, from high $500,000. **See ad page 192.**

Fairview Heights, Delco Builders, (510) 686-0169, 4-5 bedrooms, Fairview Ave., south of D St., mid $600,000.

Garin Crest, Legacy Homes, (510) 581-4880, Garin Rd., east of Hwy. 238, from low $1,000,000.

Livermore

Alden Lane, Standard Pacific Homes, (925) 373-0838, Alden Ln., between Isabel Ave. and Holmes St. Mid $700,000. **See ad page 192.**

Cooperage, Signature Properties, (925) 373-7486, Wente Rd., between East Ave. and Tesla Rd. From low $600,000. **See ad page 194.**

Cornerstone, KB Home, (925) 449-9801, Albert Way and Murdel Ln., $400,000.

Lindenwood, Greenbriar Homes, call for price, (925) 373-8883, Tesla Rd. and Wente Rd.

Los Olivos, Centex Homes, (925) 294-9797, Wetmore Rd., 3-5 bedrooms, from $800,000.

Ponderosa Legacy, Ponderosa Homes, (925) 961-9020, 4-6 bedroom executive homes, from high $900,000, Hanson Ln. and Arroyo Rd.

Sevillano, Pulte Homes, (925) 449-1637, 4-5 bedrooms, from low $1,000,000. Arroyo Rd. at Marina.

Vineyard Gate, Pacific Union Homes, (925) 455-8900, Vasco Rd., near Tesla Rd. From $800,000.

Vinsanto, Pinn Bros., (925) 245-0943, 4-5 bedrooms, from high $700,000, Arroyo Rd. at Wetmore Rd.

Oakland

Durant Place, Signature Properties, courtyard style homes, Durant at Bancroft, (510) 638-9428, from high $300,000. **See ad page 194.**

Communities of enduring appeal. And satisfaction.

RUBY HILL

In Pleasanton
Jack Nicklaus golf course,
private community. Custom lots,
custom homes, estate vineyards.
(925) 417-2250

255 BERRY

In San Francisco
Luxury residences in the
premier area of Mission Bay.
Coming Soon
(800) 300-4123

REDWOOD VILLAGE

In San Rafael
Four neighborhoods in a
master-planned setting.
Coming Soon
(800) 300-4123

STONEHAVEN

In El Dorado Hills
Great views on large lots.
(916) 941-1153

THE COOPERAGE

In Livermore
A Neighborhood of
single-family homes in
Signature's award-winning
Dunsmuir community in
the Livermore Wine Country.
(925) 373-4786

LANDMARK PLACE

New Loft-Style homes in
Downtown Oakland!
Close to employers,
entertainment and shopping.
(510) 465-9120

ASHLAND CREEK

In Folsom
A neighborhood of stylish
single-family homes within
a master-planned setting
with creeks, parks, open
space and miles of
walking/bicycling trails.
(916) 983-5822

GARIN LEGACY

In Brentwood
Great homes in a popular
master-planned setting.
(925) 513-1057

PALOMAR

In San Jose
Condominium homes in a great
location close to downtown.
(408) 292-9067

PARKVIEW

In Brentwood
Beautiful value in a
master-planned community.
(925) 240-1585

ABELLA

In San Pablo
2-3 Bedroom townhomes
and 3 to 4 bedroom
courtyard homes, with parks.
(510) 232-5222

A Tradition in Homebuilding

www.sigprop.com

Durant Village, Signature Properties, (510) 638-9428, from low $300,000. **See ad page 194.**

Landmark Place, Signature Properties, (510) 465-9120, 1-2 bedroom condos, from high $200,000, Martin Luther King Blvd. between 12th and 11th St. **See ad page 194.**

Pleasanton

Bridle Creek, Greenbriar Homes, call for price, (888) 800-8988, Sycamore Rd., south of Sunol Blvd.

Canyon Oaks, KB Home, (925) 931-1067, Bernal Ave., east of Valley Ave., from $700,000.

Carlton Oaks, Greenbriar Homes, call for price, (925) 600-8828, Sunol Blvd., west of I-680.

Pheasant Ridge, Greenbriar Homes, (925) 931-9898, call for price, Bernal Ave., west of I-680.

Ruby Hill, Signature Properties, custom homes, call for location, (925) 417-2250. **See ad page 194.**

San Leandro

Marcella Renaissance, Mission Peak Co., (888) 754-0000, Marcella at 162nd St., call for price.

Rainier at Cherrywood, Citation Homes, (510) 569-3585, Preda St. at Davis St., 5-6 bedrooms, low $600,000.

San Lorenzo

Arbor Rose, Standard Pacific Homes, Ashland Ave., south of E. 14th St., (510) 317-5769, call for price. **See ad page 192.**

Union City

Ivywood, Braddock and Logan Homes, (510) 675-9700, Alvorado-Niles Rd., east of Dowe, call for price.

Ponderosa Cove II, Ponderosa Homes, (510) 324-2563, Sloane at Ardenwood Blvd., high $700,000.

CONTRA COSTA COUNTY

Alamo

Barrington Woods, Greenbriar Homes, (925) 947-1598, call for price, south of Lavorna Rd., near Vernal Dr.

Estates of Alamo, The Castle Companies, (925) 328-1000, call for price, Danville Blvd., near Voltz Ct.

Antioch

Meadow Creek Glen, Seeno Homes, (925) 755-9270, Pruwett Ranch Dr. and Hillcrest Ave., high $300,000.

Meadow Creek Trails, Seeno Homes, (925) 522-8020, Vista Grande Dr., off Lone Tree Way, from high $300,000.

Mira Vista Ridge, Seeno Homes, (925) 755-3563, James Donan and Hummingbird, low $400,000.

Bay Point

Nantucket Cove, O'Brien Group, call for location, (800) 243-8696, from $300,000.

Brentwood

Cherry Hill at Deer Ridge Country Club, KB Home, (925) 516-8467, Foothill Dr. and St. Andrews, from $300,000.

Garin Legacy, Signature Properties, (925) 513-1057, Balfour Rd., east of Brentwood Rd., high $300,000. **See ad page 194.**

Montelena, Centex Homes, (925) 513-7023, Minnesota Ave. at Country Glen Ln., high $400,000.

Mountainside at Deer Ridge, Morrison Homes, 212 Mountain View Dr., (925) 516-9784, from low $400,000.

Parkview, Signature Properties, (925) 240-1585, Balfour Rd., east of Garin Pkwy., low $300,000. **See ad page 194.**

Ponderosa Crossroads, Ponderosa Homes, (925) 240-9760, Minnesota Ave., south of Sandcreek Rd., low $400,000.

Sagewood and Sandalwood at Shadow Lakes, Lennar Homes, (925) 516-2852, call for location, $400,000.

St. Andrews, Western Pacific Housing, (925) 634-2157, Foothill Dr. and St. Andrews, high $300,000.

Stonebrook Estates, Western Pacific Housing, Minnesota Ave., north of Sandcreek Rd., (925) 513-7410, mid $300,000.

The Fairways at Deer Ridge, KB Homes, Deer Ridge, (925) 240-7294, call for price.

The Legends, William Lyon Homes, (925) 543-7615, Chestnut St. and Sellers Ave., high $200,000.

Concord

Alberta Estates, Discovery Builders, Ygnacio Valley at Alberta, (925) 250-8181, from high $400,000.

Crystyl Ranch, Legacy Homes, (925) 687-3522, Rolling Woods and Crystyl Ranch Rd., $600,000.

Montecito, Standard Pacific Homes, (925) 288-0508, Cowell Rd. at Ygnacio Valley Rd., low $600,000. **See ad page 192.**

Parkside, Young California Homes, Monument Blvd., east of I-680, (925) 969-9977, from mid $400,000.

Discovery Bay

Horizons, Hofmann Co., (925) 634-3755, Point of Timber Rd., east of Sellers Ave., from mid $300,000.

Reflections, Hofmann Co., (925) 634-0500, Point of Timber Rd., east of Sellers Ave., high $300,000.

Stonegate at Lakeshore, Standard Pacific Homes, (925) 240-5770, Bixler Rd., south of Point of Timber, high $300,000. **See ad page 192.**

San Pablo

Abella, Signature Properties, (510) 236-8215, San Pablo Ave. between El Portal and Road 20, 3-4 bedrooms, from mid $300,000. **See ad page 194.**

Chapter 12

Fun & Games for Kids

ALTHOUGH REGIONAL amusements are popular with children, the great majority find most of their fun in their backyard or local activities.

When children are very young, parents and day-care centers or preschools will do most of the entertaining. Oh, there are other activities but generally they are of the type that demands the presence of a parent; e.g., tot swimming.

Many cities have built tot lots or installed jungle gym-type equipment in their parks. These are popular with the kids. On weekends, the petting zoo at the Oakland Zoo and the merry-go-round at Tilden Park will be clogged with children.

The Bay Area has zoos, museums, great parks, merry-go-rounds, theme parks (Six Flags Marine World, Great America), musical events (the Nutcracker is a favorite annual). All welcome children.

Activities for Youths

As the children grow older, more activities and sports come into play for the simple reason that the kids are strong enough to handle the running and kicking and throwing, etc., and mature enough to follow directions.

Alameda County and its cities and various organizations offer a great variety of sports and activities but the most popular probably are soccer, Little League baseball, basketball, Pop Warner football, softball, and swimming.

How they are played and who plays them varies by sex and age and happenstance. Sometimes, a local tradition or the presence of a facility will influence what the kids choose.

Dublin, Berkeley, Oakland and Fremont have ice-skating rinks. Ice-skating is more popular in these towns than elsewhere and when Kristi Yamaguchi of Fremont won an Olympic gold for skating, the sport got a boost.

Changes in the law have all but absolved cities for injuries incurred at public skate parks. In recent years, many cities have opened skate parks.

How Local Sports Are Organized

It's a mixed bag but once you ferret out a few networks, the rest will fall into place.

Sports are generally organized through parent groups, through traditional national groups, such as Little League, through schools and churches, through city recreation departments, through special agencies that in effect function as city recreation departments and through private groups. Some examples:

- Soccer. This sport has become very strong in the last 30 years. In many towns, the leagues are formed through parent groups but often they enlist city rec. departments and schools for help, especially in securing fields.

- Baseball. Again, parent groups, organized through Little League, which provides instructional material on how to manage, raise funds, etc.

- Basketball. For younger children, often informal leagues are organized through churches and middle schools.

- Pop Warner football. Like Little League. Very popular in California among boys. Girls often acquire cheerleading skills in Pop Warner football.

- Swimming. When the kids are young, generally through parent groups who set up and manage swim clubs. Often the clubs are built around a city or a neighborhood association pool or a school pool, leased from a school district.

  When the kids hit the teen years, generally they move into high school programs.

- Wrestling. Generally through the middle schools and high schools.

- Volleyball. The schools.

- Gymnastics. Sometimes through the schools but frequently through city programs and private businesses that open schools in converted stores.

- Skating. Through the local rinks, roller and ice.

- Dance. Through the city programs and private businesses.

- Track. Through the schools, generally beginning in junior high.

- Tennis. Schools and rec. departments. Some private.

Some Rules of the Games

- When the children are young, they all play. Soccer, baseball and football are set up to train the boys and girls in the sport. What if the kid has two left thumbs and can't kick straight? He or she will play at least two innings, at least two quarters, etc.

The more skillful kids will play more but no one is shut out. But ask about the rules, and if you don't think your kid will get a fair shake, shop for another team or league.

When the kids hit the teen years, skill and talent get rewarded more. At high school, many kids sit on the bench.

- Girls and boys play soccer and baseball together. The swim teams are mixed. Football is generally a boys' game. Many girls favor gymnastics and cheerleading.

  As the kids get older, they are broken out more by sex. At high school, after school, the girls generally play softball, the boys baseball. The girls will field their own soccer, basketball and volleyball teams. Swimming teams will still be mixed but boys race boys, and girls race girls.

  Theoretically and legally, the girls may try out for football and wrestling. In the real world, few do.

  During regular school hours, in physical education, the sexes are often mixed in a variety of sports: baseball, track, etc. But these activities are not organized for intense competition.

- Many of the teams and leagues are grouped according to age. As the children grow older, they move up into different leagues.

- Yes, you have to shell out — for uniforms and equipment. And yes, you have to volunteer for the snack shack, and the annual dance and buy tickets for this or that raffle. And eat pizza until it's coming out of your ears (because your league, for a few benefit bucks, has cut a deal with the local pizzeria). It's part — burp! — of the game.

  What if you don't have the money? Get one of the team officials aside and ask about a reduced fee. Maybe you can spend a few extra hours in snack shack. These people are not out to exclude kids.

Where to Get Information
- Start with your local recreation department, which works out of city hall. Almost all will publish a schedule of activities and sports. Here's where you get a lot of information about activities for the toddlers. Many cities offer parenting classes.

- Hayward, Castro Valley and San Lorenzo formed the Hayward Area Recreation District to provide fun and games. For information, phone (510) 881-6700.

- Check with the schools about the activities they offer.

- Some church schools, notably the Catholics and the Mormons, run their own basketball leagues and organize other activities for the kids.

- Just stop and ask. You're driving down the road and you see a soccer team playing. You want your kids to play soccer. Ask the coach for a contact phone number for signing up.

Miscellaneous

- Scouting is often run as a private activity or an activity affiliated with a church. You don't have to join the church to get your kid into the Scouts. For scouting information, call (510) 522-2772.

- Your city or town doesn't offer the sport your kid wants. The next town does. Sign him or her up in the next town; generally, no problem, except you'll have to drive farther.

- Schools still offer music instruction but many programs have been cut back. For lessons, often you have to go to private sources. Many are listed in the phone book.

- For some activities, ballet and advanced gymnastics, you have to look to the private schools that specialize in these activities — phone books.

- Fishing. Kids under age 16 fish free. Plenty of water around here.

- Skiing. The Sierra is 4-5 hours from the Bay Area. When the winters are wet, the skiing is very good. Many resorts offer training for kids.

- Ocean swimming. You can try but even in summer the water is quite cold, the result of an arctic current that bubbles up along the Northern California shore. Watch the waves! Dangerous, especially off San Francisco. City of Alameda has a public beach.

- Boys and Girls Clubs, YMCA's. Some towns have them. Good sources for activities for kids.

- Miniature golf, water slides, video game emporiums, comic book stores, book stores — they're all out there. Check the Yellow Pages.

- Community colleges. Almost all run child development programs and offer summer academic enrichment programs for kids. See list of colleges in job chapter.

- Often some activities lead to other activities. The Lawrence Hall of Science and the Chabot Space and Science Center offer activity and enrichment classes for kids. You take your kid to one of these classes, meet other parents, they tell you about other activities, and so on.

- Summer camps. Many city recreation departments put together day camps. The kids play under the supervision of an adult (often an older teen) and you pick them up in late afternoon.

Many parents send their kids away to camps for a week or two. Prices vary widely; this may be an experience you can afford. Check with YMCA or pick up a Parents Press or Valley Parent. Often they carry camp advertisements.

Fun-Educational Places to Visit

This is a partial list of attractions-amusements in or close to Alameda County. For more on parks, see Adult Fun, the following chapter.

- **Chabot Space and Science Center.** Planetarium, telescope, biology garden, classes, activities. Rebuilt and opened in 1999. If you're interested in science and want to get kids interested, good place to visit. Located at 4917 Mountain Blvd. near the MacArthur and Warren freeways. Call for schedule. (510) 530-3480.

- **Children's Fairyland.** Nestled within Lakeside Park, located off Grand Avenue at the north end of Lake Merritt in downtown Oakland. Favorite kid spot for decades.

  Featuring children's favorites — Mother Goose, Alice in Wonderland, the Cheshire Cat, the Cowardly Lion, the Owl and the Pussycat, Pinocchio, Willie the Whale, Humpty Dumpty, and Mary's Little Lamb — Fairyland is best suited to younger children. Rides include the Jolly Trolly, Lakeside Park Toy Train, the Wonder-Go-Round and Magic Web Ferris Wheel. In addition to puppet and clown shows, youngsters have myriad slides and mazes to entertain their wanderings. (510) 238-6876.

- **Magnes Museum Berkeley,** 2911 Russell St., Berkeley. Shows. Art and artifacts of Jewish culture. Library, history. (510) 549-6950.

- **Lakeside Park.** Located off Grand Avenue at the north end of Lake Merritt in downtown Oakland. Kiwanis Kiddie Korner of the park features children's attractions such as a sea horse swing or an octopus slide. The outdoor aviary and zoo holds turkey vultures, barn owls, great horned owls, hawks, sand-hill cranes, opossums, porcupines, skunks and other small animals. In addition, Lake Merritt is a wild duck refuge. Pelicans frequently entertain by diving into the lake for food.

  The Rotary Nature Center shows free nature films on occasion, in addition to its regular fare of science exhibits. An outdoor bandstand is the site of old-fashioned Sunday summer concerts, and smooth green courts provide hours of entertainment for lawn bowlers. Open year round. Details are available by calling (510) 238-3739.

- **Lawrence Hall of Science.** Great science museum for adults and children. Hands-on fun, computers, rabbits, snakes, brain games, astronomy, Nobel medals, classes, all fortified by strong connection to UC-Berkeley. Store has science toys.

  Located in the Berkeley hills. Take Highway 24 to Fish Ranch Road, right at top of hill onto Grizzly Peak Road, follow for about three miles, left on Centennial Drive. Also can be reached from Canyon Road in back of UC Berkeley, to Centennial Drive. Phone (510) 642-5132 for hours of operation.

- **Lawrence Livermore National Laboratory.** Located two miles south of Interstate 580 on Greenville Road in Livermore, is an advanced research and development complex operated by the University of California for the U.S. Department of Energy. The newly refurbished Visitors Center offers updates on scientific programs, featuring hands-on displays as well as printed materials, films, videotapes and large color photos. Call (925) 423-3272 for hours.

- **Meek Estate.** This renovated and furnished five-story 1869 national historic monument can be found at Hampton and Boston roads in Hayward. You can relive the Victorian era in the nostalgic ballroom, library, solarium, bedrooms, nursery and servants' quarters. The grounds feature acres of park and playground equipment and a barbecue in the picnic area.

- **Mission San Jose.** Located at 43300 Mission Blvd. in Fremont, Mission San Jose was founded June 11, 1797, and destroyed in the earthquake of 1868. Recently restored, this is one of the most picturesque buildings in Alameda County and possesses genuine historic value.

  Starkly simple outside, ornate within, the mission superbly captures the spirit of the Franciscans and Indians. Chandeliers, altars, statues, bells, tile floors — what was not salvaged from the old mission or from the era was accurately duplicated.

  Slide show, artifacts, some history of the Ohlone Indian, a small gift shop. For hours of operation, call (510) 657-1797.

- **Mormon Temple,** 4770 Lincoln Ave., in Oakland hills. Striking edifice, beautiful grounds. Visitor center, daily tours. Non-Mormons welcome. Phone (510) 531-3200.

- **Oakland Museum.** Located at 1000 Oak St. in downtown Oakland, the Oakland Museum focuses on California art, California history and California natural history. The excellence of its collection has given it the reputation as "California's Smithsonian."

  Art from the days of the Spanish explorers to the present is included, featuring panoramic views of San Francisco, cowboys and Indians, Oriental art and modern canvases.

  Natural sciences include exhibits on botany, birds, ecology, paleontology and geology, in addition to an aquarium and dioramas of animals in their natural settings.

  California's history begins with the Indians and walks through the rooms of history from the Spanish explorers, the Californios, the gold miners and cowboys, the pioneers and turn-of-the-century Californians. Phone (510) 238-2200.

- **Oakland Zoo.** Located at Knowland State Park at the MacArthur Freeway connection with Golf Links Road and 98th Avenue.

Underfunded for years, the zoo won state financial support and made a great comeback. The Jungle Lift takes you over the African veldt, past the high ground where elk, deer, lions, flamingo, elephants and buffalo graze in a natural setting. Fascinating acrobatics by the gibbons.

Easy viewing. One of the major features is the Baby Zoo, where children can wander and feed or pet llamas, goats, rabbits, geese, ponies and calves. Phone (510) 632-9525.

- **Sulphur Creek Nature Center.** Located at 1801 D St. in Hayward, this little-known nature center is a great place to introduce children to the wonders of nature. Hawks, foxes, coyotes and opossums are on display in outdoor cages. Plants, trees and fungus-bearing logs are neatly labelled along a nature trail.

  Museum is small but informative. Focus is native wildlife. Animal-lending library. Phone (510) 881-6747.

- **Hornet.** The carrier "Hornet" was commissioned in 1943 and saw service in World War II and other conflicts. Decommissioned, the carrier is now a museum. Located at naval station in Alameda. Open daily 10 a.m. to 5 p.m. Closed Tuesdays. Phone (510) 521-8448.

- **East Bay Regional Park District.** Runs most of the major parks in the East Bay and many nature or historic attractions. Phone (510) 562-PARK.

Chapter 13

Fun & Games for Adults

ALAMEDA COUNTY boasts professional baseball (the Athletics), basketball (the Warriors) and football (the Raiders) and college sports. It has a first-class museum and a renovated zoo.

When famous classical musicians or dance troupes tour, they often play UC Berkeley. Thanks to the foresight of its early residents, the county set up one of the first park districts in the state with the happy result that thousands of acres have been set aside in regional parks.

Within a drive of 15-20 minutes for many residents, San Francisco yields most of its cultural and artistic treasures. For Fremont, Newark and Union City residents, the San Jose Arena and professional hockey (the Sharks) are within a half-hour drive. California Cuisine was invented in Berkeley by Alice Waters of Chez Panisse. Excellent restaurants abound. Livermore and Pleasanton are part of the wine country.

As impressive as all this sounds, it needs some perspective. The average resident, looking for fun, dabbles in the above: a concert here, a Warrior game there, a night out in San Francisco once or twice a year. For the most part, people take their recreation in their back yards: in games, exercise, classes, local activities. A typical summer Saturday might include a short jog and a stop at the farmer's market. Some suggestions:

- Local recreation. Get on the mailing list of the local city or special-district recreation department. This will keep you up on the activities offered in or near your neighborhood.

- If your school district offers adult education, get on that mailing list. Adult schools, for a very reasonable fee, mix the practical (typing, bookkeeping) with the entertaining (how to dance).

- Subscribe to a local newspaper. It will carry, usually on Friday, a calendar of events, both local and regional. When you attend an event, say a local theater production, you often wind up on a mailing list and will be notified of future events.

- For regional parks, call the East Bay Regional Park District (510) 562-PARK and ask for brochures on parks, activities and trails. The district includes Alameda and Contra Costa County and owns about 53 parks covering about 69,000 acres. Golf courses, nature areas, about 800 miles of trails, lakes — a lot.

- For local parks, see city hall or the recreation district.

- For local organizations — flower societies, social and hobby clubs — chambers of commerce often will publish a directory of local groups. See also the yellow pages under Associations.

- Golf. Very popular in the Bay Area. Many courses. Yellow pages. Bookstores carry books with descriptions of courses.

Colleges and Universities

Community colleges offer a variety of courses — academic, vocational, and recreational or personal enrichment: music, art, etc.

Both California State University, Hayward, and the University of California offer many classes through their extension programs. Many of the classes are oriented toward business: how to set up a small business, bookkeeping, computer systems, etc. But many fall in the category of personal enrichment, the arts, literature.

See Chapter 14 for a list of colleges and phone numbers.

Private Groups

These include YMCA's, Nautilus exercise clubs, racquetball clubs, and so on. They fill a need; otherwise they would not be in business. Some run 24 hours daily and at 3 a.m. you'll find a few people pumping iron. Check the yellow pages.

How Things Work

Take softball, very popular in the suburbs. The city or special district provides the organizing framework (umpires, fields) but usually does not recruit the teams.

At the job or in the neighborhoods, someone will say, "Let's get a team together." A roster is submitted, practice held (according to the ambitions of the players) and they're off. Sounds simple, but someone must do the organizing.

If you're not affiliated with a team, check with the recreation department to see if some spots are open. City recreation sponsors volleyball. You show up and find in the gym that the nets have been set up and the balls provided. You do the rest: choose sides, keep score, etc.

You join the Sierra Club, get a monthly magazine, and a list of Sierra Club hikes in the Bay Area. You choose your hike.

The trick is to get a toehold in the group or activity you like, tap deeper into the information on activities and pick what you like.

Singles Clubs

Many are organized through churches and religious groups but if this is not your cup of tea there are dozens of groups in the Bay Area. The groups sponsor parties, dances and excursions. Often for a fee, some clubs are heavily into matchmaking and, in fact, if you go into almost any major job setting in the Bay Area you'll find people who have met their spouses through matchmaking services.

The clubs are too many and too diverse to list but you might start with the singles magazine, Possibilities. Phone (415) 507-9962. This is all strictly buyer-beware. McCormack's Guides does not investigate or study these clubs.

Gambling

California has lottery games and allows limited gambling at race tracks and at card parlors but the "legal" card games are few in number, usually a variation of draw poker. No Blackjack. No slots. Nonetheless, the parlors are increasing in number, quality (food, decor) and popularity. Look in the Yellow Pages under Card-Playing Rooms.

For the high-powered stuff, people head usually for Reno or the Nevada side of Lake Tahoe. There you will find the big casinos and the top entertainers. The casinos often advertise their shows in the more popular newspapers. Indian casinos with Las Vegas games and slots have opened in Sonoma County and in Placer County. The City of San Pablo, north of Berkeley, has a casino that is affiliated with a tribe and may soon offer slots and the Nevada games — a first for the Bay Area.

If you want to sample the Nevada palaces without getting behind the wheel, Amtrak and local bus companies offer gambler specials. The bus companies will usually throw in some freebie coupons to sweeten the deal. See Yellow Pages under Tours.

Skiing

On Fridays during the winter, Interstates 680 and 580 out of the Bay Area are filled with people heading for the Sierra and first-class skiing.

For tickets, information, coupons, visit local ski shops and read the Friday entertainment sections of the newspapers. Even if you don't ski, a winter trip to the Sierra is often a great frolic.

Restaurants and Dining Out

In the suburban cities, the chains are popular — Sizzler, Chevy's, etc. — but you'll have no trouble finding tablecloth restaurants and fine dining.

Berkeley is in a class itself, many excellent restaurants, and Oakland and Albany are not far behind. San Francisco, of course, has many fine restaurants. The Livermore-Pleasanton wine country is winning a reputation for fine dining.

Regional Recreation

There's a lot out there: the Napa wine country, the coast, fishing, sailing, the arts. For information in depth on what Northern California has to offer, see the guides listed in the back of this book.

Here are some of the major local attractions. Please note that almost all the large parks and many of the trails and nature attractions are in the East Bay Regional Park District. To receive a brochure about the district and its offerings, call (510) 562-PARK.

- **Chabot Regional Park.** 4,684 acres east of Oakland-San Leandro. Off Skyline Boulevard, south of Redwood Road, you reach an Equestrian Center with horses for rent and access to equestrian, hiking, jogging trails.

  Off Redwood Road between Oakland and Castro Valley, you'll find group camping areas available by reservation, a 67-acre motorcycle hill area, a marksmanship range and backpacking access to East Bay Skyline National Trail. Here you also have access to Chabot Family Camp, with 73 trailer, tent, and hike-in sites overlooking Lake Chabot with showers, self-guiding nature trails and hiking-fishing access to Lake Chabot. For more conventional activity, there is also the 18-hole Willow Park Public Golf Course and driving range.

  Off Lake Chabot Road east of Fairmont Avenue, you'll discover Lake Chabot Marina (315-acre stocked lake with rental boats), fishing, coffee shop, boat tours, picnicking, large turfed play areas, horseshoe pits, hiking, bicycling, jogging and running trails.

- **Coyote Hills Regional Park.** 1,039 acres in Fremont near the eastern approach to the Dumbarton Bridge. Take Patterson Ranch Road. Bicycling, hiking, jogging and running trails, birdwatching, picnicking, kite and radio-controlled model glider flying (requires club membership), visitor center, boardwalk view areas of freshwater marsh, self-guided nature trail and reservable group camping.

  Special features include interpretive programs and guided tours of 2,300-year-old protected Indian shell mounds and reconstructed Indian village. There's also access to Alameda Creek Regional Trail and San Francisco Bay.

- **Del Valle Regional Park.** 3,868 acres, 10 miles south of Livermore. Take South Livermore Road and Mines Road out of Livermore. Del Valle includes a 750-acre lake planted with fish on a regular basis. In season, swimming from two sandy beaches when lifeguards are on duty, visitor center, self-guided nature trail and interpretive programs.

  Year-round group picnicking and camping by reservation, four-lane boat ramp, sailboating, motor boats and rental boats. Also available are tour boat, fishing, hiking, equestrian, jogging and running trails.

Del Valle Campground offers complete family camping service year-round and connects with the Ohlone Wilderness Trail. Reservations required.

- **Redwood Regional Park.** 1,829 acres in Oakland and Contra Costa County. Take Skyline Boulevard or Redwood Road out of Oakland. Picnicking, equestrian field and trails, hiking, jogging and running trails, playfields, volleyball court, children's play area, exercise course, amphitheater fire circle, reservable group picnicking and youth group camping areas. Accessible to backpackers and horseback riders via East Bay Skyline National Trail.

- **Tilden Regional Park.** 2,078 acres in Berkeley hills, an excellent park. At Lake Anza in season, swimming, sandy beach, bathhouse complex, large turfed area, food concession. Year-round fishing.

  Environmental Education Center and Nature Area, interpretive programs, exhibits, puppet shows, Little Farm, Jewel Lake and all-weather nature trails.

  At Tilden Public Golf Course, an 18-hole course and driving range, pro shop and Tee Clubhouse restaurant.

  In other park areas, a merry-go-round, food concession and children's playhouse, Redwood Valley Railroad and Golden Gate Steamers (scale model steam locomotives), playfields, horseshoe pits, picnicking, Regional Park Native Plant Botanic Garden and Visitor Center, Inspiration Point, hilltop vistas and reservable areas for group picnicking and youth group camping.

  Hiking, jogging, bicycling and equestrian trails throughout. Backpacking access via East Bay Skyline Trail.

- **Ardenwood Regional Preserve.** 203 acres in Fremont including the former Patterson Mansion. Take Newark Boulevard north of Highway 84. A glimpse of ranch life at the turn of the century. Horse-drawn railroad and hay wagons. Picnicking.

- **Mission Peak Regional Preserve.** 2,596 acres atop Mission Peak and Monument Peak east of Ohlone College in Fremont. Climbing to the top on a clear day yields views of the entire region. Birdwatching, hiking, equestrian, jogging and running trails, kite flying, interpretive programs. Staging areas are at the end of Stanford Avenue, with space to park horse trailers. Connects with Ohlone Regional Wilderness Trail.

- **Ohlone Regional Wilderness.** 6,758 acres in southeastern Alameda County between Sunol Regional Wilderness and Del Valle Regional Park. Enter via trail from Sunol and Del Valle. Ponds, waterfalls, nature trails. Connects with Ohlone Wilderness Trail.

- **Cull Canyon Regional Recreation Area.** 360 acres in Castro Valley. Take

Cull Canyon Road. In season, swimming lagoon, sandy beach, turfed play area, bathhouse and food concession open Wednesday through Sunday. In other park areas year-round fishing, hiking and equestrian trails, picnicking.

- **Don Castro Regional Recreation Area.** 100 acres between Castro Valley and Hayward. North end of Woodroe Avenue. In season, swimming in lagoon, sandy beach, bathhouse and food concession open daily. Year-round lake fishing, hiking trails, limited horseback riding, picnicking, turfed areas, group picnic areas available by reservation.

- **Roberts Regional Recreation Area** and Redwood Bowl. 100 acres in Oakland at the western boundary of Redwood Regional Park. Take Skyline Boulevard. In season, swimming (Tuesday through Sunday) at heated outdoor swimming pool with bathhouse and food concession.

  Year-round group picnicking by reservation, family picnic areas, playfields, volleyball court, hiking, bicycling, jogging and running trails. Children's play area and wading pool.

- **Shadow Cliffs Regional Recreation Area.** 249 acres in Pleasanton. In season, swimming off a sandy beach with bathhouse, food concession and paved ramp to the lake for disabled. The Giant Rapids Waterslide operates April through Labor Day.

  Year-round fishing in the lake, picnicking, volleyball courts, horseshoe pits, hiking, equestrian, jogging and running trails. Group picnicking by reservation. Rental boats available. Connects with Alameda County bicycle trail along Stanley Boulevard between Pleasanton and Livermore.

- **Sunol Regional Wilderness.** 6,758 acres south of Pleasanton and Livermore. Take Calaveras Road to Geary Road. Picnicking, birdwatching, interpretive programs, group overnight camping by reservation, family camping, backpack loop available by reservation, hiking, equestrian, running and jogging trails.

- **Temescal Regional Recreation Area.** 48 acres in Oakland. In season, swimming off sandy beach. Crowded on hot days. Bathhouse, food concession. Year-round fishing, picnicking, turfed play areas, children's play areas, bicycling, hiking, jogging, group picnicking by reservation.

Shorelines

- **Crown Memorial State Beach.** 383 acres in city of Alameda. Bathhouse and food concession, reservable youth-group day camps, turfed play areas, beach. Estuary and reserve, wading, swimming, windsurfing, fishing.

- **Hayward Regional Shoreline.** 816 acres in Hayward at end of West Winton Avenue. Birdwatching, hiking and interpretative programs. Visitor center off Highway 92.

Trails

Lineal parkland for walking, jogging, bicycling and horseback riding. Five hundred miles of trails are within parks, plus the following 106 miles which connect the parks:

- **Alameda Creek Regional Trail.** 458 acres form parallel trails along Alameda Creek Flood Control Channel from the mouth of Niles Canyon through Union City, Newark and Fremont with several staging areas.

- **Cull Canyon Regional Trail.** This is the first portion of the Chabot to Garin Trail. Combined length of trail is 4.5 miles.

- **East Bay Skyline National Trail.** This 31-mile regional trail, suitable for hiking, backpacking and horseback riding full length and for bicycling in part, connects six regional parks. Beginning at Wildcat Canyon in Richmond, it progresses through Tilden, Sibley Volcanic, Huckleberry Botanic, Redwood and Chabot regional parks.

- **San Lorenzo Shoreline Regional Trail.** A five-mile trail connecting Hayward Regional Shoreline with San Lorenzo and San Leandro Park and Marina. Staging areas for the trail at the west ends of West Winton Avenue, Hayward, and Grant Avenue, San Lorenzo.

Around the Cities

- **Berkeley**. Theater district, Berkeley Rep, plays, foreign movies, shopping, bookstores, cafes, restaurants. Good town for strolling. For shopping, Shattuck Avenue, Telegraph Avenue, Fourth Street. Berkeley Rep, (510) 204-8901. Visitors bureau, (510) 549-7040.

- **Dunsmuir House & Garden.** A beautiful colonial revival mansion, with 37 rooms, 40 acres with garden in Oakland, available for touring for $3. Located at 2960 Peralta Oaks Ct., you can find it by taking the 106th Avenue exit from Highway 580. Phone (510) 615-5555.

- **Golden Gate Fields Racetrack.** They're off and running — from late January to June. Thoroughbred racing. Golden Gate is located in Albany — take the Gilman Street exit off Interstate 80. Phone (510) 559-7300.

- **Jack London Square.** Located at the foot of Broadway in Oakland, you'll find waterfront stores, movies, Barnes and Noble bookstore, restaurants and night clubs, and an ever-changing view of ships in the Oakland Estuary. For information about what's happening in Oakland, look at cityofoakland.com and check activities.

- **Judah L. Magnes Memorial Museum,** 2911 Russell St., Berkeley. Shows. Art and artifacts of Jewish culture. Library, history. (510) 549-6950.

- **McConaghy House,** 18701 Hesperian Blvd., Hayward, next to Kennedy Park. Furnished Victorian farmhouse. (510) 276-3010.

- **Meek Estate.** Renovated and furnished five-story 1869 mansion at Hampton and Boston roads in Hayward. Relive the Victorian era in the ballroom, library, solarium, bedrooms, nursery and servants' quarters. Park with playground equipment and a barbecue in the picnic area.

- **Mission San Jose.** Located at 43300 Mission Blvd. in Fremont, Mission San Jose was founded June 11, 1797, and destroyed in the earthquake of 1868. One of the most picturesque buildings in Alameda County. (510) 657-1797.

- **Oakland-Alameda Coliseum.** One of the premiere sports-exhibition complexes in the country, the Coliseum is located off the Nimitz Freeway at Hegenberger Road. Home of the Oakland A's, Golden State Warriors, Oakland Raiders. Site of many rock concerts and major exhibitions. (510) 569-2121

- **Oakland Museum.** 1000 Oak St. This museum focuses on California art, history and natural history. The excellence of its collection has given it the reputation as "California's Smithsonian." Art from the days of the Spanish explorers to the present is included, featuring panoramic views of San Francisco, cowboys and Indians, Oriental and modern art.

  Natural sciences include exhibits on botany, birds, ecology, paleontology and geology, and an aquarium and dioramas of animals in natural settings. California's history begins with the Indians and goes through the Spanish explorers, the Californios, the gold miners and cowboys, the pioneers and turn-of-the-century Californians. (510) 238-2200.

- **Paramount Theater.** One of best examples of "Art Deco" architecture on West Coast. Parquet floors, gold ceiling teeming with sculptured life and elegant 1930s embellishments. Used for concerts, plays. (510) 465-6400.

- **Toot-Toot**. The Pacific Locomotive Association, a group of train buffs, has rebuilt an abandoned line near Sunol and twice a month offers rides to the public on its old trains. Phone to confirm trains are running (925) 862-9063. Sunol is located off I-680, just south of Pleasanton.

- **University of California, Berkeley.** Bookstores, magnificent libraries, museums, lectures, concerts — it's one of the intellectual capitals of the world. Phone (510) 642-6000. The Campanile and Sather Gate are famous landmarks. Top dance and musical events. The Greek Amphitheater is spectacular. Great spectator sports, including football, basketball, track. Go Bears! To get on the Cal Performances mailing list, call (510) 642-6000.

Art guilds and galleries, dance schools, bands, symphonies, choral groups, little theater — Alameda County has them all. Every town is hooked to cable television. Local theaters offer a good variety of movies. IMAX (big screen) movie theater in Dublin.

Chapter 14

Job Training & Colleges

IF YOU ARE looking for a job but need training or additional education, local colleges, public adult schools and private institutions have put together a variety of programs, ranging from word processing to MBA degrees.

Many institutions have devised programs for working adults or parents who must attend the duties of school and child rearing.

In many instances, jobs and careers are mixed in with personal enrichment. At some colleges, you can take word processing, economics and music.

This chapter lists the major local educational and training institutes. All will send you literature, all welcome inquiries.

Adult Schools

Although rarely in the headlines, adult schools serve thousands of local residents. Upholstery, microwave cooking, ballroom dancing, bookkeeping, computers, cardiopulmonary resuscitation, aerobics, investing, art, music, how to raise children — these and more are offered in the adult schools.

These schools and programs are run by school districts and by cities. Many schools also run adult sports programs, basketball, volleyball, tennis. Call your local school or city for a catalog.

Getting the Older Students

As the public's needs have changed, so have the colleges. The traditional college audience — high school seniors — is still thriving but increasingly colleges are attracting older students and working people.

Many colleges now offer evening and weekend programs, especially in business degrees and business-related subjects. Some programs — an MBA — can take years, some classes only a day.

Here is a partial list of local colleges and specialty schools. As with any venture, the student should investigate before enrolling or paying a fee.

- University of California, Berkeley. High admission standards. Bachelor's, master's and doctorate degrees. Call (510) 642-6000. Also a popular extension program, all sorts of classes for the public. (510) 642-4111. Ask for catalog. The Extension service has a center in Fremont. Phone (510) 440-9090.

- California State University, Hayward. Popular with adults returning for degree or seeking master's. Day and evening classes. Branch campus in Contra Costa County. Phone (510) 885-3000.

Many extension classes. (510) 885-3605. Extension classes are popular because they are focused and short. If you need specialized training in computers or bookkeeping or dozens of other subjects, peruse a few extension catalogs.

- Mills College, Oakland. Women's college, coed grad school. (510) 430-2255 or (510) 430-3309 for graduate school information.

- Holy Names College, 3500 Mountain Blvd., Oakland, 94619. Coed. Four-year college.

Also offers weekend college for working adults. Bachelor's degrees in Humanities, Liberal Studies, Human Services, Business Administration, Nursing (for registered nurses). Master's in Business Admin., English, Education. Also many teaching credentials and certificates. (510) 436-1120.

- Armstrong University, Oakland. Primarily a business school. (510) 835-7900.

- Heald College, Oakland. Business. (510) 444-0201.

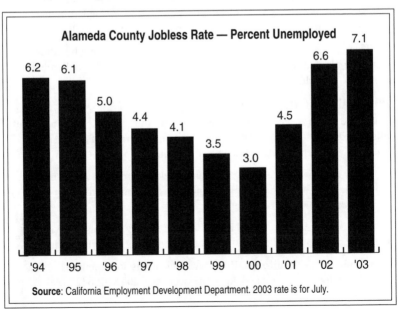

Alameda County Jobless Rate — Percent Unemployed

'94	'95	'96	'97	'98	'99	'00	'01	'02	'03
6.2	6.1	5.0	4.4	4.1	3.5	3.0	4.5	6.6	7.1

Source: California Employment Development Department. 2003 rate is for July.

- College of Arts and Crafts, Oakland. 1,100 students. Design, arts, architecture, ceramics, graphics, film. (510) 594-3600.

- Northwestern Polytechnic University, 117 Fourier Ave. Fremont. Bachelor and master degrees in computer science, computer systems engineering, electronic engineering, business. (510) 657-5911.

- John F. Kennedy University, in Orinda, draws from Alameda County, has classes in Oakland. Offers B.A. and M.A. degrees in management and B.A.'s in other fields. Also law degree. (925) 254-0200.

- University of San Francisco-San Ramon Campus. Based in San Francisco but offers bachelor's and master's programs in San Ramon. Phone (925) 867-2711.

- Silicon Valley College-Walnut Creek, 41350 Christy St., Fremont. Computer, high-tech, medical programs. 800-750-5627

- St. Mary's College. Bachelor's degrees in Liberal Arts, Economics, Business Administration, Education. Also offers special programs, including master's in business, for working adults. Credentials in education and extension programs. Phone (925) 631-4224.

Community Colleges

Many students attend these two-year public colleges then transfer as juniors to state universities or University of California schools. Community colleges also have diverse selections for people interested in occasional classes or in job-related classes.

These colleges also offer associate degrees for vocational programs and certificate and license training, e.g., registered nurses.

- College of Alameda, 555 Atlantic Ave., City of Alameda 94501. Ph: (510) 522-7221.

- Laney College, 900 Fallon St., Oakland 94607. Ph: (510) 834-5740.

- Merritt College, 12500 Campus Dr., Oakland 94619. Ph: (510) 531-4911.

- Vista College, 2020 Milvia St., Berkeley 94704. Ph: (510) 981-2800.

- Chabot College, 25555 Hesperian Blvd., Hayward 94545. Ph: (510) 723-6600.

- Las Positas College, 3033 Collier Canyon Rd., Livermore 94550. Ph: (925) 373-5800.

- Ohlone College, 43600 Mission Blvd., Fremont 94539. Ph: (510) 659-6000.

Chapter 15

Commuting

DESPITE NUMEROUS COMPLAINTS, many Alameda residents have a short commute, thanks to the presence of so many local jobs. If you take BART or buses to work and travel a long distance, you will often find the ride tiring but endurable.

In some ways, the commute is getting better. In 2002, a new San Mateo Bridge opened and in 2003, BART completed its extension to San Francisco International Airport.

Oakland International Airport is spending $1.5 billion to improve its roads and terminals. The job is far from finished but already it is much easier, from the freeway, to get to and from the airport.

Diamond (car pool) lanes are turning up more and more in Bay Area freeways. If you car pool, these lanes will speed you to your destination. Not every time. They have their choke points.

The lose-your-cool, insane commutes boil down to only two: solo drives to San Francisco or to the old Silicon Valley (San Jose, Sunnyvale, Santa Clara, etc.).

To get to San Francisco, you have to grind your way through the approaches to the Bay Bridge toll plaza, then through the metering lights, then over the bridge and into downtown San Francisco.

Damaged in the 1989 earthquake, the east span of the bridge is to be replaced over the next five or so years — construction delays. Many improvements have been made to freeways leading up to the Bay Bridge. Many more will be made. But no matter how many or how great the changes, this bridge will always snarl. Just too many vehicles trying to fit into too narrow a space.

San Francisco has never been friendly to freeways. Following the 1989 earthquake, the City decided not to rebuild the Embarcadero freeway and several heavily used ramps in the downtown.

Further, to push people into public transit, San Francisco is not building parking anywhere close to what it needs. Residents are parking on the sidewalks.

Commuter's Guide to BART
(Time in Minutes)

Station	Oakland	Berkeley	S.F.
Fremont	38	47	47
Union City	34	43	43
S. Hayward	29	38	38
Hayward	25	34	34
Bay Fair	20	29	29
San Leandro	17	26	25
Coliseum	13	22	21
Fruitvale	9	18	18
Lake Merritt	5	14	13
12th Street	1	10	12
19th Street	—	9	14
MacArthur	4	5	17
Ashby	7	2	21
Berkeley	9	—	24
N. Berkeley	13	3	26
Plaza	15	6	32
Rockridge	7	—	22
Oakland West	6	16	8
Castro Valley*	20	.	33
Dublin-Pleasanton*	36	.	49

Note: The table provides a guide to typical commuting times from BART Stations to three city-center locations — 19th Street Station in Oakland, downtown Berkeley Station and Montgomery Street Station in San Francisco. There are typically 12- to 15-minute intervals between departures on the same line but during peak hours BART runs extra trains and this cuts the waiting time. BART train schedules are available by writing 800 Madison St., Oakland, CA 94607, or you can pick one up at any BART station. Rockridge to Berkeley requires a transfer at MacArthur so times will vary. *Castro Valley and Dublin-Pleasanton times were figured to Lake Merritt (Oakland) and to Montgomery Street in San Francisco.

Nonetheless, many East Bay residents still drive solo to the City. If you are one or thinking about becoming one, at least give BART and the other alternatives a try. The mind you save may be your own.

In the 1990s and in 2000, Silicon Valley generated jobs by tens of thousands and homes by the dozens and the hundreds. Prices soared and even with the recession are still quite high.

Many people moved to places like Livermore and Pleasanton in Alameda County and Tracy and Manteca and Merced out in the Central Valley, about 75-plus miles from San Jose. Three freeways lead from these places to San Jose:

    • Interstate 580. It collects traffic from the Tracy and Central Valley and from east Alameda and Contra Costa counties and feeds it into:

    • Interstate 680. This freeway intersects I-580 at Pleasanton-Dublin and travels down the east side of Fremont to San Jose and Silicon Valley. This freeway used to be fast but as traffic increased its bottlenecks became particularly troublesome. In 2002, car-pool lanes were added between, roughly,

Pleasanton and Fremont. This has helped moved things along. Another plus, if you want to call it that, fewer jobs in Silicon Valley.

• Interstate 880, the Bayshore freeway. It travels along the shore — Oakland, San Leandro, Union City, Fremont — to San Jose and connecting freeways. Road from hell. Always being improved, always jamming. Too popular. Serves Oakland Airport and Coliseum complex and, over the Hayward-San Mateo Bridge, San Francisco International Airport and nearby job centers.

Other Improvements

• After years of work, the rebuilding of the freeway interchange at Dublin-Pleasanton was completed in 2002. Big difference.

• FasTrak, automated tolls. Now installed at all bridges in the Bay Area. Proving popular and a time saver.

• BART to SFO. As popular as Oakland Airport is, many East Bay residents depend on SFO or work at the airport or in the vicinity.

• Altamont Commuter Express, from Stockton to San Jose with stops in Livermore, Pleasanton and Fremont. A new service, it recently added a train and is proving popular.

• More money. In 2000, Alameda County renewed a half-cent sales tax to pay for transit projects and Santa Clara County passed a half-cent sales tax for transit. Much of the Santa Clara tax will go to extending BART from Fremont to San Jose and the remainder for local jobs.

As for the Alameda tax, it's going to fund a variety of jobs around the county, some long-term, some immediate.

Shortcuts and Commuting Strategies

Nothing ventured, nothing gained. Do some experimenting.

• Change routes. If the Bay Bridge is driving you batty, take BART or drive the Hayward-San Mateo Bridge.

Switch freeways. Instead of I-880, try I-680.

• Buy a good map book and keep it in the car. The editor favors Thomas Guides. Sooner than later you will find yourself jammed on a freeway or about to be jammed and in dire need of an alternate route. They're out there.

San Pablo Avenue will get you through Berkeley, Emeryville and Oakland; Hesperian Boulevard parallels I-880 through the south county; Mission Boulevard in Fremont will take you off I-880 and place you on the usually faster I-680.

For people shopping for new homes, Thomas is indispensable. Many

Driving Miles to Bay Bridge

City/Location	On I-580	On I-880
Alameda	NA	9
Albany	NA	5
Berkeley*	5	4
Castro Valley	20	NA
Coliseum	NA	9
Dublin	29	NA
Emeryville	NA	2
Fremont	NA	23
Hayward	20	17
Livermore	37	NA
Newark	NA	22
Oakland Airport	NA	10
Pleasanton	29	NA
San Leandro	17	11
San Lorenzo	NA	15
Union City	NA	21

Note: These are approximations. A traveler from Fremont, a large city, could easily add another five miles depending upon his starting point within the city. Of bridges, the Bay Bridge is a little over 8 miles long, the San Mateo about 7, the Dumbarton about 3. **Key:** NA, not applicable. Either exits were not available or the freeway was judged to be too distant for a reasonable measurement. *I-580 route applicable mostly to residents in south and southeast Berkeley who use Highway 24.

foldout maps sold locally are several years old. Often they don't show the new tracts.

- Listen to traffic reports on radio. The info is timely and will give you a chance to take alternate routes.

- Buy your BART tickets at Safeway or Albertsons. This will speed you through the gate. BART is studying new ways to ticket riders.

- Join a car pool. The Bay Bridge and local freeways have set aside "diamond" lanes for car pools (two or three people). No toll; you shoot right through to the head of the line. So popular are these lanes that drivers, shy a body or two, cruise BART stations in search of riders.

The Dumbarton and San Mateo bridges also have diamond lanes for poolers.

RIDES, phone 817-1717, will help you find a car pool in your town — no charge. In the typical arrangement, passengers meet at one or two spots and are dropped off at one or two destinations in Oakland, Silicon Valley or San Francisco.

The pools go all over; all that's needed are passengers and a driver. If you want to set up your own pool, RIDES will help you find passengers and obtain a van.

- Use Park-and-Ride lots. Built by Caltrans, the state transit agency, about 160 lots are scattered around the Bay Area. Many are located near bus stops or set aside for patrons of a particular transit service, for example, BART. Call 817-1717 for a list.

- Take a ferry to the City. Ferries run to San Francisco from Oakland and the City of Alameda. For info, (510) 522-3300.

- Avoid the peak hours. If you can leave home about 6 a.m. and get on the freeway before 3:30 p.m., your life might become easier.

- Take BART. Breakdowns are few, the cars clean, the ride smooth.

  Passengers from Fremont, Albany-Berkeley and Dublin-Pleasanton, among the last stops in Alameda County, can usually secure seats on the way in. On the way home, it's first come, first served. For schedules and information, call (510) 465-2278.

- Amtrak. Known for long-distance service, Amtrak also runs commute trains, called Capitols, from Sacramento to Silicon Valley. Discounts tickets available. Phone (800) 872-7245.

- Take a bus. You can leave the car in the garage, avoid a parking fee, and read the paper on the way home.

  AC-Transit is the major bus company in Alameda County. Phone (510) 839-2882 for transit information.

  Livermore, Pleasanton and Dublin are served by a separate company, WHEELS. Phone (925) 455-7500.

  Union City Transit, (510) 476-1500. Around Union City and to south Hayward BART station.

- Universal transit number, for buses, BART, etc., and highway conditions. 817-1717.

- Oakland International Airport. It is not as large as San Francisco International but if you can fly out of Oakland, you'll probably save time. It's just closer. A shuttle bus will take you from the airport to the BART station, about two miles to the east.

- If forced to pull off onto the freeway shoulder in fog, shut off your lights. In fog, motorists often line up on the lights ahead. Get out of your car and off to the side. Slow down in fog.

Excuses

Heard by toll collectors on the Bay Bridge

* "Someone hit me over the head and took my wallet."

* "I spent all my money buying gas."

* "I left my purse/wallet at home/work (most used)."

* "I am broke, I just don't have it (second most)."

* "My wife/ husband took all my money out of my wallet/purse."

* "My grandma is dying."

* "My money blew away."

* "This is my first time … do I have to pay?"

* "I never carry cash. Will you take credit cards?"

* "I forgot."

* "I just got robbed."

* "I didn't know there was a bridge here."

* "My dog ate my money."

* "I just had the money. It disappeared."

* "I just spent all my money buying this BMW."

Toll takers get an average 200 "no pays" a day. They will issue an emergency payment notice. If you don't pay within 5 days, you get another bill for $12 (includes $10 fine).

Chapter 16

Weather

THE WEATHER of Alameda County can be accurately described as almost delightful. The qualifying "almost" is necessary because there will be days when you will curse the heat, bewail the fog and wish the rain would cease. But these days will be few and the days of balm many.

Broad Weather Patterns

Although erratic, Alameda weather does hold to broad patterns. Rain almost never falls in the summer. September and October will usually usher in winter with several spells of heat. Snow every few years will powder the mountain tops.

Livermore in the summer will be warmer than Newark and Newark will be warmer than Berkeley. In the winter, the reverse will show: Berkeley cool, Newark cooler, Livermore coolest.

Understanding how the weather works — an easy task — will make you appreciate it all the more. There is a perverse but charming logic to the play of the elements.

If you are shopping for a home in the Bay Area, knowledge of the weather can save you from buying in a place unsuitable to your temperament.

Five actors star in weather extravaganza: the sun, the Pacific, the Golden Gate, the hills and the Central Valley.

The Sun's Role

In the spring and summer, the sun moves north creating a mass of ocean air called the Pacific High. The Pacific High blocks storms from the California coast and dispatches winds to the coast.

In the fall the sun moves south, taking the Pacific High with it. The winds slough off for a few months, then in bluster the storms. Toward spring, the storms will abate as the Pacific High settles into place.

The Fog Machine

Speeding across the Pacific, the spring and summer winds pick up moisture and at the coast, strip the warm water from the surface and bring up

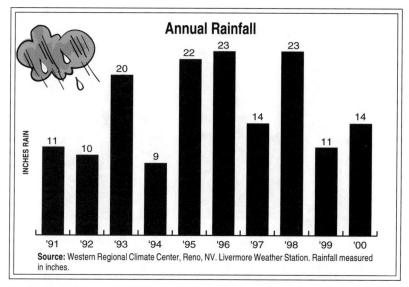

Annual Rainfall

INCHES RAIN

Year	'91	'92	'93	'94	'95	'96	'97	'98	'99	'00
Inches	11	10	20	9	22	23	14	23	11	14

Source: Western Regional Climate Center, Reno, NV. Livermore Weather Station. Rainfall measured in inches.

the frigid. Cold water exposed to warm wet air makes a wonderfully thick fog.

In summer months, downtown San Francisco often looks like it is about to be buried by mountains of cotton candy. This candy entrances many and depresses not a few coastal residents. Week after week of chilly fog, which happens occasionally, wears on some nerves.

The Golden Gate

This fog would love to scoot over to the East Bay but Mount Tamalpais and the hills running up the San Francisco peninsula stop or greatly impede its progress — except where there are openings. Of the half dozen or so major gaps, the biggest is that marvelous work of nature, the Golden Gate.

The fog shoots through the Golden Gate in the spring and summer, visually delighting motorists on the Bay Bridge, and bangs into the Berkeley-Albany hills. Some of the cooler air will drift toward Oakland, and the other gaps will admit the cool air to the lower Bay. But Berkeley gets the most, which is why Berkeley and Oakland in the summer are cooler than Newark.

A Mountain Barrier

A mile or so inland, the east shore ascends to a mountain range, which traverses Alameda County. These mountains perform the same function as the coastal mountains: they impede the cool air and fog from traveling on to Pleasanton and Livermore.

The next summer day you drive Interstate 580 from Hayward to Pleasanton, let your hand hang out the window. As you crest the ridge and descend, the air will become noticeably warmer. You have left the coastal pattern and entered the continental, warmer and dryer — which is why, in

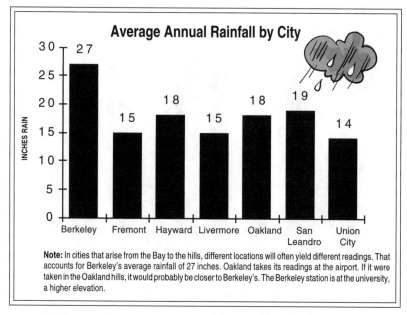

Average Annual Rainfall by City

Note: In cities that arise from the Bay to the hills, different locations will often yield different readings. That accounts for Berkeley's average rainfall of 27 inches. Oakland takes its readings at the airport. If it were taken in the Oakland hills, it would probably be closer to Berkeley's. The Berkeley station is at the university, a higher elevation.

summer, Livermore is warmer than Newark or Berkeley (see chart).

But although weakened, the coastal pattern retains enough strength to take the edge off the Livermore-Pleasanton-Dublin summer. As with the coastal range, the East Bay range has its gaps, foremost the Carquinez Strait near Martinez, and the Hayward gap, which opens to Pleasanton-Livermore. Into these gaps runs the cooler air, hurried along by the last actor, the San Joaquin Valley.

Valley Air Pump

The San Joaquin Valley is also known as the Central Valley. Located about 75 miles inland, the vast Central Valley lies within the continental pattern. In the summer, this means heat. Hot air pulls in cold air like a vacuum. The Central Valley sucks in the coastal air through openings in the East Bay hills, and even over the hills.

You are driving down Interstate 680 south approaching Dublin. The sky is blue, the temperature high. To your left, the horizon is clear. To your right, a great surprise: snow white fog billowing over the hills and through the gaps, cooling the air while you gawk in wonder.

When the cool coastal air neutralizes the Central Valley heat, the Valley says to the coast: no more cool air, thank you. The suction disappears and the winds taper off.

With the winds down, the ocean fog stays offshore, and San Francisco, Berkeley and the East Bay shore towns enjoy some sunny days. Livermore and

Pleasanton, in the grasp of the continental pattern, endure considerably more heat.

Meanwhile, lacking the cooling fog, the Valley heats up again, creating the vacuum that pulls in the cool air and renews the cycle. This cycle has its daily counterpart. As the sun's rays weaken in the late afternoon, the fog will often steal across and down the Bay to be burned off the following morning by the robust sunlight.

In the fall and winter, the temperatures are reversed. The Central Valley grows colder and the Pacific Ocean, which is warmer than the land in winter, sends its balmy breezes over the coast. Again the hills impede the coastal flow. San Francisco, in the winter, is warmer than Berkeley, which is warmer than Newark, which is warmer than Livermore (see temperature chart).

Also in the winter, Central Valley fog, attracted to warm air, moves toward the shore cities but, except at openings like the Hayward gap and the Carquinez Strait, is blocked by the hills.

Rain Patterns

Besides blocking the fog, the hills greatly influence the rain pattern.

When storm clouds rise to pass over a mountain, they cool and drop much of their rain. Mt. Diablo, a landmark of the region, gets an average of 25 inches annually at its summit, 3,849 feet. But at the ranger station about a 1,000 feet lower, the amount drops to 22 inches.

For the most part, the average rainfall ranges between 14 and 19 inches for most Alameda County cities. But in cities that rise from the Bay to the mountains, different locations will often yield different readings. That accounts for Berkeley's average rainfall of 27 inches.

Oakland, which averages 18 inches, takes its reading at the airport. If it were taken in the Oakland hills, it would probably be closer to Berkeley's. (The Berkeley station is at the University, a higher elevation.) Berkeley, opposite the Golden Gate, also gets visited by more rain-bearing clouds than Oakland, which is sheltered by San Francisco.

Drenched by Fog

Fog drip can sometimes be as heavy as rain. One of the editors recalls attending a summer picnic in a redwood grove in the Oakland hills. He and his family arrived about 11 a.m. to find the air cold and the drip heavy enough to soak their clothes. Parents bundled up children, plastic tablecloths were used as rain jackets. Two hours later the fog had burned away and they were playing softball in a hot sun.

In this instance, the trees were squeezing the fog, forcing it to give up its moisture, another example of the neighborhood diversity of Bay Area weather. Fog drip in the Berkeley hills has been measured over 10 inches in a summer.

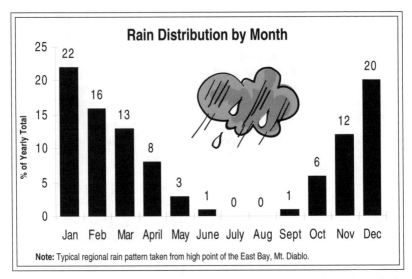

Rain Distribution by Month

% of Yearly Total

Jan 22 | Feb 16 | Mar 13 | April 8 | May 3 | June 1 | July 0 | Aug 0 | Sept 1 | Oct 6 | Nov 12 | Dec 20

Note: Typical regional rain pattern taken from high point of the East Bay, Mt. Diablo.

That, basically, is how the weather works in the Bay Area (see, that wasn't hard). But unfortunately for regularity's sake, the actors often forget their lines or fail to show up. Rainfall over the 10 recent seasons shows how undependable nature can be (see chart).

Up and Down Years

During the drought years of 1975 through 1977, rainfall averaged 14 inches or less and dropped as low as 8 inches in 1976.

Between 1981 and 1983, El Niño tricked the Pacific into forgetting the summer fogs. The Bay Area enjoyed unusually warm summer weather. Rainfall also zoomed to 35 inches in 1983, causing widespread flooding and damage. Then years of droughts followed. Then two years ago the rains came back.

Even when erratic, however, the weather is almost always mild. Rainy winters cause slides and road washouts but Bay Area residents count their blessings when they sit in front of the television and see what havoc Nature raises in the rest of the nation.

Weather Tidbits

- When San Francisco built Candlestick Park, it chose, in its civic wisdom, the junction of several wind funnels coming through a gap in the Pacific hills. Pop flies, when they could be seen, flitted around like demented bugs. The new baseball stadium, Pac Bell Park, is sheltered by the coastal hills. It may catch some fog but it will not be as wild as Candlestick.

   Conversely, Candlestick is a great football stadium. Winter breaks down the fog, abates the winds.

- September and October are the best months to go swimming in the ocean.

Average Daily Temperatures

City	Ja	Fb	Mr	Ap	My	Ju	Jy	Au	Sp	Oc	No	De
Berkeley	50	53	54	56	59	62	63	63	64	62	55	51
Livermore	47	51	54	58	63	68	72	72	70	63	54	47
Newark	50	54	56	60	63	66	68	69	67	64	56	49
Oakland	51	55	56	59	61	63	65	66	66	64	57	51

Note: Figures derived from 1971-2000 records, National Climatic Center, Asheville, North Carolina.

The upwelling of the cold water has stopped. Often the fog has gone. Sunshine kisses the water and the coast.

While cooler, the coast is also delightful in April and May. Winter has departed. The summer fogs have yet to arrive.

- Like sunshine? You are in the right place. Records show that during daylight hours the sun shines in New York City 60 percent of the time; in Boston, 57 percent; in Detroit, 53 percent; and in Seattle, 43 percent.

In San Francisco, the sun shines during 66 percent of daylight hours. Atop Mt. Tamalpais in Marin County, where conditions are comparable to Alameda County, the sun shines 73 percent of daylight hours.

- Of Alameda County's two types of fog, one is much more dangerous than the other.

The coastal fog often forms well above the Pacific and, pushed by the wind, generally moves at a good clip. In thick coastal fog, you will have to slow down but you can see the tail lights of a car 50 to 75 yards ahead.

In winter, valley or tule fog blossoms at shoe level when moist air rests atop the cold ground. Tule fog rarely penetrates west of the Berkeley-Oakland-Fremont mountain ranges. But it is a problem east of the hills.

When you read of chain accidents in the Altamont area (east Alameda County) or in the Central Valley, tule fog is almost always to blame.

- During the summer and fall, the Pacific High will occasionally loop a strong wind down from Washington through the Sierra and the hot valleys, where it loses its moisture, and into the Bay Area.

Extremely dry, these northeasters, which are now called "Diablos," will tighten the skin on your face, cause wood shingle roofs to crackle and turn the countryside into tinder.

The October 1991 fire that destroyed 2,500 homes and apartments in the Berkeley-Oakland hills and killed 25 was caused by a Diablo.

On Sept. 27, 1923, a northeaster fire roared down upon North Berkeley, destroying homes, libraries, students' clubs, hotels and boarding homes —

Temperatures for Selected Cities
Number of Days Greater than 90 Degrees in Typical Year

City	Ja	Fb	Mr	Ap	My	Ju	Jy	Au	Sp	Oc	No	Dc
Berkeley	0	0	0	0	0	0	0	1	0	0	0	0
Fremont	0	0	0	0	0	3	4	10	5	0	0	0
Livermore	0	0	0	0	1	6	14	21	11	0	0	0
Oakland	0	0	0	0	0	0	1	0	0	0	0	0

Temperatures for Selected Cities
Number of Days 32 Degrees or Less in Typical Year

City	Ja	Fb	Mr	Ap	My	Ju	Jy	Au	Sp	Oc	No	Dc
Berkeley	2	0	0	0	0	0	0	0	0	0	0	4
Fremont	1	0	0	0	0	0	0	0	0	0	0	6
Livermore	11	2	0	0	0	0	0	0	0	0	0	12
Oakland	0	0	0	0	0	0	0	0	0	0	0	1

Source: National Weather Service

584 buildings in all.

If you buy in the hills, take a look at fire prevention tactics.

- Allergies. They often kick in during the spring and in October. During the spring, the grasses pop their buds and many trees release pollen.

  In the fall, the Diablos dry out the trees and cones and pollen fills the air. Hanky time.

- Frosts are rare but one in 1973 killed almost all the eucalyptus trees in the Berkeley hills. A fire hazard, the trees were cut down but, as a drive through Tilden Park will prove, the eucalypti came back.

  In December, 1990, several nights of below-freezing temperatures killed countless plants throughout the Bay Region, froze water lines and burst many pipes. When the forecast says frost, you can save at least some of your plants and trees by wrapping them in plastic.

- Although moist, the coastal climate is rarely muggy. The fog keeps the temperature too low.

- Rain is rain, generally welcome all the time in dry California. But some rains are more welcome than others. Storms from the vicinity of Hawaii turn Sierra slopes to slush and, in the upper elevations, deposit soft snow that sinks under the weight of skis. Alaskan storms bring snow to the lower mountains and deposit a fine powder, ideal for skiing. When snow caps Mt. Diablo and the mountains above Fremont, thank Alaska.

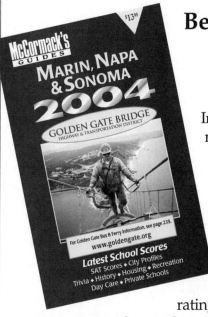

Chapter 17

Crime

EVERY neighborhood or city in this country suffers from some crime. Even communities surrounded by gates and patrolled by guards will on occasion see domestic violence or pilfering by visitors.

So the question to ask when shopping for a home or apartment is not: Is this neighborhood safe? But rather, how safe is it compared to other places?

In California, crime often follows demographics: High-income neighborhoods generally have low crime, middle-income places middling crime, and low-income towns and neighborhoods high crime.

For these guides, we label towns with fewer than 40 crimes per 1,000 residents over a year as low in crime. Towns with 40 to 70 crimes per 1,000 residents are placed in the middling category. Towns with over 70 crimes per 1,000 are labeled high in crime or worrisome. The statistics are supplied by the FBI and the California Dept. of Justice.

In many instances, these figures mislead. You can probably take every high-crime city in the country and find within it low-crime neighborhoods.

The demographic connection also can mislead. Many peaceful, law-abiding people live in the "worst" neighborhoods. But these neighborhoods also contain a disproportionate number of the troubled and criminally inclined.

A town low in homicides and violent crime might have a high crime rate, if it has a lot of stores. Theft is the most common crime.

Why does crime correlate with income and demographics? In many countries, it doesn't. Japan, devastated after World War II, did not sink into violence and thievery. Many industrialized nations with lower standards of living than the U.S. have much less crime. In 1990, according to one study, handguns killed 10 people in Australia, 22 in Great Britain and 87 in Japan. The count for the U.S. was 10,567. (But in recent years Europeans have seen more burglaries, robberies, etc. In fact, in some categories, the U.S. is doing better than some European nations. The big exception: handgun deaths.)

Sociologists blame the breakdown of morals and the family in the U.S, the pervasive violence in the media, the easy access to guns, and other forces. Any

Crime Statistics by City

City	Population	Rate	Homicides
Alameda	74,600	41	2
Albany	16,750	50	0
Berkeley	104,600	91	1
Dublin	33,500	22	1
Emeryville	7,300	185	3
Fremont	208,600	29	0
Hayward	144,300	38	10
Livermore	76,700	28	0
Newark	43,650	45	0
Oakland	408,800	68	84
Piedmont	11,150	26	0
Pleasanton	66,200	26	0
San Leandro	81,300	55	1
Union City	70,200	37	3
County Total	1,486,600	51	108

Crime in Other Northern California Cities

City	Population	Rate	Homicides
Concord	123,900	45	0
Danville	43,000	14	0
Fairfield	100,200	46	3
Mountain View	71,600	34	1
Palo Alto	60,500	31	2
Richmond	101,100	72	18
Sacramento	426,000	73	40
San Francisco	793,600	37	62
San Jose	918,000	27	22
San Ramon	46,250	24	0
Stockton	253,800	78	30
Sunnyvale	132,800	20	0
Vacaville	92,300	26	0
Vallejo	118,600	61	4
Walnut Creek	65,900	39	0

Source: California Crime Index from State Dept. of Justice, 2001 data, with population estimates from Calif. Dept. of Finance, Jan. 1, 2002. Rate is all reported willful homicide, forcible rape, aggravated assault, burglary, motor vehicle theft, larceny-theft and arson per 1,000 residents. Homicides include murders and non-negligent manslaughter.

one of these "causes" could be argued into the next century but if you're shopping for a home or an apartment, just keep in mind that there is a correlation between demographics and crime.

How do you spot a troubled neighborhood?

Crime is a young person's game, particularly boys and men. In one of its annual studies, the FBI determined that 61 percent of all the people arrested

Crime in Other Cities Nationwide

City	Population	Rate	Homicides
Anchorage	263,588	50	10
Atlanta	426,511	123	144
Birmingham	243,762	86	73
Boise	189,671	46	2
Boston	591,944	63	65
Chicago	2,866,191	NA	628
Cleveland	479,263	69	77
Dallas	1,215,553	91	240
Denver	569,653	53	45
Des Moines	198,468	64	11
Hartford, Conn	122,274	88	25
Detroit, MI	956,283	94	395
Honolulu	885,605	55	20
Jacksonville	754,679	68	75
Las Vegas	1,117,763	45	133
Little Rock	184,413	91	34
Milwaukee	601,229	76	127
Miami	371,863	95	66
New York City	8,023,018	33	*3,472
New Orleans	484,289	75	213
Oklahoma City	507,517	90	45
Pittsburgh, PA	331,414	58	55
Phoenix	1,366,542	77	209
Portland, OR	537,081	80	21
Reno	190,218	58	6
St. Louis, MO	350,336	150	148
Salt Lake City	184,723	89	18
Scottsdale, AZ	209,686	47	10
Seattle	572,345	81	25
Tucson	503,461	99	42

Source: Annual 2002 FBI crime report, which uses 2001 data. Population estimates are based on updated estimates from 2000 census. Key: NA (not available). *Note: New York City's homicides includes 2,792 people killed on Sept. 11, 2001 at World Trade Center.

were under age 30. For every female arrested four males were arrested, the same study noted.

Take a look at the academic rankings of the neighborhood school. Very low rankings indicate that many children are failing or dropping out, that they will have difficulty finding jobs — conditions that often breed crime.

In middle-scoring towns, the failures are fewer. In higher scoring towns, fewer still.

Drive the neighborhood. The signs of trouble are often easily read: bars on many windows, security doors in wide use.

Should you avoid unsafe or marginal neighborhoods? The troubled neighborhoods often carry low prices or rents and are located near job centers. In the East Bay, some of the best commute neighborhoods are run down and have crime problems. Some landlords have made their complexes safer and more assuring by hiring guards and installing cameras and security devices.

Crime in States

States	Population	Rate	Homicides
Alabama	4,464,356	43	379
Alaska	634,892	42	39
Arizona	5,307,331	61	400
Arkansas	2,692,090	41	148
California	34,501,130	39	2,206
Colorado	4,417,714	42	158
Connecticut	3,425,074	31	105
Delaware	796,165	41	23
Florida	16,396,515	56	874
Georgia	8,383,915	46	598
Hawaii	1,224,398	54	32
Idaho	1,321,006	31	30
Illinois	12,482,301	41	986
Indiana	6,114,745	38	413
Iowa	2,923,179	33	50
Kansas	2,694,641	43	92
Kentucky	4,065,556	29	191
Louisiana	4,465,430	53	501
Maine	1,286,670	27	18
Maryland	5,375,156	49	446
Massachusetts	6,379,304	31	145
Michigan	9,990,817	41	672
Minnesota	4,972,294	36	119
Mississippi	2,858,029	42	282
Missouri	5,629,707	48	372
Montana	904,433	37	34
Nebraska	1,713,235	43	43
Nevada	2,106,074	43	180
New Hampshire	1,259,181	23	17
New Jersey	8,484,431	32	336
New Mexico	1,829,146	53	99
New York	19,011,378	29	*3,752
North Carolina	8,186,268	49	505
North Dakota	634,448	24	7
Ohio	11,373,541	42	452
Oklahoma	3,460,097	46	185
Oregon	3,472,867	50	84
Pennsylvania	12,287,150	30	651
Rhode Island	1,058,920	37	39
South Carolina	4,063,011	48	255
South Dakota	756,600	23	7
Tennessee	5,740,021	52	425
Texas	21,325,018	52	1,332
Utah	2,269,789	42	67
Vermont	613,090	28	7
Virginia	7,187,734	32	364
Washington	5,987,973	52	179
West Virginia	1,801,916	26	40
Wisconsin	5,401,906	33	192
Wyoming	494,423	35	9
Washington D.C.	571,822	77	232

Source: FBI 2001 Figures. *Includes 2,792 people killed on Sept. 11, 2001.

Crime In Other California Cities

City	Population	Rate	Homicides
Anaheim	334,700	33	8
Bakersfield	257,900	41	22
Fresno	441,900	80	40
Huntington Beach	194,600	23	0
Riverside	269,400	54	20
Los Angeles	3,807,400	50	588
San Diego	1,255,700	40	50
Santa Ana	343,700	35	24
Santa Barbara	90,700	32	3

Source: California Crime Index from State Dept. of Justice, 2001 data, with population from Calif. Dept. of Finance, Jan.1, 2002. Rate is all reported willful homicide, forcible rape, aggravated assault, burglary, motor vehicle theft, larceny-theft and arson per 1,000 residents. Homicides include murders and non-negligent manslaughter.

Many towns and sections are in transition; conditions could improve, the investment might be worthwhile. What's intolerable to a parent might be acceptable to a single person. If you don't have the bucks, often you can still buy safe but you may have to settle for a smaller house or yard.

Whatever your neighborhood, don't make it easy for predators.

Lock your doors, join the neighborhood watches, school your children in safety, take extra precautions when they are called for.

U.S. Statistics

• In 2001, the FBI reports, 13,752 people were murdered in the United States. Of these, 8,719 or 63 percent were shot, 1,796 stabbed, 661 beaten with blunt instrument, 925 assaulted with feet, hands or fists, 10 poisoned, 104 killed by fire, 23 drowned and 152 strangled. Narcotics killed 34 and asphyxiation 112. In 1,212 homicides, weapons were not identified. (These numbers and the following do not include the 2,792 people lost on Sept. 11, 2001 at World Trade Center)

• Of total murdered, 10,503 were male, 3,214 female and 35 unknown.

• In murders involving guns, handguns accounted for 6,790 deaths, rifles 389, shotguns 497 and other guns or type unknown 1,043.

• Of the 13,572 murdered in 2001, the FBI reported that 4,007 lost their lives in violence stemming from arguments or brawls. The next largest category was robbery victims, 1,042 homicides. Romantic triangles led to 118 homicides, narcotics 558, juvenile gang violence 865, gangland violence 74, rape 59, arson 70, baby-sitter-killing-child 37, burglary 73, prostitution 5, gambling 3.

• In 2001, there were 585 justifiable homicides in the U.S. — 370 by police officers, 215 by private citizens.

• In 1995, the U.S. recorded 20,232 homicides. In 1996, the number took a big drop, 16,967. The following year they decreased to 15,837 and the next year to 14,276. In 1999, the FBI tallied 13,011 homicides and in 2000, the amount shrunk again, to 12,943. Among possible reasons for decline: better emergency-trauma care, locking up more people, prosperity, more cops. Although 2001 homicides, minus the September 11 deaths, showed an increase, they are still well below the 1995 figures — 13,752 vs. 20,232.

California Crime

In 2001, the California Dept. of Justice recorded 2,201 homicides, a slight increase over 2000, which had 2,074 homicides. The counts for the preceding years are, 2,006, 2,170, 2,579 and 2,910. In 1980, over 20 years ago, the state recorded 3,405 homicides.

Of the 2,201 homicides in 2001, guns accounted for 1,568 deaths, or 72 percent of the total, knives 298, blunt objects such as clubs 95, hands and feet other personal weapons 103, and unidentified weapons 110.

Subject Index

Advertisers' Index

Developers

Hospitals-Medical Centers

Information Services

Private Schools

Realtors & Relocation Services

To advertise in McCormack's Guides, call 1-800-222-3602

Before you move ... buy

$13⁹⁵
SINGLE COPY
VOLUME DISCOUNTS

McCormack's Guides are published for:
- ALAMEDA • CONTRA COSTA-SOLANO
- SANTA CLARA-SANTA CRUZ-SILICON VALLEY
- SAN FRANCISCO-SAN MATEO • MARIN-NAPA-SONOMA
- SAN DIEGO • LOS ANGELES • ORANGE COUNTY
- GREATER SACRAMENTO-CENTRAL VALLEY
- RIVERSIDE-SAN BERNARDINO • SANTA BARBARA-VENTURA

New from McCormack's Guides:
How California Schools Work
California Almanac
www.mccormacks.com
1•800•222•3602

BUY 10 OR MORE & SAVE!

If you order 10 or more guides, the price drops to $6.25 per book. 100 or more, $5.50 per book. Phone orders 1-800-222-3602. Or fill out form and send with check to: McCormacks Guides, P.O. Box 1728, Martinez, CA 94553. Or fax order to (925) 228-7223. To order online go to www.mccormacks.com

1-800-222-3602

Next to title, write in number of copies ordered and total below:

No.	McCormacks Guide	Single	Bulk
___	Alameda County	$13.95	$6.25
___	Contra Costa & Solano	$13.95	$6.25
___	Los Angeles County	$13.95	$6.25
___	Marin, Napa & Sonoma	$13.95	$6.25
___	Orange County	$13.95	$6.25
___	Riverside & San Bernardino	$13.95	$6.25
___	Sacramento & Central Valley	$13.95	$6.25
___	San Diego County	$13.95	$6.25
___	San Francisco & San Mateo	$13.95	$6.25
___	Santa Barbara & Ventura	$13.95	$6.25
___	Santa Clara & Silicon Valley	$13.95	$6.25
___	How California Schools Work	$15.95	$7.95
___	California Almanac	$12.95	$6.50

_____ Books @ $ _____ (Price) = $ _____

CA sales tax (8.25%) _____

Shipping* _____

Total Amount of Order: $ _____

*For orders of 10 or more, shipping is 60 cents per book. For orders of fewer than 10, shipping is $4.50 for first book, $1.50 per book thereafter.

VISA MasterCard [▢] *Circle one: Check/Visa/MC/Am.Exp. or Bill Us*

Card No. _____ *Exp. Date* _____

Name _____

Company _____

Address _____

City _____ *State* _____ *Zip* _____

Phone: (_____) _____ Fax (_____) _____

[▢] **Check here to receive advertising information**